Higher Education in Ethiopia

Global Perspectives on Higher Education

Series Editors

Philip G. Altbach (*Center for International Higher Education, Boston College, USA*)
Hans de Wit (*Center for International Higher Education, Boston College, USA*)
Rebecca Schendel (*Center for International Higher Education, Boston College, USA*)
Gerardo Blanco (*Center for International Higher Education, Boston College, USA*)

This series is co-published with the Center for International Higher Education at Boston College.

VOLUME 52

The titles published in this series are listed at *brill.com/gphe*

Higher Education in Ethiopia

Themes and Issues from an African Perspective

By

Wondwosen Tamrat

BRILL

LEIDEN | BOSTON

Cover illustration: Addis Ababa University Main Gate, photograph by Mesay Getnet

All chapters in this book have undergone peer review.

The Library of Congress Cataloging-in-Publication Data is available online at https://catalog.loc.gov

Typeface for the Latin, Greek, and Cyrillic scripts: "Brill". See and download: brill.com/brill-typeface.

ISSN 2214-0859
ISBN 978-90-04-51346-4 (paperback)
ISBN 978-90-04-51347-1 (hardback)
ISBN 978-90-04-51348-8 (e-book)

Copyright 2022 by Koninklijke Brill NV, Leiden, The Netherlands.
Koninklijke Brill NV incorporates the imprints Brill, Brill Nijhoff, Brill Hotei, Brill Schöningh, Brill Fink, Brill mentis, Vandenhoeck & Ruprecht, Böhlau and V&R unipress.
All rights reserved. No part of this publication may be reproduced, translated, stored in a retrieval system, or transmitted in any form or by any means, electronic, mechanical, photocopying, recording or otherwise, without prior written permission from the publisher. Requests for re-use and/or translations must be addressed to Koninklijke Brill NV via brill.com or copyright.com.

This book is printed on acid-free paper and produced in a sustainable manner.

Contents

Preface XI
Series Editors' Preface XII
Acknowledgements XIII
List of Acronyms XIV
About the Author XV

Introduction 1

PART 1
Access and Equity

1   Linking Female Students' Access to Success   15

2   Gender Parity and the Leaking Pipeline   18

3   Disability in Higher Education: From Policy to Practice   21

4   Responding to the Needs of Eritrean Refugees in Ethiopia   24

5   A New Refugee Law: Implications for Higher Education   27

6   Closing the Gender Gap in Higher Education Leadership   30

7   Perpetuating Inequity Despite Higher Education Expansion   33

PART 2
HE Governance and Management

8   Government-University Relations: A Troubled Marriage   39

9   The Shifting Sands of University Management in Ethiopia   43

10   Do Students Have a Say in University Governance?   46

11   University Boards: Visibility, Efficiency and Accountability   49

12 Towards More Achievable University Vision Statements   53

13 What Next for a Partially Differentiated Higher Education System?   56

PART 3
University Systems and Resources

14 HE Financing Reforms: Intentions and Realities   63

15 Challenges of Ensuring Quality Education   66

16 Towards a Uniform System of Academic Promotion   69

17 Imperatives for a Functioning Information System at HEIS   72

18 University Resources: Imperatives for Efficient Utilization   75

19 Unlocking the Potential of ICT in Higher Education   78

PART 4
Private Higher Education and Privatization

20 Emerging Contours of African Private Higher Education   85

21 Unusual in Growth and Composition: Ethiopian Private Higher Education   88

22 Family Owned PHEIs in Africa   91

23 African Private Higher Education: Progressive Policies and Ambivalent Stances   94

24 Overcoming the Public-Private Divide in HE Law   97

25 Perils of Unregulated Privatization in Public Universities   100

26 Improving the Knowledge Base on Private Higher Education   103

PART 5
Quality Assurance in Higher Education

27 Towards a Diversified System of Quality Assurance   109

28 Beyond the Establishment of Quality Assurance Agencies   112

29 Internal Quality Assurance: Key to Maintaining Quality   115

30 From Gate Keepers to Gate Crashers: Corruption among University Faculty   119

31 The Scourge of Unscrupulous Private HE Institutions   122

32 Academic Credential Fraud: In Search of Lasting Solutions   125

PART 6
Internationalization of Higher Education

33 Disparities and Parallels in Internationalization: The Ethiopian Experience   131

34 Medical Education and the Ethiopian Exodus of Talent   134

35 Foreign HE Outposts: Navigating Risks and Opportunities   137

36 Foreign Qualification and Credential Evaluation   140

37 Cross-Border Higher Education: Regulating the Benefits and Risks   144

38 The Challenges of Attracting and Retaining Foreign Faculty   147

39 Internationalization Now a Deliberate Undertaking   150

PART 7
Research and Outreach

40 Towards a More Productive and Aligned Research System   155

41 Catalyzing R&D: The Need for More Government Funding   159

42 The Meager Output of Ethiopian PhDs   163

43 Increasing the Visibility of Local Journals   166

44 Towards a National System of Journal Accreditation   169

45 Re-Engaging with Community Service in Universities   172

46 University-Industry Ties: The Need for Good Management   175

PART 8
The Link between TVET and Higher Education

47 When TVET Fails to Provide the Answers   181

48 Universities vs TVET: Are Attitudes the Problem?   184

49 Applied Universities: A Viable Path to Higher Education   187

50 The TVET Sector's Challenge to Recruit, Retain Competent Trainers   190

51 Gains and Challenges for Women in the TVET Sector   193

PART 9
Graduate Employability

52 Education and the Workplace: Addressing the Yawning Gap   199

53 Graduate Employability: Whose Responsibility?   202

54 Producing Work-Ready Graduates Requires Strong Partnerships   205

55 Job Creation Plan: What Role for Higher Education?   208

56 Employment Gender Gap also a Higher Education Issue   211

57 Students Face Challenges on Route to Self-Employment   214

58 Advancing Employability through a Labor Market Information System   217

PART 10
COVID-19 and Its Impact on Higher Education

59 COVID-19 Threat to Higher Education: Africa's Challenges, Responses, and Apprehensions   223

60 COVID-19 – Private Higher Education Faces Precarious Future   227

61 The Shift to Online Learning Calls for Global Cooperation   231

62 Stemming the Impact of COVID-19 on Employment   235

63 Defying the Notion of the Ivory Tower in the Aftermath of COVID-19   239

References   243

Preface

The developments, changes and challenges experienced by the African higher education system in the past few decades reflect the fast-changing global higher education ecosystem of which it is part. Having identified higher education as a primary tool for development, many countries on the continent have embarked on the expansion of the sector at tremendous speed. The complex realities unfolding in the past few decades indicate that despite some encouraging developments, African higher education is still beset by a variety of challenges.

There is a paucity of studies on the various dimensions of African higher education. This is particularly true of Ethiopia, which has one of the continent's largest and fastest-growing higher education systems. There are few publications on the sector in general or proper documentation of the changes and reforms that have taken place over the past two decades. This book is a modest contribution to fill this void by presenting key themes and issues in Ethiopian higher education from an African perspective.

The book brings together 63 articles published by the author from 2017 to 2020 in *University World News, Inside Higher Education* and *International Higher Education*. Some were re-published in different local, regional and global fora and a number of readers and academics have requested that they be reproduced in book format for easy reference and research purposes. The articles included were selected based on their timeliness and relevance to global and regional higher education themes and are grouped in ten parts. Efforts have been made to update and revise the content of some articles for relevance and timeliness.

It is hoped that the book will provide a comprehensive review of the diverse dimensions of Ethiopian and African higher education, drawing on the knowledge and expertise of the author as a long-time educator, researcher, practitioner and institutional leader. In doing so, it will hopefully serve as a reference point for those that seek to learn more about the African higher education system in general and the changes that are affecting the continent and Ethiopia in particular. While the brevity, organization and variety of the topics and individual articles are expected to attract readers, the nature and content of the book are also expected to be of significant interest to researchers, academics and post-graduate students in Africa and beyond.

Series Editors' Preface

Higher Education in Ethiopia: Themes and Issues from an African Perspective by Wondwosen Tamrat is Volume 52 in our book series 'Global Perspectives on Higher Education'. This book – an updated compilation of previously published work by the author, a leading Ethiopian scholar and experienced institutional leader and practitioner – brings valuable insight concerning the developments and trends of higher education in Africa's second most populous country and positions them in a broader African context and perspective.

> *Philip G. Altbach, Gerardo Blanco, Rebecca Schendel and Hans de Wit*
> Series Editors

Acknowledgements

Several people have provided their unreserved assistance towards the publication of this book which brings together articles published by the author from 2017 to 2020. First and foremost, I wish to express my heartfelt thanks to Professor Damtew Teferra, Founding Director, International Network for Higher Education in Africa, without whose help the preparation of the book would not have been possible. His assistance during the planning, design and editing process was unparalleled. I also wish to recognize his contribution as a co-author of some of the articles.

Special thanks go to Professor Philip Altbach, Research Professor and Distinguished Fellow, and Professor Hans de Wit, Distinguished Fellow, both from Center for International Higher Education, Boston College, for their kindness, continuous encouragement and follow up during the preparation and publication process.

I am grateful to the respective editors of *International Higher Education*, *Inside Higher Education* and *University World News* for their constructive engagement and incisive comments during the write up and publication of individual articles. I also wish to acknowledge the Brill team for their dedication and professional assistance toward the production of the book.

Acronyms

AAU	Association of African Universities
ARRA	Administration for Refugee and Returnee Affairs
AUC	African Union Commission
DAFI	Albert Einstein German Academic Refugee Initiative
EAS	Ethiopian Academy of Sciences
ESDP	education sector development program
ETHERNET	Ethiopian Education and Research Network
FDRE	Federal Democratic Republic of Ethiopia
GER	gross enrollment rate
GPI	gender parity index
HE	higher education
HEIS	higher education institutions
HERQA	Higher Education Relevance and Quality Agency
ICT	Information Communication Technology
IFC	International Finance Corporation
MoE	Ministry of Education
MoFED	Ministry of Finance and Economic Development
MoSHE	Ministry of Science and Higher Education
NER	net enrollment rate
PHE	private higher education
PHEIS	private higher education institutions
R&D	research and development
STISA	Science, Technology, and Innovation Strategy of Africa
TVET	Technical and Vocational Education and Training
UIS	UNESCO Institute of Statistics
UN	United Nations
UNESCO	United Nations Educational, Scientific and Cultural Organization
UNHCR	United Nations High Commissioner for Refugees
UNISA	University of South Africa
WBESE	World Bank Enterprise Survey Ethiopia
WHO	World Health Organization

About the Author

Wondwosen Tamrat is an associate professor and founding President of St. Mary's University, Addis Ababa, Ethiopia. He has taught at Kotebe Metropolitan University, Addis Ababa University and St. Mary's University in Ethiopia for more than two decades. He is a PROPHE (Program for Research on Private Higher Education) Partner. At the continental level he serves as the coordinator of the private higher education sub-cluster of the higher education main cluster set up to achieve the Continental Education Strategy for Africa (CESA 2063). He has participated as a team member and reviewer of many policy documents developed by the Ethiopian Ministry of Science and Higher Education. Tamrat has presented and published several papers on Ethiopian higher education both at national and international fora. He is a member of the International Advisory Board of the International Journal of African Higher Education (IJHEA) and serves as a reviewer for various international peer reviewed journals.

Introduction

Higher education in Africa has a long history. Arguably, the earliest higher education institutions (HEIs) on the continent are older than those found in the West. Examples include the Qarawyyin in Fes, Morocco, which started as early as 859, Al Azhar in Egypt which was established in 975 AD, Timbuktu (in modern-day Mali) which began in the fifteenth century, and the Ethiopian monasteries which date back to the fourth century (Teferra, 2017). People traveled to these centers in search of knowledge and scholarship.

Modern higher education in most of Africa has been heavily influenced by the continent's colonial and post-colonial history. However, there were significant differences in the colonial powers' education assumptions and practices. The most important of these powers, Britain and France, had by far the most lasting impact on African higher education in terms of the organization of academe, and language of instruction and communication (Teferra & Altbach, 2004). Francophone higher education developed quite differently from British-led universities, and Portugal's colonial higher education policy mirrored that of the French, reserving higher education for the elite few, while the Belgians prohibited higher education in their colonies (Collins, 2014). The colonialists' assumptions and practices had severe limitations in terms of developing the African higher education system. To begin with, the colonial masters were more interested in training a limited cadre of local staff to assist in administering the colonies than in enabling widespread access to higher education to benefit individual countries and society. Other barriers included ethnocentric curricula that mirrored the colonial administration, the language of instruction which was limited to the language of the colonizer, and restrictions on academic freedom (Teferra & Altbach, 2004; Collins, 2014).

Although ties to former colonizers remain strong after independence, there were expectations that African HEIs would respond to the many challenges the continent was facing. However, political independence from the 1960s did not necessarily lead to the creation of a higher education system reflective of continental orientation and needs. Consequently, the African higher education system continues to be accused of being a mere replica of the West and failing to address African realities and developmental needs.

Given the expectation that higher education across the continent would serve as a tool for poverty reduction and economic development, attempts were made to develop the sector from the 1960s to the 1980s. In the late 1990s and the 2000s, fresh emphasis was placed on this mandate (Collins, 2014) and many countries promulgated reforms to drive the changes required to ensure that the African higher education system is more responsive to continental needs and the demands of the fast-changing global higher education system. While these ongoing efforts offer much promise, there is meagre documentation of and research on unfolding changes and developments. Notwithstanding the newness and evolving nature of higher education research across the globe, the state of affairs in Africa leaves much to be desired.

1 Outline of the Book

This book brings together a variety of issues and themes grouped into ten parts. The issues raised are fundamental to understanding the Ethiopian higher education sector as well as typical manifestations of the African higher education system. The ten major parts cover access and equity; higher education governance and management; university systems and resources; private higher education (PHE) and privatization; quality assurance; internationalization, research and outreach; Technical and Vocational Education and Training (TVET), graduate employability, and the impact of COVID-19.

Although generalization is always difficult in the context of a large and diversified continent, each chapter contains five to seven short articles under a single theme and provides sufficient content and analysis on the trajectory of the Ethiopian higher education ecosystem in light of continental and global higher education developments. A brief overview of the themes included in the book is presented below in the interests of providing appropriate context and background.

1.1 *Issues of Access and Equity*

As noted by Altbach (2016), 'massification' of higher education is the central driver of academic change in the past century. Demand for higher education has increased tremendously in Africa over the past few decades. This has been triggered by the growth of lower levels of education, demand for more higher education, the increasing importance attached to higher education as a driver of Africa's socioeconomic development and donors' influence. In 1970, there were approximately 200,000 higher education students in sub-Saharan Africa which increased to 4.5 million in 2008 and 6.3 million in 2011 (USAID, 2014). Although Africa's higher education growth rate is one of the fastest in the world, perhaps second to Asia, the continent has the lowest per capita access to higher education with the current tertiary enrolment rate standing at just over 12% – well below the global average of 32%. While a few countries have much higher enrolment rates, with Egypt standing at around 33%,

INTRODUCTION

South Africa at 20%, and Ghana and Nigeria at 14%, this signifies the need for further expansion of the sector. However, despite encouraging advances in the expansion of higher education, the continent continues to face many challenges. Among others, significant inequalities persist in gender representation and between different socioeconomic, ethnic and regional groupings (British Council, 2014). Little is known about students with disabilities who are not well-accommodated in the current systems. Without mitigating such challenges, the African higher education landscape cannot claim to be making significant improvements.

The articles included in the first part of the book explore the Ethiopian higher education system's major achievements and challenges in addressing access and equity by capitalizing on issues such as gender parity at both student and leadership levels, female students' access and success rates, disability in higher education and the needs of refugees seeking to attend HEIs. In addition to outlining and analyzing the specific challenges under each area of focus, the articles suggest possible mechanisms for mitigation.

1.2   *Higher Education Governance and Management*

The value of governance and management systems in running successful academic institutions cannot be overemphasized. This is more so at a time when the growth of higher education systems in many countries has rendered tertiary education institutions large and complex enterprises. The concept of university governance embodies a variety of concepts but mainly pertains to issues such as relations between universities and governments; financial oversight; provision of sector-wide services; adoption of funding models to give institutions greater flexibility; developing new sources of income; the establishment of external agencies to monitor educational quality; affirmation of governing boards as the institution's highest decision making body; the state's gradual withdrawal from direct decision-making; and appointment of university governing board members and chief executives (Fielden, 2008).

In particular, issues of academic freedom, autonomy and accountability continue to draw significant attention in the continental education system due to their critical role in the running and development of HEIs. Despite some encouraging changes, African HEIs continue to be a microcosm of the wider political systems of individual countries. In many countries, governments regard universities as centers of opposition. Strong controls are exercised that restrict the authority and discretion of institutional leadership and academic freedom. Authoritative governments seek to ensure that the manner in which presidents and other functional segments of a university are organized does not pose threat to their administration, resulting in highly centralized and autocratic structures. This not only limits institutions' ability to exercise their freedom, but also seriously constrains their development and functional efficiency.

There is growing realization that changes in this area are one of the most critical reforms that modern, effective higher education requires. The articles included in the second part of the book emphasize the need to improve government-university relations, adopt meaningful governance and management reforms and infuse the required governance changes at board and student levels.

1.3 *University Systems and Resources*

Efficient university systems and resources are of vital importance to the productivity and effectiveness of academic institutions. This is more so in the African context where, with the exception of few countries, these systems and resources are poor, underfunded and the cause of continued deterioration of higher education (Teferra & Altbach, 2004). Most of Africa's higher institutions are dependent on governments that provide the bulk of their operating budgets with limited experience and capacity to generate internal income. Economic and political challenges that result in inflation, devaluation of the currency exchange rate, economic and political turmoil, and structural adjustment programs continue to strain the financial stability of institutions and systems (Teferra & Altbach, 2004). The rapid growth of student enrolment is thus posing a serious challenge to resources, public expenditure per student and sustainable financing of higher education through government coffers.

The financing mechanisms and strategies on the continent exhibit a variety of patterns. In most countries, budgetary practices remain largely traditional (Collins, 2014). Faced with inadequate public financing, some countries have, however, adopted a strategy of shifting the cost of higher education from the government and taxpayers to parents and students. Strategies to increase funds and internal efficiency involve steps to reduce or moderate public expenditure, greater economy in the use of resources and mobilizing additional resources to achieve sustainability. The latter requires strategies that include different forms of cost sharing; limiting enrollment in public institutions and channeling excess demand to private providers; embracing low cost delivery modes such as distance teaching and short-cycle programs and funding formulas based on average or target costs per student (USAID, 2014).

In light of the above continental developments, the articles in Part 3 of this book highlight the issues of financial reforms, efficient utilization of resources, and the use of ICT and other systems that enhance the growth of academic institutions in Ethiopia with implications for other institutions on the continent.

1.4 *Private Higher Education and Privatization*

Private higher education has become an essential part of national systems in much of the world (Altbach, 2016, p. 230). The privatization of African higher education emerged in the 1980s. Private higher education has been used by many countries to cope with the challenges of higher education delivery. It has been spurred by factors such as favorable policies and market-friendly reforms, burgeoning demand from students for access, the declining capacity of public universities, pressure by external agencies in the form of structural adjustment, and other related global developments (Fielden & LaRocque, 2009). Private Higher Education Institutions (PHEIs) offer a variety of advantages over public dominated systems. They provide critical support in responding to increased demand for high level training and education, and the need to develop the continent's economies and enhance nation building. They help to conserve Africa's scarce foreign exchange by creating alternative opportunities to study at home. These institutions also infuse some element of competitiveness in the public dominated sector due to their dynamic and entrepreneurial features.

Private institutions in Africa are mainly established by religious organizations, foundations, for-profit agencies and individuals/families. They can be secular as well as sectarian and can be broadly categorized into for-profit and non-profit institutions. Most of the non-profit institutions in Africa are affiliated to Christian or Islamic institutions while most secular and for-profit private institutions depend on student tuition and fees for revenue. In religious based private institutions, responsibility for funding falls heavily on the founding religious organizations or their affiliates. Governments do not provide financial support to private institutions in most African countries. Although Africa's religious institutions have a long history, the proliferation of for-profit and non-for-profit institutions and the introduction of a commercial orientation within the sector are new developments.

Private HEIs are free from the obligations that constrain public institutions whose responsibilities span wider and broader national objectives. They provide relatively low cost, skills-based courses that are closely aligned with the needs of the labor market. The most common courses are computer science and technology, accounting, management, banking, finance, marketing, and secretarial science. Most private institutions hire academic staff from public institutions, rarely engage in research and enroll a small number of students, usually those that do not gain entry to public institutions. This influences perceptions of private institutions. Issues that continue to plague the development of PHE include matters relating to their legal status and national policies, quality assurance, the cost of their services, lack of infrastructure and resources, outdated accreditation criteria, and their limited ability to set fees at market rates (Fielden & LaRocque, 2008).

Although Africa is dominated by demand-absorbing PHEIs, it also hosts institutions that are achieving "semi-elite" status. These are institutions with quality programs, research endeavors, and innovative delivery – defying the generally unfavorable characterization of PHEIs on the continent (Tamrat, 2017). In some countries the reputation of these institutions is such that gaining admission is increasingly difficult. Some PHEIs pursue foreign partnerships to enhance their quality and attract students from other countries.

Part 4 of the book addresses the aforementioned developmental issues and concerns by drawing on various examples and experiences across the continent. In addition to tracing the growth of PHE at continental and national level, the articles examine the nature of policies that promote or hinder the growth of the private sector and the need to do so through ethical practices and an enhanced information and knowledge base.

1.5 *Quality Assurance in African Higher Education*

Despite longstanding concerns, there appears to be broad consensus among various stakeholders that the quality of African higher education has declined. This is the case regardless of how quality is defined or measured (Seddoh, 2003). Several factors have been identified to explain this challenge including rapidly rising enrollment, insufficient numbers of qualified academic staff, poor infrastructure, brain drain, and poor governance and leadership (Collins, 2014).

Internal and external quality assurance schemes have been introduced in many African countries to address quality challenges in higher education. National quality assurance agencies have been established to coordinate such efforts. Continental/regional initiatives that focus on improving the quality of education such as the Arusha Convention, Regional Recognition Conventions, Continental Education Strategy of Africa (CESA) (2016–2025), and other initiatives of the African Union and African Association of Universities have also been introduced (Ayoo et al., 2020). There are also sub-regional, national and institutional initiatives that focus on improving the quality of higher education and the perennial quality concerns that abound across the continent. However, such structured processes at the national level are a very recent phenomenon in most African countries and their impacts on the system have yet to be seen.

In addition to outlining the key areas where quality appears to be compromised, Part 5 of the book examines the nature of internal and external quality schemes that are used in the Ethiopian context as well as various alternative schemes by drawing on experiences from outside the continent.

1.6 Internationalization of Higher Education

The past few decades have witnessed a global increase in the internationalization activities of universities in terms of volume, scope and complexity (Altbach, 2016). It is posited that internationalization will play a central role in sustaining Africa's growth due to its potential to strengthen the international dimension of teaching, research and community outreach. Africa has embraced internationalization through student and staff mobility, research and publication partnerships, cross-border higher education, etc. However, such schemes are less common within the region and across the Global South. With the partial exception of South Africa, the African continent exhibits the fewest international and cross-border initiatives (Altbach, 2016). This is due to the fact that the continent takes on the process of internationalization not from a position of strength but one of weakness emanating from the confluence of historical, economic, educational, financial, and paradigmatic contexts (Teferra & Knight, 2008).

Factors such as the lack of resources; dependence on foreign resources; the use of foreign languages; poor educational quality and quality assurance mechanisms; the tension between localization and internationalization; substandard cross-border provisions; limited partnership schemes and related factors continue to inhibit the internationalization process. Addressing these and related challenges is urgent since Africa cannot remain outside internationalization initiatives across the globe.

In addition to identifying the nature of internationalization in the Ethiopian context, Part 6 of this book addresses its various dimensions that include brain drain, foreign branches, foreign qualifications and credentials evaluation, cross-border higher education and attracting and retaining foreign faculty. It examines internationalization policies and practices that have wider meanings for neighboring countries and the region.

1.7 Research and Outreach

The notion that universities are at the forefront of the production and consumption of knowledge and information is emphasized in Africa (Teferra & Altbach, 2004). However, African universities' involvement in research activities has been limited. Over the past decade, it has significantly improved the quantity and quality of its research output, citations and citation impact although its share of global research still accounts for less than 1% of the world's research output. The percentage of the GDP devoted to research is also less than 0.5% compared to the world average of around 1.7%. This is in contrast to Africa's share of the global population at 15% (World Bank & Elsevier, 2014). The only exceptions are South Africa and Egypt which together account for half of Africa's scientific publications, followed by Kenya, Morocco, Nigeria, and Tanzania that account for an additional 25%. Overall, research in Africa is plagued by various challenges that include inadequate infrastructure and facilities, a lack of qualified personnel, poor incentive and remuneration schemes, brain drain, limited funding, etc.

Higher education is expected to be more responsive to the various challenges and problems faced by African communities, which calls for public engagement. As centers of learning and development, Africa's tertiary institutions are expected to acquire theoretical and practical information about issues and concepts relevant to the African community, process this information through systematic categorization, and transmit this categorized knowledge to their students (World Bank & Elsevier, 2014).

Part 7 of this book which focuses on the major themes of research and outreach, includes articles on the challenges and mechanisms of enhancing research and development, journal production, university-industry linkages and community service. In addition to analyzing current challenges within the Ethiopian system, efforts are made to indicate mechanisms that could help to address the major inhibitors in the sector.

1.8 *Technical and Vocational Education and Training (TVET) in Africa*

TVET is receiving increasing recognition across Africa due to its potential to enhance competitiveness, social inclusion, decent employment, and poverty reduction. The African Union's Continental Technical and Vocational Education and Training (TVET) Strategy recognizes TVET as the most practical avenue to acquire readily employable skills for the world of work. In light of this, many countries are reforming their technical and vocational skills development system and linking training to employment.

However, many constraints limit TVET's impact and growth in Africa. There are missing links between national development policy and the role of TVET; and between TVET institutions and universities; industry's skills needs and educational curricula; and formal training and firm-based or informal training (Kingombe & Wagner, 2008). The lack of a coherent strategic approach to the sector has resulted in fragmented efforts, and wasted resources, making it difficult for private actors and donors to adequately promote the development of technical skills. The experience of successful African countries suggests that TVET strategies need to be informed by a clear vision, fully integrated into national development strategies and actions, and focused on sectors with promising employment prospects. Furthermore, partnerships with the private sector, employers and civil society are regarded as crucial in ensuring that the training offered is relevant. Finally, additional resources need to be secured to finance TVET (Kingombe & Wegner, 2008).

INTRODUCTION

Part 8 of the book is dedicated to articles that addressing TVET as a post-secondary education system with wider implications for employment and tertiary education. The articles examine the major challenges relating to successful delivery of TVET and the transition towards tertiary education.

1.9 Graduate Employability

Employability is often defined as the possession of relevant knowledge, skills and other attributes that enable one to gain and maintain worthwhile employment. Despite Africa's promising economic outlook, creating sufficient jobs for its growing population continues to be a major challenge (British Council, 2014). While around 11 million young people enter the job market each year, only three million formal jobs are created every year on the continent. This suggests the risks associated with growing numbers of urban youth without meaningful occupations.

Despite the rapid expansion of higher education enrolment, there are serious concerns about African universities' ability to produce the right type of graduates who can drive the region forward. Given the pressure for higher education expansion and the gains made thus far, absorption of graduates into the labor market will not be an easy task. Graduate unemployment rates are high in many countries and employers across the region complain of a lack of basic, technical and transferable skills which graduates need to find work.

High-quality university education is hence central to the task of enabling successful transition to the labor market. Failing to do so will hamper economic growth and create a generation without opportunities to pursue a better future (British Council, 2014). Universities cannot solve the jobs crisis alone, and co-ordinated action is necessary across all sectors, including at the level of macroeconomic policy.

Against the above backdrop, Part 9 of the book examines the nature and wider implications of graduate employability, self-employment and the link between preparation of graduates and the demands of the job market in Ethiopia. It emphasizes the role of higher education in employment creation and the changes required for it to meet the demands of the time.

1.10 COVID-19 and Its Impact

More than in any other part of the world, the African higher education sector has been heavily challenged by the COVID-19 pandemic. The shift to online learning which has been perceived as an immediate solution has not been easy to implement due to the continent's infrastructural challenges and limited preparation and readiness prior to the pandemic. In its immediate aftermath, only 29% of African HEIs were able to move teaching and learning online, compared to 85% in Europe (Koninckx et al., 2021). This has been mainly due to the lack of infrastructure, resources and facilities that continue to plague the sector.

Although COVID-19 is said to have provided new opportunities in terms of facilitating acceptance and the shift toward online education, accelerating the digitalization process requires concerted efforts to address the multifaceted challenges the sector is experiencing. Access to power and the Internet, data costs, faculty and students' knowledge and readiness to use the ICT platform and other related factors are seriously affecting university education across the continent. Many students who lack technological access or financial wherewithal have been forced to terminate their education, exacerbating the gender and class inequalities that characterize the sector.

African countries must ensure that technology does not further amplify existing inequalities in access and the quality of learning in universities. Changes in this direction require improvement in areas such as accelerating the digitalization of curricula and establishing a real culture of online training and distance education, while simultaneously strengthening teachers' capabilities in techno-pedagogy; investment in digital infrastructure; and offering targeted programs to bridge remaining gaps (Koninckx et al., 2021).

The last part of this book discusses the challenges of COVID-19 by examining the changes that have occurred in the public and private higher education spheres since the onset of the pandemic. These include the shift to online learning and the challenges of employment and linking with the community during such difficult times. Beyond identifying the challenges, the articles suggest possible ways to address them.

References

Altbach, P. G. (2016). *Global perspectives on higher education.* John Hopkins University Press.

Ayoo, P., Tamrat, W., & Kuria, M. (2020). QA in higher Education in Africa: A synoptic view. In S. Karakhanyan & B. Stensaker (Eds.), *Global trends in higher education: Challenges and opportunities in internal and external quality Assurance.* Brill Sense.

Collins, C. S. (2014). An Overview of African higher education and development. *The Development of Higher Education in Africa: Prospects and Challenges*, 21–65. http://dx.doi.org/10.1108/S1479-3679(2013)0000021005

Fielden, J. (2008). *Global trends in university governance.* Working Paper Series, The World Bank.

Fielden, J., & La Rocque, N. (2008). *The evolving regulatory context for private education in emerging economies.* Discussion paper. The World Bank.

Kingombe, C., & Wegner, L. (2008, November). *Technical and vocational skills development in Africa* [Paper]. DSA Annual Conference: Development's invisible hands.

Koninckx, P., Fatondji, C., & Burgos, J. (2021). COVID-19 impact on higher education in Africa. https://oecd-development-matters.org/2021/05/19/covid-19-impact-on-higher-education-in-africa/

Materu, P. (2009). *Higher education quality assurance in Sub-Saharan Africa: Status, challenges, opportunities, and promising practices.* Working Paper 124. World Bank.

Seddoh, K. F. (2003). The development of higher education in Africa. *Higher Education in Europe, 28*(1), 33–39. DOI: 10.1080/0379772032000110080

Teferra, D., & Altbach, P. (2004). African higher education: Challenges for the 21st century. *Higher Education, 47,* 21–50.

Teferra, D. (Ed.). (2017). *Funding higher education in sub-Saharan Africa.* Palgrave Macmillan.

Teferra, D., & Knight, J. (2008). *Higher education in Africa: The International dimension.* Center for International Higher Education, Boston College and Association of African Universities.

USAID. (2014). African higher education: Opportunities for transformative change for sustainable development.

World Bank & Elsevier. (2014). *A decade of development in sub-Saharan African science, technology, engineering and mathematics research.* Elsevier.

PART 1

Access and Equity

∵

CHAPTER 1

Linking Female Students' Access to Success

An earlier version of this chapter appeared in *University World News, Africa Edition*, 17 November 2017, https://www.universityworldnews.com/post.php?story=20171114092145811

While significant improvements have been made in female students' access to universities in Ethiopia, high attrition rates remain a challenge. Since 2000 the Ethiopian higher education sector has experienced expansion unprecedented in the country's history. Against its earlier elitist leanings, the sector is fast transforming itself, following a 'massification' path which is opening up new opportunities and confronting tremendous challenges.

When the incumbent government assumed power in 1991, policy directions primarily sought to tackle what were considered to be the major deficiencies of previous systems – lack of access, equity, quality and relevance. Higher education was identified as a tool for poverty reduction and sustainable development that demands the participation of all sections of society. A 20-year plan (now succeeded by five-year plan), the Education Sector Development Program, was crafted to guide national efforts with the aim of effecting fundamental changes in major areas of concern.

Over the past two decades, the number of public universities has grown from two to 51 and that of private higher education institutions (PHEIs) from none to nearly 300. The gross enrollment ratio which was below 1% two decades ago now stands at around 12%, for the first time surpassing the sub-Saharan average of around 10%. Female students' access rate has also gradually changed. While in 2003–04 females represented 20% of university students, this figure now stands at nearly 40%. In 2003–04 female students represented only 7% of the 2,560 postgraduate students that attended universities. The plan for 2019–20 was to raise female enrolment to 45% and 35% at undergraduate and postgraduate levels, respectively.

Significant gains have been made in the discipline-specific participation rate of female students. The highest percentage of female students (42%) is found in medicine and health sciences, which is exemplary even when compared with other countries in sub-Saharan Africa. This is followed by business and economics (37%), social sciences and humanities (32%), agriculture and life sciences (31%), and natural and computational science (31%). Although engineering comes last at 29%, trailing the other disciplines, the government aimed to raise female participation in science and technology subjects to 45% by 2019–20 (MoE, 2015). Some progress has been made with regard to the number of female faculty at universities, albeit far from satisfactory. Female faculty make up around 12% of the more than 40,000 academic staff% – very low in terms of the desired equitable participation and the potential value such faculty have in terms of encouraging female students' success (MoE, 2018). The plan for 2019/20 was to raise this figure to 25% (MoE, 2015). In light of these developments, how do female students fare in terms of completing their studies?

1   The Link between Access and Success

Disadvantaged populations enrolled at universities are usually confronted with a multitude of challenges that may derail their efforts to complete their studies. It has been widely argued that the whole concept of equitable access can be questioned if tolerance at the point of entry is not supplemented by active assistance to enable such students to stay the course.

Ethiopian universities have not been as successful in addressing the challenges of female completion rates as they have been in creating the required access. When the Higher Education Relevance and Quality Agency (HERQA) conducted its first quality audits of the older public universities between 2007 and 2009, the situation was quite alarming. The attrition rate of female students in the faculty of medicine at Gondar University was, for instance, more than 50%. The same was true of Haramaya University where the departments of cooperatives, education, biology, and history lost 75%, 56%, 65% and 66% of their female students respectively, in just one semester. While female students made up only 20% of the intake in the first semester of Arba Minch University, they constituted 54% of dropouts from the university.

This situation did not show any significant improvement during the 2014 quality audit reports of HERQA as exemplified by the findings in universities like Debre Berhan, Debre Markos and Wolaita Sodo. While the rate of student attrition at Debre Berhan University is 17%, it more than doubles for female students to 38%. Female enrolment in the regular programs of Wolaita Sodo University amounts to only 20% of the total, but the dropout rate is 45% while the withdrawal rate shoots up to 54.4%. The rate of female attrition goes from bad to worse as we move from social science subjects to the hard sciences. The highest attrition rate at Debre Markos (50%) was recorded in the department of mathematics while the lowest was in the department of history (3%). At Debre Berhan, higher dropouts were reported in the department of engineering while lower rates were observed in social science and health programs. The low participation and high attrition rates of female students are explained by a variety of factors that continue to impinge on the national policy of equitable access.

2 Reasons for Low Female Success Rates

One of the major obstacles to female students' success is their poor academic background that pervades the whole system. Other educational and social problems include the challenge of adjusting to a new teaching-learning system and new social environment – loneliness, inability to balance social and academic life, lack of role models, sexual harassment and violence, and financial problems. A shortage of basic facilities such as dormitories and toilets, scarcity of water, lack of recreational amenities and space in libraries have also been identified as common problems faced by female students, especially in the newly-established universities. Another challenge is related to the type of institutional support which has not always been organized, focused and forthcoming. Female students often complain about the lack of training in study skills and foreign languages, absence of tutorial services and ineffective guidance and counselling services that would have improved their likelihood of success.

3 Implications for Policy and Practice

Addressing inequality in the education sector is an aspiration and commitment shared by many countries, educational systems and individual institutions. While political commitment has been made to ensure the success of disadvantaged students, and policies have been adopted, challenges persist. Efforts to expand access to female students in Ethiopia are commendable, though not devoid of bottlenecks. A lot remains to be done at both national and institutional level in terms of investing, planning, implementation and rigorous follow-up to help female students to succeed.

While improvements in terms of retention are evident over the past few years, such changes are partly the result of leniency in grading rather than genuine efforts to fix the problem. Nurturing the alliance between equity considerations and female success rates thus remains one of the major priorities that Ethiopian HEIs should continue to address in earnest. Universities' quest to address this challenge in a sustainable manner should continue unabated without necessarily compromising institutional quality.

CHAPTER 2

Gender Parity and the Leaking Pipeline

An earlier version of this chapter appeared in *Inside Higher Education*, 16 December 2019, https://www.insidehighered.com/blogs/world-view/gender-parity-and-leaking-pipeline-0

In the 2019–20 academic year, the Ethiopian Ministry of Science and Higher Education (MoSHE) planned to ensure that female students make up no less than 43% of enrollment in public universities. This was a significant development from the 2018 figure of 37% and closer to government's target of 45% for that year. It is perhaps the first time the government came close to ensuring gender parity in higher education. The success rate of similar plans has been far below government intentions in the past. The Education Sector Development Program, ESDP III (2004–05 to 2009–10) aimed to increase female enrollment from 24% to 39%, but by the end of the period the rate stood at less than 30%. During ESDP IV (2010 to 2014–15), the plan was to increase female enrollment from 29% to 40%, but participation only approached 32%.

The latest drive to increase female participation in higher education might be an indication of the ministry's resolve to bridge the persistent gap, but the broader goal of gender parity is still far from being achieved. Despite improvements in the gender parity index in Ethiopian higher education from 0.22 in 1991 to the current 0.37, the figure remains among the lowest in the world. Addressing this challenge requires a closer look at the lower levels of education and its root cause.

1 The Gender Fault Line

The continued gender imbalance at Ethiopian HEIs is partly explained by the increasing underrepresentation of females at the lower levels of education. This can be understood by closely studying current figures for gross enrollment rate (GER), net enrollment rate (NER) and gender parity index (GPI) that are often used to measure achievements at the lower levels. The GER compares the percentage of students (irrespective of age) at a particular grade level to the corresponding school-age population. The NER looks at children who are of the correct age (in the Ethiopian context the proportion of 7-year-olds who enroll in Grade 1) while the GPI is the ratio of female to male students at a given level.

The 2018 Annual Education Statistics Abstract of the Ministry of Education shows that the GER for elementary level (Grades 1-8) in 2017–18 was 103.5 for female and 115 for male students, respectively. In the same year, the NER for males in elementary schools stood at 115 while that of females was 95.4. Gender parity at the elementary level was 0.90 and 0.89, indicating a limited gap in participation. The completion rate to eighth grade does not reflect a huge gap between male and female: in 2017–18 it was 55.9 for female and 59.5 for male students, respectively. Secondary school appears to be the point where the education pipeline begins to leak significantly. The GER for Grades 9-10 in 2017–18 was 45.2% for female students and 50.1% for males. The exceptions were two regions (Amhara and Addis Ababa), where more females were attending secondary education compared to males. The NER for females at secondary grades (Grades 9-12) was around 31%, which indicates the challenges female students are facing in transitioning from primary to secondary education.

The fault line widens further after the Grade 10 secondary school completion examination, when females begin to be significantly underrepresented. Out of a total of 1,205,789 students who sat for Grade 10 examination in 2017–18, 47.2% were female. While 64.78% of those who took the exam scored the passing mark – 2.0 or above – female students constituted only 43.7% of those who passed. The number of female students goes even lower after they take the university qualifying exam at the completion of Grade 12. Among those who sat for the Grade 12 exam in 2017–18, 52.9% scored 350 (the pass mark set for the year), and among these only 39.5% were female. Currently, the percentage of female students within the public higher education sector stands at around 37% at undergraduate and 18% at postgraduate level (MoE, 2018). While government proposed to increase the postgraduate participation to 35% during 2019–20, this was quite unlikely since the figure for 2017–18 stood at around 24%.

According to the MoE (2015), gender disparities at the lower levels are widely attributed to gender roles and related household tasks, an unfavorable cultural environment including negative attitudes toward girls' education, harmful traditional practices such as child marriage, school-related gender-based violence, a lack of adequate role models and the distance to schools. Some of these difficulties continue to be a challenge at the tertiary level. Factors such as misconceptions about gender-related academic ability, economic conditions, gender bias, sexual abuse and classroom interactions that favor male participation are often cited as challenges that young women face in adapting to university life.

2 Addressing the Root Causes

A variety of policies, strategies and special support schemes have been designed at both ministry and institutional levels to address gender disparity in educational institutions. However, as conceded by the ministry (MoE, 2015), implementation of these policies is "challenging, insufficiently supported, or insufficiently integrated with regional or local conditions affecting enrollment and completion", indicating the need to address the specific constraints female students face in general and in higher education in particular. Addressing the challenge of gender parity through policy and practice should begin in earnest at the lower levels of education, at the root cause of the problem. This remains the key to improving the participation and success rate of female students at a higher level.

CHAPTER 3

Disability in Higher Education

From Policy to Practice

An earlier version of this chapter appeared in *University World News, Africa Edition*, 9 March 2018, https://www.universityworldnews.com/post.php?story=20180307105907347

Equity considerations in higher education assume a variety of dimensions including gender, socio-economic background and disability. While the expansion of higher education across the globe has been seen as a means to address these issues, the reality has not been as straightforward. While major and relatively successful efforts have been directed at addressing the gender imbalance in the form of improving female representation in HEIs, disability issues continue to be overlooked or sidelined, both in terms of practical considerations and scholarly attention.

According to the World Health Organization (2011), there are over one billion people with disabilities in the world, about 15% of the global population. In Africa, the proportion of disabled people is estimated at approximately 40%, including 10–15% who are school-age children. This roughly translates to 300 million people with disabilities in Africa. In Ethiopia, as elsewhere, there is a lack of organized and up-to-date data on disability. Available figures diverge widely, depending on who is issuing the numbers. The last national census in 2007 reported only 805,492 persons with disabilities – 1.09% of the total population of 86 million. Many regard this as underreporting caused by the design of the census. On the other hand, the WHO puts the figure at 15 million persons, representing 17.6% of the total population at the time. A more realistic estimate of 10% continues to be widely used in the country, although the Ministry of Education claims to be using the WHO figure for its planning purposes.

The number of disabled students attending, mainly public, Ethiopian HEIs rose from 398 in 2009–10 to more than 1,000 in 2015. While this number is still low, what is more worrying are the challenges that still exist for those pursuing their studies in unaccommodating environments.

1   Policy and Practice Trajectories

The issue of disability in Ethiopia is widely reflected in a variety of policy documents, plans and commitments. The government is a party to the UN Convention on the Rights of the Child (1990), the United Nation's Convention on the Rights of Persons with Disabilities (2010), and the African Charter on Human and Peoples' Rights (1981) – all of which recognize the rights of disabled people to equal treatment. While Ethiopia's Constitution gives due recognition to this issue, other specific policies and plans embody provisions on rights and opportunities that should be made available to the disabled. For instance, the Growth and Transformation Plan II (MoFED, 2015/16–2019/20) establishes the need to ensure disabled people's participation in political, economic and social activities including the creation of wider educational opportunities. Specific guidelines have also been issued to HEIs on how to address issues of disability.

The Ethiopian Higher Education Proclamation (2009) stipulates that institutions should ensure that their facilities and programs are accessible and 'friendly' to physically challenged students. Building designs, the campus physical landscape, computers and other infrastructure should take into account the interests and needs of these students. In addition to relocating classes, developing alternative testing procedures, and providing different educational auxiliary aids, institutions are required to ensure that disabled students receive the necessary academic assistance, including tutorial sessions, extra examination time and deadline extensions. As indicated in education sectoral plans, universities are expected to implement the national policy on facilities and infrastructure by adapting their campuses to provide full access to all students. Three universities are also set to receive additional support to establish facilities to provide services to students with the most severe needs. This experience will guide later improvements across the higher education subsector in terms of facilities as well as teaching skills and adaptations required to support all students with special educational needs effectively. Despite these commitments, much remains to be done in terms of implementation.

2   Barriers to Participation

Local studies indicate that a range of barriers hamper disabled students from meaningful participation in higher education. The built environment in most Ethiopian universities continues to pose serious hurdles, forcing disabled students to seek support from others. A lack of adequate educational materials, assistive devices and computers, the absence of curricular or material adaptations, rigid assessment techniques and examination procedures are critical barriers that continue to affect the success of disabled students.

Most institutions are ill-prepared to provide the necessary support to disabled students. Policy statements on disability, support units with fully-fledged staffing, and viable structures are rare. Even where such amenities are said to exist, they appear to be meagre, fragmented and still at a nascent stage. Limited assistance is available from faculty members and administrative staff, most of whom have little awareness and preparation in terms of accommodating the needs of disabled students. In addition to restricting their choice of where and what to study, these challenges frequently result in an understandable aversion to study and greater social isolation of the disabled. This in turn has the effect of hampering the development of their capacities and the realization of their educational and professional goals.

3 Beyond Policy

Despite signs of progress in terms of policy considerations, disabled students' participation in Ethiopian higher education is still marked by many difficulties. In the globalized higher education context which includes the developing world, addressing issues of social justice in earnest remains a major challenge. Ethiopia's quest for more equitable higher educational opportunities cannot succeed without responding to the many challenges faced by disabled students.

To begin with, more research is required on the subject to gain insights that will not only increase public understanding of the problems, but also inform policy directions and ways of overcoming existing barriers at national and institutional levels. The government should play a leading role in addressing current challenges and lend its weight to the involvement of a broad range of pertinent stakeholders to ensure improved participation and success of disabled students in higher education, so that they are not deprived of the most powerful instrument they have at their disposal to extricate themselves from poverty and social inequity.

CHAPTER 4

Responding to the Needs of Eritrean Refugees in Ethiopia

An earlier version of this chapter appeared in *Inside Higher Education*, 21 January 2018 (with Samuel Dermas), https://www.insidehighered.com/blogs/world-view/responding-needs-eritrean-refugees-ethiopia

The refugee crisis around the world has been described as one of the worst challenges humankind has confronted since the end of World War II. According to 2016 UNHCR data, 65.6 million people are forcibly displaced globally because of persecution, conflict, violence, or human rights violations. While more than 40 million of these are internally displaced, 22.5 million are identified as refugees. Contrary to common suppositions, 84% of the world's refugees or 14.5 million people are accommodated in developing countries.

The five countries that host the highest number of refugees are Turkey, Pakistan, Lebanon, Islamic Republic of Iran, and Ethiopia, in that order. Currently, Ethiopia hosts more than 850,000 people – the largest in Africa – from South Sudan, Somalia, Eritrea and the Sudan. Eritrean refugees account for 160,000 or 19% of the total. As a signatory to the 1951 Refugee Convention, the 1969 OAU Refugee Convention, the Covenant on Economic, Social and Cultural Rights and many other international legal instruments Ethiopia is obliged to provide the necessary support to the refugees it hosts.

1   Initiatives and Opportunities

One of the refugee schemes Ethiopia has adopted since 2010 is known as the out-of-camp scheme. It allows refugees to live and move freely across the country, opening opportunities to further their education and engage in gainful employment. As a result of this scheme alone, around 17,345 refugees live in Addis Ababa. Another scheme for refugees, especially of Eritrean origin, is the provision of free scholarships at Ethiopian public HEIs.

While the global average for higher education enrollment exceeds 30%, only 1% of refugees worldwide are said to have access to higher education. Even in countries like Afghanistan, that is afflicted by long-term conflict, the rate is around 9%. A number of global initiatives – in some cases country specific – by national and international organizations aim to help refugees fulfil their higher education aspirations, although provision is far from meeting demand. For instance, demand for the United Nations High Commissioner for Refugees (UNHCR)'s global scholarship program is said to be so high that for every successful application, between 10 and 30 are rejected.

The Ethiopian free higher education scheme has so far enabled 1,600 Eritrean refugees to pursue their studies at various public universities across the country. While 1,300 are sponsored by the Ethiopian government, the remaining 300 are supported by the UNHCR's Albert Einstein German Academic Refugee Initiative (DAFI) scholarship program. Self-sponsored Eritrean refugees also attend HEIs, with medical science being the most popular program for this group. With these degrees, the refugees hope to secure better employment opportunities if they are able to migrate to the west. Self-sponsored students cover their college fees mainly through financial assistance from family members who likely reside abroad, often in Europe and North America.

2 Barriers and Challenges

Despite the new opportunities, the educational aspirations of Eritrean refugees are challenged by barriers they encounter before and after joining Ethiopian HEIs. One such challenge is the lack of academic transcripts required to gain admission. Most of the refugees do not possess these documents due to Eritrean rules that restrict issuance of original school certificates or diplomas to any citizen who cannot present evidence of having completed national service or having been exempted. Those who already have college diplomas also face the challenge of securing recognition from the Higher Education Relevance and Quality Agency (HERQA) in Ethiopia because of the difference in the educational systems of the two countries. This challenge is mitigated by a placement examination for refugees coordinated by the Administration for Refugee and Returnee Affairs (ARRA) and the Ministry of Education. On the basis of their scores, refugees are issued a letter of cooperation they can use to register at the HEI of their choice.

The major challenges faced by refugees after joining HEIs are academic, psychological and socio-cultural. The academic challenges are caused by disruptions to prior schooling, a lack of academic skills, poor language proficiency, hesitance to participate in class, and differences in the school ethos. The most common psychological challenges relate to the traumatic experiences of fleeing their country; safety concerns; low self-esteem; and anxiety about their future success due to UNHCR's cumbersome resettlement processes. The socio-cultural challenges are complicated by communication problems caused by poor knowledge of Amharic, Ethiopia's official language. On a positive note, refugees appreciate the advantages they gain as a result of the similarity between the Eritrean and Ethiopian cultures.

The final challenge relates to the lack of support given the plethora of challenges refugees face. The lack of academic and psychological support is a glaring gap. The exceptions are ARRA interventions to arrange placement at HEIs and help the refugees to gain the same treatment as Ethiopians. Despite the aforementioned challenges, it is estimated that around 85% of the Eritrean refugees successfully complete their studies. The major reason for discontinuing their studies is resettlement opportunities in Europe or other western countries. The transient nature of their stay in Ethiopia has a significant influence on both their academic performance and their readiness to stay after graduation.

3 Conclusion

Schemes such as out-of-camp living, and providing education and employment opportunities are immense challenges in a country like Ethiopia whose own burgeoning youth population demands similar benefits. In a situation where assistance may not be forthcoming from outside, resources that could be used to alleviate the problems of native citizens are shared with refugees.

Notwithstanding the various hurdles, Ethiopia's commitment to free higher education for refugees is defended by the government. In addition to helping to improve the lives of refugees, success might also be seen as an indication of what can be done to address a growing global humanitarian crisis, even in countries with meager resources. The initiative has been welcomed by donors and international partners as exemplary practice that could be emulated in similar contexts. However, some within the local and refugee community regard the measure as a political gimmick. Whatever the political dimensions, the pedagogical implications of providing higher education to refugees call for more than opportunities; various forms of academic and non-academic support are required to help refugee students achieve their aspirations.

CHAPTER 5

A New Refugee Law

Implications for Higher Education

An earlier version of this chapter appeared in *University World News, Africa Edition*, 23 August 2019, https://www.universityworldnews.com/post.php?story=20190819132407160

Due to its geographical location, and the political instability and humanitarian crises in neighboring countries, Ethiopia has become one of the largest refugee-hosting countries in the world and the second largest in Africa, providing refuge to close to a million refugees from some 24 countries. While the South Sudanese are the largest group with a total of 422,240 refugees, Somalis number 253,889; Eritreans 173,879; and Sudanese 44,620.

The urban-registered refugee population is also considerable, numbering close to 23,000 individuals, and includes those transferred from the refugee camps to cities on medical and protection grounds – refugees like the Yemeni with no designated camps, university students on sponsorship programs and beneficiaries of the out-of-camp living scheme. According to available data, 80% of the urban refugee population comprises Eritreans, followed by Yemenis at 8.3%, Somalis at 4.7%, South Sudanese at 2.3% and the remaining 5.4% from the Great Lakes region.

1 A New Legislative Regime

The various agreements and conventions signed by Ethiopia and its hospitality to refugee populations are evident of its commitment to the protection of refugee rights. Until recently, refugee affairs were administered through Refugee Proclamation No. 409 of 2004 which restricted moving out of camps, access to employment and education outside camps. A new refugee law that incorporates significant policy and legal reforms was ratified by parliament in January 2019. This gives refugees the right to engage in wage-earning employment, and acquire and transfer property and assets under the same circumstance as "the most favorable treatment" accorded to foreign nationals; and exempts them from any duty, charge or tax higher than that imposed on Ethiopian nationals.

In addition to allowing refugees access to national health and education services on the same basis as Ethiopian nationals, the law gives them access to telecommunication, banking, financial and judicial services, identity and travel documentation and driver's license certification. Similar to other foreign nationals, the new law further grants refugees or asylum seekers liberty of movement and freedom to choose their residence, which is expected to encourage a move away from the existing camp-based approach to "an integrated model of refugee assistance". The right to integrate locally into Ethiopian society is, however, restricted to refugees who have lived in the country for a very long period of time. The law also makes reference to the existing Nationality Law of Ethiopia which allows foreign nationals, including refugees, to acquire Ethiopian nationality by fulfilling the necessary requirements.

2   Implications for Higher Education

The Ethiopian government is known for providing educational access to refugees, although most of these provisions have mainly been offered in refugee camps. However, opportunities for higher education were also extended through the out-of-camp and UNHCR scholarships that offered the best opportunity for those wishing to attend university.

Support from the UNHCR, whose Education Strategy 2012–16 sets higher education as one of its priorities, is mainly through the worldwide DAFI scholarship. In 2017, the majority of DAFI scholarships (41%) were awarded to candidates from 30 sub-Saharan African countries including Ethiopia which ranks top among the three largest country programs. A total of 28 HEIs in Ethiopia host DAFI scholarship students with an annual budget of US$499,096, with the average scholarship standing at $685 (UNHCR, 2019). Among the 729 students enrolled through 2017 DAFI scholarships, 388 came from Somalia, 169 from Sudan, 88 from South Sudan, 63 from Eritrea, 13 from Yemen, seven from Congo Brazzaville, and one from Burundi (UNHCR, 2018).

The provision of free university scholarships at Ethiopian public HEIs, especially for refugees of Eritrean origin, has thus far enabled 1,500 Eritrean refugees to pursue their studies across the country (UNHCR, 2018). With its new commitments the Ethiopian government has pledged to increase enrolment in primary, secondary and tertiary education, including adult literacy and technical and vocational education and training without discrimination and within available resources. The targets set by government are to increase enrolment of pre-school-aged refugee children from 46,276 (44%) to 63,040 (60%); primary school-aged children from 96,700 (54%) to 137,000 (75%); secondary school-aged refugees from 3,785 (9%) to 10,300 (25%); and higher education enrolment from 1,600 to 2,500.

3   Opportunities or False Promises?

The new legislation can be regarded as a significant step in the protection of refugee rights including widening opportunities for higher education. The UNHCR, which participated in the drafting of the law, called the move "historic", and Filippo Grandi, United Nations High Commissioner for Refugees, said: "By allowing refugees the opportunity to be better integrated into society, Ethiopia is not only upholding its international refugee law obligations, but is serving as a model for other refugee hosting nations around the world".

However, the political, demographic and economic implications of the plan cannot be underestimated as these factors can affect the social, economic and educational opportunities available to refugees. For instance, immediately after its ratification, the Anuak people in Gambella Regional State protested that the law was ratified without their consent and that the equal rights given to refugees threaten their existence since they are outnumbered by refugees. Moreover, the mechanisms to achieve the commitments enshrined in the law remain fuzzy and, given Ethiopia's limited capacity, its goals cannot be attained without significant strain and meaningful external assistance. Among new initiatives in this regard is a plan to harness foreign assistance to expand the number of industrial parks across the country to create 100,000 jobs, 70% for Ethiopians, and 30% reserved for refugees. However, the size and sustainability of such assistance should be examined in light of the increasing needs of refugees and the extent to which the country can meet them.

The same is true of government efforts to host refugees in public universities. Currently, the UNHCR provides only 25% of the total cost of education for refugees pursuing higher education in Ethiopian universities while the government covers the remaining 75% through its subsidies to public universities (UNHCR, 2015). Giving more opportunities to refugees in a country that provides access to higher education to only 12% of its own eligible student population is no easy task in the absence of additional resources – about which no clear strategy seems to exist.

While the current move towards the protection of refugee rights is commendable, realization of this intention will most likely depend on addressing issues of political sensitivity and strengthened economic capacity which call for wider participation and substantial assistance from the local and international community. Where this is lacking it is difficult to see how the promises made in the new legislation can be realized in a meaningful way.

CHAPTER 6

Closing the Gender Gap in Higher Education Leadership

An earlier version of this chapter appeared in *University World News, Global Edition*, 12 December 2019, https://www.universityworldnews.com/post.php?story=20191209065455348

Until very recently the number of women leaders at Ethiopian HEIs was dismally low or literally non-existent. However, this appears to be changing for the better thanks to the concerted efforts of the Ministry of Science and Higher Education.

1   Sectoral Targets and Progress

Supported by the government's Education Sector Development Program, ESDP V (2015), efforts to improve female representation at leadership position started with the development and implementation of guidelines on the composition of university boards and top leadership which incorporated criteria that favor greater representation of women. The ministry set a target of 50 females in top leadership positions, with at least one woman president in public universities. This has not been achieved as the presidents of all 51 public universities are still male, although observable changes have been made at the level of vice-presidents and below.

From a limited number of female vice-presidents a few years ago, the number has now risen to 29 (16.27% of top leadership positions). Women also represent 11.8% of middle-level leaders and 17.29% of lower-level managers, although this is below the ESDP V (2014–15 to 2019–20) goal of raising the same from 5% to 30%. A similar change has recently been witnessed in female representation at the level of university boards where 32.5% are now women, including the board chair of the country's flagship university. The latter is a significant achievement and well above the ESDP V target of 25% representation at board level.

2 Capacity-Building Initiatives

In addition to addressing policy deficiencies and recruiting more female leaders, an important development within the sector is the ministry's capacity-building initiatives aimed at improving women's leadership capabilities. Two recent initiatives include training programs on transformative leadership and university governance. The training on transformative leadership was organized in partnership with UN Women and held from 12 to 16 June, 2019 in Debre Zeyit (Bishoftu). A total of 29 female vice-presidents from 19 public universities participated in the training which aimed to expose participants to the practical skills necessary for leadership. The second training program was held at Zhejiang Normal University in China between 8 and 27 September, 2019, and was organized by the Ethiopian Ministry of Science and Higher Education in collaboration with the Ministry of Commerce of the People's Republic of China through the China Aid Program. A senior female advisor to the Ministry of Science and Higher Education and 13 female university vice-presidents participated in the training that focused on university governance and was delivered through seminars, on-site training, field visits and cultural experiences.

It is expected that the knowledge and skills acquired from such trainings will improve the individual performance of female leaders and overall institutional capacity in the sector. Further plans by the ministry appear to be underway to provide a series of similar training programs at local level in collaboration with the recently established Ethiopian Institute for Higher Education in order to enhance the capacities of women in lower, middle and higher academic positions. These developments are indicative of positive changes aimed at promoting gender equality within the higher education sector. The ministry's capacity-building efforts are also in line with government plans, although they still fall short of ESDP V's plan to establish a "female talent cultivation centre" to inspire and support women to participate and succeed in leadership and management at all levels.

3 Sustainability

Furthermore, while national and institutional efforts are encouraging, more needs to be done to produce the desired results and ensure the sustainability of initiatives through continuous follow-up, coordination and support. In addition to closely evaluating their contribution to the achievement of broader goals the Ministry of Science and Higher Education needs to examine its success against specific targets set at national and institutional levels. For instance, the fact that the ministry's plan in terms of the number of female teaching staff, and female enrolment in HEIs, both at undergraduate and graduate level, are behind national targets set in ESDP V should be a source of concern.

One of the regulations in the Higher Education Proclamation against which HEIs' strategic plans are measured is the level of assistance institutions provide to disadvantaged sections of their student community, and their ability to meet social goals such as increasing the proportion of women in senior positions (FDRE, 2019). In addition to monitoring institutions' performance, the ministry should consider mechanisms to recognize those that are responding positively to the task of promoting gender equity. The limited representation of women both as students, and as leaders at the lower levels, should also be a focus for the ministry because it is from these cohorts that future leaders will be recruited.

Last but not least, studies should be conducted on the experiences of past and current women leaders in order to learn more about their challenges and success stories. Understanding the journey of Ethiopian women leaders into leadership roles can help identify the factors that contribute to improved female representation in leadership positions, and the most effective strategies to enhance their promotion. In addition to encouraging gender diversity across institutions, such efforts will assist in moving the needle towards more balanced leadership in the system.

CHAPTER 7

Perpetuating Inequity Despite Higher Education Expansion

An earlier version of this chapter appeared in *Inside Higher Education*, 17 July 2018, https://www.insidehighered.com/blogs/world-view/perpetuating-inequity-despite-higher-education-expansion

Despite encouraging strides in the expansion of higher education across the globe, the challenge of equity is far from being addressed. Disparities in access and opportunities among students from different economic backgrounds remain of major concern. Against the claim of being an equalizer, higher education is blamed for perpetuating inequity and not serving as a channel to equal opportunity and social mobility. Drawing a clear distinction between participation and equity is thus important when assessing the impact of higher education expansion. Celebrating changes in the participation of a given group may not always speak to the success of mediating equity challenges that are more complex than they appear. In many sub-Saharan African countries, students from households in the highest income quintiles continue to dominate tertiary enrollment. Ethiopia is no exception in this regard.

Discussions on equity in higher education mainly focus on four target groups: females, individuals from lower income groups, individuals from groups with a minority status defined on the basis of their ethnic, linguistic, religious, etc. background, and people with disabilities. Strategies to address equitable access in Ethiopia have mainly concentrated on increasing the number of public institutions distributed across the country, the establishment of private institutions, rapid increases in student intake, and a gradual increase in female participation. A variety of strategies to address the different dimensions of inequity have also been initiated, from special admission requirements for disadvantaged groups to providing various forms of student support at individual HEIs. While the achievements thus far appear to address some equity goals, challenges persist. The system's continued failure to address equity related to students' socioeconomic background is one such challenge.

1 Public Spending and Beneficiaries

Total expenditure on education in Ethiopia is in the range of 4–4.5% of annual GDP. Higher education receives more than 40% of the total budget allocated for education. Recurrent public expenditure per student is reported as 557 ETB (~USD 20) at the primary level, 1,398 ETB (~USD 50) at the secondary level, and 14,493 ETB (~USD 518) at the level of higher education.

The system is vastly subsidized by the government, especially at the lower levels of education. The only exception is a cost sharing scheme for students attending public universities. According to the Higher Education Cost Sharing Regulation (FDRE, 2003), graduates from Ethiopia's public universities are obliged to repay the full cost of board and lodging, and a minimum of 15% of tuition related costs in the form of a graduate tax. The wealthiest households benefit more from the government subsidized system than the poorest households. The Ethiopia Welfare Monitoring Survey (2016), Ethiopia Public Expenditure Review (2016) and related studies found that the benefit they obtain increases with an increase in grade levels.

Data obtained from the aforementioned sources reveal that children from the poorest and wealthiest income quintiles are equally represented in the first cycle of primary education – 19% of children in Grades 1-4 are from the poorest 20% of the population. However, 20% of the poorest households comprise only 15% of the student population in the second cycle of primary education (Grades 5–8). This group is overwhelmingly sidelined as it moves higher up the educational ladder. The wealthiest households account for 87% of student participation at the level of Technical and Vocational Education and Training (TVET) and 82% in higher education. While the poorest represent 1% of the student population in TVET, in higher education, they comprise 2% of the student population. Related findings further indicate that the proportion of students from the highest income quintile over the proportion of students from the lowest quintile (known as the disparity ratio) in Ethiopia is one of the highest in sub-Saharan Africa.

On-going disparity between the poor and the wealthy is explained in large part by poor attendance/transition and completion rates. For instance, children from the highest income quintile have a threefold higher probability of entering the second cycle primary (Grades 5-8) by age 11 than those from the poorest income quintile. Those from the poorest quintile have the lowest completion rate at postsecondary level due to challenges they face in their academic progress.

The expenditure patterns in the system also favor the wealthiest households. Data from Ethiopia Welfare Monitoring Survey (2016) and Ethiopia Household

Income, Consumption and Expenditure Survey (2005) indicate that the poorest contribute more to education financing than they benefit from it.

2   Towards Addressing Inequity

Counteracting existing inequities will not be simple. Responding to the complex realities behind equity challenges is not easy, especially in the context of a young, rapidly 'massifying', and under-resourced system. However, a range of measures could be deployed to bridge existing gaps. The experience of countries in East Europe and Central Asia that have been relatively successful in tackling similar challenges is worth emulating. Addressing various dimensions of inequity should begin with what is often known as 'equity mindedness'. Promotion of policies and practices that facilitate better access to and completion rates of disadvantaged groups from the lower levels upwards should be given increased attention. Equal consideration should be given to the quality of education offered to students from such backgrounds. Mechanisms by which the rich contribute more to the education of their children should also be explored. This could extend to the arduous task of addressing the structural determinants of inequity across society. Since these goals cannot be achieved overnight, long-term planning, allocating the necessary resources and concerted follow-up and improvement of the system will be necessary to address existing inequity in the various strata of the education sector.

PART 2

HE Governance and Management

CHAPTER 8

Government-University Relations
A Troubled Marriage

An earlier version of this chapter appeared in *University World News, Global Edition*, 12 October 2018 (with Damtew Teferra), https://www.universityworldnews.com/post.php?story=20181009144147891

In 2018, Ethiopia unveiled a draft education roadmap to provide strategic direction for the next 15 years following the end of its 20-year Education Sector Development Program in 2020. The roadmap covers the entire education sector, including higher education. Government-university relations – as an umbrella theme incorporating elements of academic freedom, autonomy and accountability – appear to have been overlooked in the roadmap, although issues of autonomy are marginally noted. We argue that a strong, vibrant and competitive higher education system cannot thrive without the cultivation of healthy government-university relationships.

Successive governments in Ethiopia have been at loggerheads with academia, which has seriously impeded the emergence of effective, robust and dynamic institutions that are critical to development. Although government-university relations have been precarious since the founding of the first University College of Addis Ababa in 1950, they were substantially eroded over the past four decades subsequent to the military takeover in 1974.

The remarkable transformation of the higher education sector following the defeat of the Dergue (the Provisional Military Government of Socialist Ethiopia) in the 1990s has not brought about the requisite adjustment in the relationship. In a stunning move, the incumbents summarily fired more than 40 senior academics and professors from Addis Ababa University not long after assuming power, shattering promises and expectations, while setting unsettling tone for the future. Ethiopian HEIs continue to be the subject of unfettered political and administrative interference, beyond the expected norms of such engagements. This calls for a clear definition of government relations with universities and institutionalized mechanisms for practice and compliance.

1 The Status Quo

In Ethiopia, the government plays a dominant role and wields unlimited power in HEIs, mainly through legislation and resource allocation. Limited research and substantial anecdotal evidence indicate a serious lack of freedom to critique government policies, establish and participate in independent student-teacher associations and openly criticize institutional policies and practices. Although universities are established as autonomous institutions by law, their policies and priorities are excessively influenced by the wishes and wide-ranging whims of the government. Higher education institutions have a very limited scope in resisting direct external interference; an example is the presence of armed and plainclothes security forces operating on their premises and/or intervening in their internal administrative and management affairs.

Internally, staff representation on governing bodies, their participation in internal policy-making processes and their contribution to major policy dialogues have been dismal. Admittedly, the threat to institutional autonomy in some institutions emanates from the lack of capacity to exercise powers enshrined in legislative frameworks such as the Higher Education Proclamation (FDRE, 2009). The overall trend has, however, been the overbearing influence of the government, which is commonly described in the literature as a state-controlled system.

Over the past decade, mandatory mechanisms to account to government have multiplied. The Higher Education Proclamation of 2009 dictates various forms and tools of accountability – such as financial management, financial audit, strategic plan agreement, reporting and supervision, self-evaluation, academic audit and accreditation – yet Ethiopian universities continue to be poorly rated in terms of transparency, financial management, effective public communication, commitment to excellence, transparent and open accounting, and efficient use of resources. This is attributed to low levels of compliance and enforcement, in contrast to excessive scrutiny of matters pertaining to academic freedom and institutional autonomy.

2 Effects and Challenges

The steep decline in academic freedom and autonomy in Ethiopian HEIs has had deleterious manifestations. As noted above, professors were fired for exercising academic freedom and expressing political views. Until recently, wider anti-government movements, student protests, class boycotts, campus takeovers by security forces and brutal crackdowns on protesters have been common. The government has frequently been accused of direct and wide-ranging interference in academic and administrative matters, conducting surveillance, propping up favorable political orientations, recruiting party members and sowing divisive views. These have resulted in apathy, silence, self-censorship and fear across virtually all universities.

The decline in faculty influence in institutional governance has further led to poor motivation and engagement in the most important tasks of institutional development and national dialogue. The yawning gap between legal and legislative pronouncements and actual practices has been another stark reality. The concepts of academic freedom and autonomy will remain elusive as long as they continue to be the mere pronouncements of lofty declarations, without regard to their practice by institutions and academics. The lack of translation of intention into real practice as a result of negligence, lack of capacity and state interference points to a nagging mismatch between the two. This has harmful implications for the rule of law and realization of the aspirations of institutions and the academic community.

Although the government receives the lion's share of blame for the gradual deterioration of its engagements with universities, the university community may be partially culpable for obfuscating the complex interplay between academic freedom, autonomy and accountability. Over the years, the government has erroneously viewed the university as an integral part of its political system and one of its appendages. In contrast, the academic community has largely considered the university a fully independent entity that determined its own fate, without the tutelage of the government. There is need to reconcile these divergent views, which often co-exist in perennial tension.

3   Where to From Here?

A new dawn of hope has broken in Ethiopia in the sphere of politics, governance and admission of guilt since the new prime minister, Dr. Abiy Ahmed, assumed power. In addition to opening up the political space, his government has been trying to redefine its relations and interactions with a host of institutions that include academic, religious, civic and business organizations.

The historical coincidence of the unveiling of the draft education roadmap (2018) and the renewed spirit in the country offers a rare opportunity to redefine relations between the government and universities. This must be used to build strong and viable institutions to encourage not only the embodiment of a new institutional culture, but enhancement of the country's ambition to emerge as an economic powerhouse and knowledge hub in the sub-region and beyond. Indeed, a system that chooses to silence its powerhouses of knowledge and disenfranchise its university community may find it immensely difficult to achieve its national development goals. Given that critical role played by universities in the development endeavor, the government should respect their academic freedom and institutional autonomy. The open apology extended by Abiy to academics who were dismissed without due process may be regarded as a good – and encouraging – start.

4   Putting Mechanisms in Place

In view of the critical role that higher education plays and the huge government resources allocated to it, it is imperative to put in place effective mechanisms that guarantee external accountability without stifling autonomy. In particular, a healthy balance between university autonomy and accountability must be created so as to provide the requisite assurance to the government on the proper utilization of public resources, while reminding the university community of the exigencies of accountability in discharging their responsibilities. We cannot anticipate a better opportunity to chart these ideals and the practical components of a viable higher education system, than the new education roadmap (MoE, 2018) under consideration.

CHAPTER 9

The Shifting Sands of University Management in Ethiopia

An earlier version of this chapter appeared in *Inside Higher Education*, 22 October 2017 (with Damtew Teferra), https://www.insidehighered.com/blogs/world-view/shifting-sands-university-management-ethiopia

Dictated by the unprecedented demands of massification and other shifting trends, HEIs are under constant pressure to implement new management modalities. These developments have, however, created tensions between the traditional models of collegial governance and new managerial leanings. In this article, we examine how Ethiopia navigated this exercise in light of the phenomenal growth of its higher education sector.

Ethiopia has entertained a number of university reforms that involved, among others, the redesign of policies, systems, and organizational structures. Key among these was the reform of the management modalities in the public higher education sector – a shift that has drawn significant research attention. Research on the universities of Addis Ababa, Aksum, Haramaya, Jimma and Mekele (all, except Aksum, belonging to the old group of universities), focuses on the processes, challenges and outcomes of a variety of public management tools employed to steer university reforms. We draw on the findings of these studies to examine the nature of the reforms.

1 Rationales for University Reforms

When the Ethiopian higher education sector identified broader access as one of its major goals, the need for university reform was unequivocally established. If institutions were to respond to evolving external demands, it was necessary to change the manner in which they were structured, governed and managed. Since the end of the 1990s, new policy directions have been set by the government and aggressively pursued. However, given the very nature of universities – widely recognized as change averse – the choices were not that simple.

Ethiopian universities have embraced national reforms introduced within the civil service. The first in 1997, took the form of Civil Service Reform Program (CSRP), in line with the changes from a centralized to a free market economy.

Regarded as part of the civil service, universities were required to implement reforms to respond to the new demands of the sector. Although this was the first far-reaching step in questioning how traditional public universities were led, the inclination to use earlier CSR tools, like strategic planning, did not last long. Another modality came into being in 2006 in the shape of Business Process Reengineering (BPR) – in keeping with the spirit of new public management theory whose influence was on the rise. Introduced with new vigor, BPR caused huge upheaval across the country, once again generating the exigency of transforming public organizations, including universities. It has been in decline since 2008, giving way to what is called the Business Score Card (BSC), Kaizen, and currently "deliverology" – an emerging business management approach used to manage, monitor and implement reform initiatives. Although these changes are presumably driven by the desire to improve efficiency, accountability and performance at all levels of the civil service, including higher education, the significance of this wave of management reforms remains elusive, and at times messy; hence, the need for closer scrutiny.

2 The Lessons of Experience

Some changes have elevated the autonomy of academic units within universities, especially in the areas of financial, human and physical resource management. Another achievement has been the shift from collegial management to that based on the college, institute and school. Research on these reforms, however, demonstrates meager success. Even changes observed in terms of restructuring the work process and academic units seem to be merely symbolic compliance with government demands. Changes so far seem to be reflective of superficial rather than functional gains, effected for the purposes of attaining legitimacy and resource acquisition from the government.

Reasons abound for the derailment of the reform process. Reforms have invariably been initiated from outside and followed a top-down approach with limited room for customization, resulting in glaring gaps in understanding the context and culture of individual institutions. The new management tools fell short in aligning with the values, norms, practices and policies of universities and their academic units. They also lacked integration with the other interventions imposed on the sector. Further challenges included the poor composition and turnover of reform teams; inconsistent and limited support from leadership; the lack of an incentive system; inadequate performance measurements; poor communication on the essence of the reform; and reports to outsiders that masked the actual progress of implementation. Other challenges pertain to a lack of enthusiasm punctuated by frustration over paltry business process outcomes; poor utilization of information technology; lack of strategic leadership at all levels; undue influence by the authorities; a lack of in-depth understanding of the innovation process among leaders and staff; the lack of team spirit and shared understanding of the implementation process; aversion to risk taking with a lack of flexibility; and the obvious tension between the traditional and new institutional cultures.

The reform initiatives had many drawbacks. Among these were the external imposition of change for the presumed sake of efficiency and effectiveness, and the pressure on university leadership to maintain the right balance between the values and norms of academia and mediate prevailing negative perceptions. These were further compounded by the formation of a hierarchical governance structure with power concentrated at the top and the sidelining of the internal stakeholders, particularly academics, who should have been key champions for success.

3 The Virtues of Inexperience

The ideological and pragmatic changes leading to the unprecedented growth of Ethiopian higher education have subjected the sector to a multitude of challenges. Chief among them has been the reform of university management. Available data suggest that the huge resources, time and energy spent on country-wide reforms have fallen far short of the anticipated results. The imperative of learning from past weaknesses while consolidating gains made prior to moving further in the same direction remain paramount.

The government is currently pushing "deliverology" as the newest management tool for the higher education sector. The blanket imposition of this new trend on universities, and enclaves of "organized anarchy" that tend to be averse to business-orientated models for higher learning management, may trigger new challenges. Before vigorously pursuing "deliverology", as the latest effort to improve efficiency, the Ethiopian government may first need to seriously and systematically analyze the fitness of the new tool for application to the academic sector. Ethiopian social, cultural, economic, infrastructural, and political realities ought to be taken into account prior to the deployment of any new management models. While the lessons of experience imply learning from the past, the virtues of inexperience potentially unleash curiosity about new possibilities in the present and into the future. It is hoped that the virtues of experience and curiosity might both be deployed prior to imposing new management approaches on the universities.

CHAPTER 10

Do Students Have a Say in University Governance?

An earlier version of this chapter appeared in *University World News, Africa Edition*, 4 May 2018, https://www.universityworldnews.com/post.php?story=20180501094l0779

One of the principles of good governance in higher education is the concept of shared governance or distributed leadership. This requires the representation of various stakeholders, including students, in universities' decision-making processes. Compared with the representation of faculty and administrators, student representation fails to receive the required attention in higher education governance, both in theory and practice.

It can be argued that student participation in university governance has a variety of advantages that can extend to the individual student, the institution and society at large. Involving students in university governance is considered to be instrumental in the creation of improved trust and understanding in the university community. Conversely, its lack could result in student unrest and apathy. Those who consider universities 'sites of democratic citizenship' and platforms to develop the individual student argue in favor of encouraging students' participation in the decision-making process in order to develop democratic values and a sense of democratic citizenship.

Students' personal growth is also considered to be a result of this engagement and the practical learning that comes with it. For those who view students as consumers or clients, it follows that students should be given some place in the administration as they can be affected by what goes on in the institution. From the point of view of students themselves, their motivation for engaging in university decision-making may be dictated by factors such as the chance to improve university governance, to gain experience, and the desire to serve other students. Universities' conception of and adherence to any of the above principles can eventually determine the type of student participation that might be encouraged within their governance systems.

1   Resistance and Lip-Service

Student participation in university governance has become a universal trend. However, demands for such participation continue to be met with various forms of resistance ranging from ambivalence to outright rejection. While there are genuine efforts by many institutions to promote student participation, levels of resistance and lip service to the concept abound in many others. Those who wish to discourage student participation usually put forward arguments such as students' lack of sufficient knowledge (student incompetence), inexperience, apathy, transience or the need to exclude students from sensitive decision-making and the need for confidentiality.

Some institutions permit student participation not out of a genuine acceptance of the need for student involvement but out of concern to remain politically correct. In this case, student participation may be limited to advisory roles rather than decision-making functions. Students are thus involved in consultation rather than partnership. The way in which students exercise their rights is critical and revolves around questions about what kind of representation they have, what type of decisions they are part of, how meaningful their participation is, and whether their rights are legislated by law.

2   Legislative Frameworks

Ethiopia's Higher Education Proclamation (FDRE, 2009) makes no provision for students to participate at the level of university boards. The board has seven members, excluding students. Below board level, the president of a university is expected to ensure that the institution's academic community (including students) is appropriately represented. With regard to current forms of involvement, the Higher Education Proclamation (2009/2019) dictates that student representation should be exercised through student unions established to promote and protect students' common interests.

A review of university legislation and a variety of quality audit reports generated by Ethiopia's Higher Education Relevance and Quality Agency, reveals that Ethiopian university students are currently represented at the level of the senate, faculty academic commissions, and ad hoc and standing committees such as the academic standards and curriculum review committee, food committee, discipline committee and other committees – although the precise focus of the committee and student representation on it may differ from university to university.

While participation at senate level is achieved through two representatives, student involvement at the level of the faculty academic commission is in most cases restricted to a single representative. Surprisingly, student representation at the department level, where students would be expected to make contributions and where there is a corresponding high level of expectations on the part of students themselves, is literally non-existent.

A significant number of students feel that the governance and administrative system of Ethiopian universities is not sufficiently democratic and participatory. They contend that existing systems are mainly dictated by the interests of the administration and faculty – to the detriment of students. Where representation is granted, students are numerically outnumbered. Students complain that even where they are fairly represented they are not always able to table their own agendas, which suggests that student affairs are of relatively low importance. Students find it particularly challenging that matters of direct concern to them are rarely discussed in appropriate fora.

The reports of the Higher Education Relevance and Quality Agency also suggests that, with very few exceptions, student participation – where it exists – is predominantly passive. While student representation can theoretically provide students with a say on many matters that concern them, students report that committee membership does not necessarily ensure them an opportunity to influence decision-making. In addition to being a minority on committees, they feel that there is no guarantee that even reasonable requests by students will be decided in their favor. This implies that current participatory arrangements may not always be sufficient for genuine student participation unless there are efforts to ensure their relevance to student interests.

3   The Way Forward

Genuine student participation in university governance is still a long way from receiving the attention it deserves in the Ethiopian higher education sector. I suggest that changes should focus on creating the necessary alignment between legislation and policies, and actual practices; promoting more student representation in governance structures; improving existing attitudes towards student representation; improving the quality of student participation; and stepping up the assistance provided to students to realize their ambitions. Since the type and quality of participation are important components of the improvement scheme, the overall emphasis should shift from a consultative version of student participation to more active participation that allows enough space for student concerns and issues to be freely aired and properly addressed.

CHAPTER 11

University Boards

Visibility, Efficiency and Accountability

An earlier version of this chapter appeared in *University World News, Africa Edition*, 17 May 2019, https://www.universityworldnews.com/post.php?story=20190515184852404

University boards serve as key agents of higher education governance in many countries, including Ethiopia, and are frequently conceived of as a buffer between the state and HEIs. The largest role in external governance of the higher education sector in Ethiopia is played by the Ministry of Education, now the Ministry of Science and Higher Education. The various strategic roles and functions of the ministry outlined in the Higher Education Proclamation (FDRE, 2009/2019) ensure the implementation of national policy and strategy on higher education, the determination and issuance of standards, approval and implementation of the strategic plans of public institutions, and facilitation of coordination among universities and other external entities. Internal governance of universities, on the other hand, is entrusted to governing and advisory bodies, academic units, administrative and technical support units, and other relevant offices (FDRE, 2009/2019).

In Ethiopia, university boards have served as a key component of higher education governance for decades and appear to be situated somewhere between the ministry and the internal governance structures of the university. The university board is currently designated "the supreme governing body of the institution" with a plethora of responsibilities from monitoring to supervising the overall operations of the university (FDRE, 2009/2019). Despite their importance in the achievement of effective and transparent university governance, boards seem to be the least reformed, researched and accountable of all university structures.

1 Historical Precedents

Strikingly, boards set up during the past six decades under three different governments bear close resemblance to one another, both in terms of the number of members and their composition. When the University College of Addis

Ababa (UCAA), the first institution of higher learning in the country, was established in 1950 the board of governors consisted of six members appointed by the emperor and the UCAA president. The only exception was an elected student representative who was supposed to join the board as an additional member when the growing alumni body numbered 200. The first board members were recruited from the ministries of justice, defense, education, and foreign affairs. The board of the Haile Selassie I University (formerly UCAA, and currently Addis Ababa University), established in 1961, assumed all the powers vested in the UCAA board but membership was augmented to eight members, three of whom were drawn from the ministries of education, agriculture and public health.

When the Dergue assumed power in 1974, a Higher Education Commission with a higher education council took over most of the responsibilities previously assigned to the university board. The members of the higher education council, which was chaired by the education minister, were the ministers of health, agriculture and settlement, industry, and the commissioners of planning, science and technology, as well as five persons appointed by the government.

After the new government assumed power in 1991, the Higher Education Proclamation (FDRE, 2003) reinstituted the board with similar powers as in the past. However, the power to designate the chairperson for the board was assigned to the Ministry of Education. The proclamation did not specify the members of the board, stating only that "representatives from the Regional Government, representatives of the beneficiaries of the products and services of the institution, notable personalities as well as members from the management organs of the public institution" (Article 36.2) would be appointed. The second/third Higher Education Proclamation (2009/2019) did not introduce any fundamental changes to the way in which university boards were composed.

2   Government Influence

The board is accountable to the ministry and is composed of seven voting members. In addition to the virtual lack of representation from internal stakeholders, the board is heavily dominated by government officials with little room for other external stakeholders. Many view the representation of government officials as useful for facilitating institutional success through access to enhanced government and community support, resources and influence. Such heavy government representation is despite the promise in the legislation that members will be selected for their "exceptional knowledge, experience and commitment that enable them to contribute to the attainment of the mission of the institution and the objectives of higher education" (HEP, 2009/2019).

The chair of the board and three voting members are appointed by the minister. The remaining three are nominated by the university president in consultation with the University Council and the Senate, but still they need to be approved by the minister. The ministry has full authority to reform and change the board (FDRE, 2019, Article 49.5) whenever it deems it necessary.

3 Deficiencies

Although the composition of boards is expected to be based on merit and gender equity, most boards are still dominated by men. University boards have been criticized for lack of clarity of purpose, micro-management, poor understanding of their role, misunderstanding of the unique nature of the university, and in some cases having limited capacity to meet obligations. These deficiencies are partly influenced by the nomination process which does not necessarily consider the personal qualities, professional attributes and commitment of members. They are further compounded by a lack of effort to fill gaps in awareness and training.

A discussion paper prepared by the Ministry of Education as an input to the Ethiopian Education Development Roadmap (2018) notes that many university boards' performance leaves much to be desired. It highlights the lack of communication between board members and the university community and indicates that most boards are weak in developing their own work plans and following up on university operations and strategic matters. The level of leadership provided by boards to solve institutional problems is in most cases, meager or non-existent. The lack of comprehensive and timely follow-up by boards is known to have further exacerbated problems. Specific institutional matters such as program expansion, research strategy and university-industry relations at times run contrary to government plans when boards fail to provide the necessary direction and follow-up.

4 The Need for Reform

While the benefits of a board are not in contention, in their current form most university boards in Ethiopia are far from meeting many of the expectations of internal and external stakeholders. It is high time the sector looks at reforming existing boards in order to shore up their capacities, combat their deficiencies, and create a vibrant, knowledgeable and informed body that can lend assistance and direction to the fledgling higher education sector where governance continues to be a critical factor for success. Areas of improvement may include broadening membership of the board, improving the quality and capacity of its members, establishing clear lines of accountability and, importantly, creating sufficient distance between the ministry and the board so as to strengthen the intermediary role it can play between the interests of the government and those of universities.

CHAPTER 12

Towards More Achievable University Vision Statements

An earlier version of this chapter appeared in *University World News, Africa Edition*, 6 April 2018, https://www.universityworldnews.com/post.php?story=20180403140626471

Overly ambitious and unrealistic vision statements will not be able to move Ethiopian universities higher up the regional and international ranking ladders. Instead, universities might be better off focusing more seriously on what they can achieve locally. A vision statement is a concise description of where an organization aspires to go or what it wants to achieve. Vision statements reflect institutional priorities or promises articulated in the form of a 'vision' concerning a future desired state. As descriptive statements of what awaits an organization when it has completed a certain stage of its journey, vision statements should be distinguished from slogans or wishful thinking.

Ethiopia is currently home to 51 fully-fledged public universities and nearly 300 PHEIs which cater for the higher education needs of nearly a million students. The system accommodates more than 40,000 teachers. As is the practice elsewhere, Ethiopian HEIs customarily craft vision statements that are designed to guide their current engagements and future aspirations. These statements are widely communicated in their publications and on their websites. Some aspirations are quite specific. Among the first-generation universities in the country, Addis Ababa and Bahir Dar universities aspire to be among the top 10 universities in Africa, while Mekelle University wants to be among the top 25. Haramaya and Jimma universities seek, more generally, to be among the premier universities in the region, but do not stipulate a specific ranking. The more cautious Hawassa University aims to be "competent in the region" – although what that means is not clear. Arba Minch University has set its sights on becoming a center of excellence in water technology, a relatively focused vision. Some universities have timeframes to achieve their visions. A quick glance reveals that this currently extends from 2017–18 to 2025. While three out of nine institutions aspire to meet their visions by 2020, one intends to do so by 2023, and the remaining five have chosen 2025 as their target year. At this juncture it is important to explore how much the facts on the ground differ from or coincide with the vision statements.

1   Regional Performance

A comparison of the aspirations of Ethiopian universities against regional rankings offers a plethora of interesting findings. According to the Ranking Web of Universities (July 2017), no Ethiopian university made it to the top 20, despite their desires. The African ranking list is overwhelmingly dominated by South Africa, which has 12 institutions among the top 23. Egypt follows with three institutions, while Nigeria, Kenya and Uganda have one each. No Ethiopian university comes close to the rankings they desire. Furthermore, the chances of improving their current positions appear to be extremely remote given the limited number of years to achieve the target and the gap between where the universities are and where they aspire to be. Addis Ababa University, the country's flagship university, which aims to become one of Africa's top 10, is way behind its aspirations. The rest are similarly far from achieving their goals.

2   Global Performance

Five out of the nine Ethiopian universities have set their goals at a global level, aiming to garner an international reputation. This is despite the fact that the performance of African universities is dismal when it comes to global rankings. The number of African universities that make it to the global charts of the QS World University Rankings (2018) did not exceed 20 and most of these institutions were again from South Africa and Egypt. While South Africa dominates with 11, Egypt has three universities on the list. Morocco, Kenya, Ghana and Uganda each have one university among the top 1,000 institutions in the world. None of the Ethiopian universities appear on the list of first 1,000 institutions. Even in the African rankings, only four of Ethiopia's universities make it into the top 400. The results from the Times Higher Education World University Rankings (2018) do not show a substantially different pattern.

Global rankings are a source of perennial interest and contention across the globe. Universities in the developing world, including those in Africa, complain about being left out due to the combination of criteria used by the rankings systems which do not accurately reflect their nature and contributions. It can be argued that HEIs in developing countries should explore some of the options they have to excel and make a positive impact at a local level rather than aspiring to achieve what is unachievable from the start.

3   Local Goals and Aspirations

Since their inception, African universities have been viewed as institutions of national pride and have played a significant role in fostering national development through the cultivation of a skilled workforce. This lofty goal is usually expressed in government policies and regulations but continues to be sidelined or under-emphasized when it comes to the vision statements of Africa's universities. In the Ethiopian context the Higher Education Proclamation (FDRE, 2009) and the government's Education Sector Development Programs justify the continued expansion of the public sector by emphasizing universities' role in local development. The Ministry of Education has also introduced its own mechanisms to compare and recognize public universities on the basis of their performance and in terms of the strategic plan they themselves devise. Despite these clear directions, local goals and aspirations appear to be under-emphasized by local institutions when compared with regional or international aspirations.

While the ambitions of many of the Ethiopian universities' vision statements need to be acknowledged, the fact that they are not tempered by reality will dent their credibility. Despite ongoing competition for better slots on the global charts, institutions in the developing world have choices with regard to their aims and would do well to consider the importance of local goals and aspirations when it comes to setting visions, particularly in their early stages of development.

CHAPTER 13

What Next for a Partially Differentiated Higher Education System?

An earlier version of this chapter appeared in *University World News, Africa Edition*, 1 October 2020, https://www.universityworldnews.com/post.php?story=20200929080901365

Steps taken towards the establishment of a differentiated higher education system in Ethiopia should be seen as a major achievement. However, successful implementation of such a system requires much more than identifying institutions in terms of new institutional categories. Triggered by a variety of academic and non-academic factors, the differentiation of the Ethiopian higher education system has been one of the major operational areas with which the Ministry of Science and Higher Education (MoSHE) has been preoccupied in the past two years. A study commissioned by the ministry (2020) on differentiating the higher education system has been published, leading to the classification of Ethiopian universities into three groups. While this is a welcome development, the differentiation process appears to be incomplete and requires further consideration to address gaps and possible implementation challenges.

1   Rationale

From only two universities at the end of the 1990s, Ethiopia established 51 public universities and over 300 PHEIs in less than two decades. Corresponding changes in capacity have enabled the system to accommodate nearly a million students, from only tens of thousands in the 1990s. Despite these changes, Ethiopia's new public universities have been widely accused of being replicas of the oldest universities in terms of structure, focus and even program offerings. Besides questioning its rationale, excessive homogeneity within the system has become a source of concern due to its failure to create a more responsive and competitive system that promotes excellence and value for money.

2 The Process and Outcome

The differentiation scheme approved is an outcome of a study commissioned by MoSHE. The study was conducted by Ethiopian scholars drawn from the various universities and the Higher Education Strategy Center. It generated a huge set of data to determine the type of differentiation scheme to be introduced within the higher education system. The process included examining the current system, studying 43 public institutions, and drawing experiences from both the developing and developed world. While primary data were collected from these sources through the field-based administration of questionnaires, secondary data were drawn from an extensive desk review. International visits were used to draw on experiences from countries where similar systems exist. Public consultative workshops were held with a wide range of stakeholders comprising university presidents, members of university change councils, teachers, academic staff, student representatives, state ministers of education, and university communities. The final output is a classification model with specific criteria to categorize universities on the basis of their current status and future potential. A three-category differentiation system that comprises research universities, universities of applied sciences and comprehensive universities was conceived.

According to the proposed scheme, research universities are those that undertake research and teaching with a special focus on program offerings at postgraduate level. Their teaching staff is supposed to comprise at least 50% PhD holders with annual publications in reputable journals. While educational facilities commensurate with their teaching and research missions are expected to be available, at least 5% of research universities' annual budget is to be allocated to research. These institutions are expected to establish strong academic and research collaborations with local, regional and international partners and to build high level research centers and facilities. Eight universities, almost all of which are first generation universities in Ethiopia, have been assigned to this group.

The second category, universities of applied sciences, are supposed to offer professional, practice-oriented teaching in varied programs, forge strong linkages and engage in collaborative applied research with industry and business. The staff profile of universities of applied sciences is expected to constitute 20% or more PhDs, with at least 5% having industry and/or business experience. These universities are primarily expected to align their curricula with the job market, and collaborate closely and establish strong linkages with the world of work. They are also expected to promote a 'culture of innovation', by dedicating at least 30% of their facilities to innovation-related tasks. Fifteen universities that are assumed to fulfil these criteria have been classified as universities of applied science.

The third type of universities, comprehensive universities, are expected to undertake teaching and research in equal proportions with a greater focus on teaching. They are expected to offer multi-disciplinary programs. Eighty percent of students at comprehensive universities are expected to be enrolled at undergraduate level and at least 3% of the university budget is to be allocated for research. A total of 21 universities fulfilling these criteria have been assigned to this group.

3   Missing Elements

The differentiation document itself admits that there are some limitations to the proposed scheme. It is clear that what has been created is a partial system that requires further work and refinement in order to be considered a fully-fledged national framework. To begin with, there are institutions that were not part of the design of the differentiation model. These includes institutions such as Addis Ababa Science and Technology University and Adama Science and Technology University which were groomed to achieve a specialized function and status within the system long before the differentiation project was initiated. The same is true of teacher training colleges and private institutions of higher learning. Given the nature of the first two types of institutions, the differentiation scheme could have included a fourth category of 'specialized universities' which could have responded to existing gaps and handled similar needs in the future.

The initial focus on public universities has also excluded private institutions from the scheme but it is clear that this sector, which is responsible for nearly 17% national higher education enrolment, cannot be neglected in a fully-fledged national system that needs to accommodate the diverse features of all forms of institutions. There is limited information on how the lower education system should be aligned with the scheme proposed at the higher education level. The proposed differentiation scheme also lacks clarity on the articulation that should operate within the types of institutions created and the implications thereof.

4   Next Moves

The move towards the establishment of a differentiated higher education system in Ethiopia should be regarded as a major achievement of MoSHE, given long-standing demands and the need for such a framework. However, successful implementation of such a system requires much more than identifying institutions by their new categories. Among other things, it requires responding to the aforementioned and related gaps and making the necessary preparations for successful implementation of the proposed changes.

As recognized by the study team entrusted with this task, the implementation of the differentiation scheme needs to address the most important issues of policy support, structural changes and resource allocation. Among other things, the next phase demands that MoSHE galvanizes universities, their communities and relevant stakeholders towards achievement of the goals, responsibilities and specific functions crafted for the universities. Individual universities should also adjust their systems and structures in a manner that enables them to respond to their new or modified roles. Achieving such a huge and ambitious agenda requires clear, workable strategic and operational plans that should promote the accomplishment of the proposed scheme. It also demands rigorous follow-up and corresponding support until such time as the system begins to operate in the required way. Without such plans and concrete effort, the differentiation proposal which has attracted interest as a promising move will remain a change in name only.

PART 3

University Systems and Resources

CHAPTER 14

HE Financing Reforms

Intentions and Realities

An earlier version of this chapter appeared in *University World News, Africa Edition*, 25 July 2019, https://www.universityworldnews.com/post.php?story=20190715121430316

The Ethiopian higher education sector is growing in leaps and bounds due to the aggressive expansion scheme the government embarked upon in the past two decades. Among other achievements, this has created many new institutions and a sizeable student population that has reached nearly a million. With further expansion under way, Ethiopia is set to join the list of countries with the highest number of university students on the continent in the next half a decade. One of the challenges presented by a growing system is making available resources that can match the growth. Thus far, the major burden of financing the sector has been shouldered by the government with little assistance from foreign sources and internal income generation schemes that appear to be in their nascent stages. Government funding of the sector has, among other things, produced the required infrastructure for many of the new universities built from scratch. However, the amount of money dedicated to the sector has had little impact in delivering the envisaged quality of education. Higher education institutions continue to be blamed for churning out half-baked graduates who perform way below expectation and are shunned by the job market. The sustainability of a financial strategy that is fully dependent on the government has also been questioned in light of competing national developmental needs.

In response, government has sought to facilitate diversification of resources. For example, in addition to introducing a cost-sharing scheme within the public sector, HEIs have been encouraged to set up their own research and innovation funds, engage in consultancy and supplementary activities and establish income-generating enterprises. However, despite some encouraging moves, the limited financial autonomy accorded to Ethiopian public institutions has become a serious challenge that conspires against the success of any efforts along these lines.

1 Inflexible Policy

Currently, Ethiopian universities receive government budget allocations that are based on criteria such as student and staff numbers, programs and previous annual budgets. Once they receive their annual budget, they have to strictly follow the budget line allocations which are defined a priori. Moving one budget line to another when the need arises is near impossible, necessitating a lengthy and bureaucratic procedure which is discouraging for many institutions. Having experienced the various limitations of this inflexible policy, Ethiopian public universities have been calling for financial reform. The most promising initiative directed towards this end has been the block grant system that was promised in the Higher Education Proclamation of 2009. According to this scheme, HEIs would be given the right to adapt and allocate the funds they receive from the government on the basis of institutional objectives and particular needs. The proclamation stipulated that the block grant funding system will be based on a strategic plan agreement with the government. The agreements that individual institutions will have to establish with the Ministry of Education (now the Ministry of Science and Higher Education) take into account a variety of considerations, including:

- Strategic objectives, academic priorities, learning outputs, and institutional and human resources development;
- Planned research projects and programs;
- Study and diversity of programs and continuing, distance and virtual education;
- Number of students and number and qualifications of academic staff;
- Social goals such as increasing the proportion of senior positions held by women, and assistance to disadvantaged students;
- Indicative block-grant budget commitments made by the government and the institution's commitment to make up, through other sources of income, the financing gap that may occur;
- The indicative allocations of the block grant budget and the funds to be mobilized by the institution for each year of the strategic plan period;
- Contingency plan in the event of non-fulfilment of the anticipated strategic plan budget; and
- Appropriate mechanisms of accounting, monitoring, evaluation and reporting.

The greater flexibility the block funding would bring and the legislative objective of moving towards performance-related funding are considered to be critical in solving current budget challenges in the areas of teaching and learning, and research activities. This scheme is also considered to have the advantage of improving institutions' overall performance and efficiency. However, despite the fact that this innovative model has been in the air for more than a decade, it has not yet translated into practical action. A shift to the model requires sufficient capacity on the part of institutions in terms of financial and educational management which the law assumes they have. However, no such preparation seems to have been made thus far, which hints at the possibility of challenges in the future. The third Higher Education Proclamation of 2019 echoes the same plan and aims to promulgate a more flexible system in years to come. However, it still falls far short of addressing accompanying challenges that need to be addressed in reforming the financing of the sector.

2   Additional Challenges and Changes Needed

Although most universities have been augmenting their efforts to generate internal income, they do not yet have the right to spend such income as they see fit. The law requires that such money is spent on capital budget expenditures and only with the approval of the university board. Aside from discouraging universities to make additional efforts, this can limit their capacity to spend money on activities that have a direct impact on the quality of education provided and what the institutions consider to be important. While the current plan to move towards performance-oriented funding may be encouraging, the question is whether the system reform goes far enough to address the bottlenecks that can hinder planned changes.

How can universities be granted full autonomy to use their internally generated income within established schemes of accountability? What challenges are public institutions facing in running private companies and how can the system address this? Should the financial administration of universities continue to fall under the Ministry of Finance and Economic Development, which is the central government body that administers the budget of all government ministries and organizations, or should the system seek a better arrangement? Attempts to reform the financing of the higher education sector require not only that the issue of introducing a block grant system be addressed, but also responses to these and related areas of concern that universities are experiencing and wish to see improved.

CHAPTER 15

Challenges of Ensuring Quality Education

An earlier version of this chapter appeared in *University World News, Africa Edition*, 5 October 2018, https://www.universityworldnews.com/post.php?story=20181001111308979

Ethiopia is at the crossroads in terms of choosing between consolidating current higher education achievements – by moving its budget focus to academic activities that improve the quality of tertiary education – or continuing with the old model of expansion that created an impressive number of new universities, but failed to promote quality output.

The success of a higher education system is partly judged by the strength of its financing. In terms of budget allocation, the share of GDP allocated by a government to education and how this is divided among subsectors – primary, secondary and post-secondary – is commonly used to determine the extent of a country's financing commitment to its education sector. The budget allocation pattern within each subsector also relates to positive or negative changes to an education system. It therefore impacts on critical issues such as the quality of education.

1 Government Commitment

Unlike many developing countries where reliance on foreign sources is common, higher education financing in Ethiopia continues to be covered almost entirely by government, drawing just 0.02% of income from external sources. The expansion of Ethiopia's education system over the past two decades has mainly been attributed to the government's political and financial commitment. Although this has wavered at times, it is ongoing. Over the years, the total education budget – specifically for higher education – increased substantially. In 1991, education expenditure constituted 2.4% of the country's GDP and 9.4% of total government expenditure. From 2002–05 the figure rose to 6.1% and 17.5%, respectively. While Ethiopia now spends around 4.5% of its GDP on education – less than the sub-Saharan African average of 4.7% – in the past decade, education's share of education of the total annual budget has hovered around 20% and above. This is higher than the global average for low-income and developing countries. From 2005–06, 25% of the national education budget was dedicated to higher education. It rose to its current figure of 42%, with primary education receiving 46% of the budget. It could be expected that the amount dedicated to higher education should result in improved quality, but this has not been the case, and the sector continues to be blamed for a deteriorating quality of education. A possible answer to this conundrum resides in the spending patterns of the higher education budget.

2 Unchanging Spending Patterns

Despite Ethiopia's huge financial commitment to education, the higher education sector is dominated by capital spending. This trend, which has continued to grow since the sector was reformed at the end of the 1990s, appears to have negatively affected areas that impact provision of quality education. According to 2003 World Bank figures, in 1997, capital spending consumed 35% of the sector's budget. In 2003, the combined student welfare expenditure of Ethiopian universities was as much as 20% of recurrent budget (including student feeding, which took 15% of the budget). Forty percent of the overall recurrent university budgets, was allocated to salaries, 8% to services, 5% to maintenance, and 4% to grants, leaving just 10% for educational materials and 11% for other supplies. Fifteen years later, this spending pattern seems to have remained unchanged.

3 Growth in Capital Spending

The growth in the number of public universities from two at the end of the 1990s to the current 46 explains the increasing focus on capital investment, with capital spending in this sector growing from 35% in 1997 to nearly 75% from 2010–16. Seventy percent of capital expenditure is allocated to the construction of new universities around the country. A substantial investment by any means, this budget allocation dwarfs that of other subsectors. The current spending pattern in the recurring budget also reveals that more than half goes to food, housing subsidies and other administrative costs, which have no direct link to the quality of education. Nearly 40% of the recurrent budget is allocated to staff salaries. There is little evidence that this pattern will change significantly. For instance, the Education Sector Development Program V (2015–16 to 2019–20) aimed to increase the higher education gross enrolment ratio from 9.4% in 2014–15 to 15% by 2019–20, and to 22% by the end of 2025. This date is set down in Ethiopia's Growth and Transformation Plan for the country's attainment of middle-income status. This implies that any slowing down of the current expansion drive will be inconceivable in the next decade.

4   Different Approach Needed

Like any other developing country, the issue of higher education financing in Ethiopia is regarded as critical to the success of the sector. In 2003, the World Bank noted that Ethiopia's financing strategy would hold the key to succeeding in the major challenges of expansion and maintenance of quality while major reforms were being introduced to the sector. "If the bold vision contained in the new Higher Education Proclamation is to have any chance of success, the solution to this double challenge will have to be found in the financing strategy that underpins and supports these reforms", it said. With mounting national concern about the poor quality of higher education – and Prime Minister Abiy Ahmed repeatedly vowing to improve the situation – it is clear that the system cannot move forward with the continued use of old assumptions and models. Some commentators have suggested the need for a period of respite from unabated expansion in the sector that has dictated spending patterns over the past two decades. This, however, is unlikely, given the government's future plans.

5   Need to Augment the Higher Education Budget

Another suggestion is to augment the higher education budget allocation with an increase in public financing and/or budget trade-offs in favor of the education sector. Given the increasing strain on the system, the sector may not receive any meaningful increment in its current share or secure possible trade-offs with other sectors in its favor – at least in the short term. Although government encourages internal revenue generation by universities, this has not yet reached a level where it can supplement substantial fiscal deficiencies, notwithstanding the limited financial autonomy that public institutions have in spending available internal income on activities that contribute to improving the quality of education. While possible alternatives are reducing the pace of creating new public institutions, diversifying university income and improving their resource utilization, reconciling demands for access and quality will require the introduction of new modalities distinct from the brick-and-mortar university model that continues to consume a huge amount of the subsector's budget. Therefore, other options should be encouraged. These include distance and online education, expanding a specific segment of the private higher education (PHE) sector and other innovative modalities that allow the absorption of more students without the quality of education being compromised.

CHAPTER 16

Towards a Uniform System of Academic Promotion

An earlier version of this chapter appeared in *University World News, Africa Edition*, 12 March 2020, https://www.universityworldnews.com/post.php?story=20200311100448733

When Ethiopia's higher education system comprised only a handful of colleges and universities until the end of the 1990s, the process of academic promotion was relatively simple, requiring adherence to clearly defined institutional regulations that were mostly copied from the legislation of Addis Ababa University, the country's flagship university, and some guidance from the 2003 Higher Education Proclamation. However, the phenomenal growth of higher education over the past two decades and the commensurate growth in academic staff (now sitting at more than 40,000) have meant that the process is now much more complicated, requiring due diligence and some element of uniformity across the system.

Anecdotal evidence suggests that the process of academic promotion has steadily faltered over the past decade, becoming a target of criticism and allegations of unethical practices due to a variety of reasons. One of the reasons relates to the variety of promotion requirements prescribed by individual institutions. This has led to discrepancies in applying rules and regulations, especially at the lower levels of university administrations. The major criteria often considered for promotion in Ethiopian universities include length of service after a given academic rank, effectiveness in teaching and research, active participation in the affairs of the university, public service and publication numbers. While universities have shown limited discrepancies in many of these areas, variations have been noted, particularly with regard to publications, both in terms of the requirements set and the procedures followed.

While the requirements are stringent in some universities, they appear to be lax in others. For instance, the 2013 legislation of the Addis Ababa University stipulates that at least four publication points, earned by publishing five articles in reputable journal(s) since the last promotion, are sufficient to be considered for promotion to full professorship. The 2014 legislation of Bahir Dar University, on the other hand, requires the publication of 12 articles in reputable journal(s), while the University of Gondar and Hawassa University require the publication of four articles in reputable journal(s) since last promotion. It is not clear how individual institutions decided on these variations, especially when faculty moved from one university to another but it is likely that the lack of uniformity had an impact on academic and institutional recognition schemes.

Until 2009, promotion to all ranks of professorship required the approval of the university senate, which followed rigorous steps. However, things began to change after Ethiopia's second Higher Education Proclamation of 2009 delegated responsibility for granting the rank of associate professorship to the college or institution rather than the senate. As a result, while some institutions continue to be rigorous in their approach, others are criticized for offering quick promotions based on sub-standard work, including publications in unrecognized local journals and predatory journals published outside of Ethiopia. Promotions based on favoritism and various forms of corruption have also been raised as additional challenges.

In 2013, a harmonized academic policy was developed for all Ethiopian public HEIs. Its major purpose was to narrow the gaps between the academic promotion policies and practices of universities and reduce discrepancies within the sector. However, this does not appear to have worked as planned since the policy was neither strictly adhered to by universities, nor enforced by the Ministry of Science and Higher Education.

1 New Directive

A new directive issued by the Ministry of Science and Higher Education (Directive on Academic Publishing and Promotion, January 2020) could bridge this gap and respond to additional concerns raised in the promotion of academic staff across the sector. One of the most notable features of the new directive is its demand for both local and international recognition of published work. In addition to addressing previous deficiencies, this will hopefully help in laying the foundation to prevent unethical and illegal academic promotion. However, the directive also makes some changes to the status quo, which could be a source of genuine concern and controversy.

The values accorded to various types of publications is one potential source of discord. For example, the new directive appears to favor full-length journal articles as compared to a book, textbook or a book chapter, all of which were more favorably regarded in previous rating schemes. The new directive assigns a full-length journal article 100 points, a book 150 points, a textbook 100 points and a book chapter 25 points. This differs significantly from previous practice at most universities. For instance, the legislation of Addis Ababa University considers a book based on original research as equivalent to four articles (400 points) or two textbooks. The University of Gondar's 2013 legislation states that a book based on original research is regarded as equivalent to three journal articles (300 points) while a textbook is rated as equal to two journal published articles (200 points). In the same legislation a chapter in a book is given 30 points.

The rating proposed in the new directive appears to be controversial, not only because it seems to disregard the level of effort required to produce different kinds of products, but also because it does not seem to recognize the importance of outputs such as locally-produced books and textbooks. While the new directive from the Ministry of Science and Higher Education is long overdue and has the potential to positively influence the quality of publications coming out of the higher education sector, caution should be exercised to prevent it from having a negative impact on academics' productivity and the types of work they produce, some of which make a serious contribution to enhancing the teaching and learning process within Ethiopian universities. It is incumbent upon the Ministry of Science and Higher Education to offer stakeholders additional opportunities to improve the content of the new directive and to maximize the benefits of what is being planned with a view to ensuring the quality and integrity of research. Furthermore, beyond determining the requirements for promotion, the ministry is also expected to ensure proper implementation of the directive and establish clear accountability lines to achieve uniformity of academic promotion across the sector.

CHAPTER 17

Imperatives for a Functioning Information System at HEIS

An earlier version of this chapter appeared in *University World News, Africa Edition*, 14 December 2018, https://www.universityworldnews.com/post.php?story=20181210122656577

The collection, retrieval and dissemination of data related to HEIs' core academic, research and outreach activities are key to achieving institutional, sectoral and national goals. Furthermore, the availability of a well-organized information system to capture data and assist in planning, monitoring and appraising the progress of HEIs helps university leaders to make informed, timely and reliable decisions. Aside from their internal needs, the availability and dissemination of a well-functioning higher education management system can also strengthen HEIs' accountability by increasing their transparency in reporting plans and performance. It appears that despite the importance of an information system at all levels of institutional operations, many higher education systems and institutions are deficient in building such systems and recognizing their strategic importance.

1   Policy Directions

The importance of data management and reporting is emphasized in Ethiopia's Higher Education Proclamation (2009/2019) which stipulates the duties of HEIs regarding the organization and use of institutional information and making such information available to internal and external users. For instance, production of reports for the Ministry of Education and other external users such as the Higher Education Relevance and Quality Agency requires a range of data on institutional profiles and progress in accreditation, quality audit and annual performance. Accordingly, all institutions are required to establish efficient systems for statistical data collection and information exchange among themselves, their units and with the Ministry of Education to which they are accountable. Higher education institutions are also required to publish accurate, detailed and comprehensive annual educational and financial statistical data at a prescribed date (i.e., three months) after the end of an academic year. For most of the Ethiopian universities that have undergone institutional reform and are using management tools such as the Balanced Scorecard, the availability of an integrated information system appears to be critical. Communication and implementation of HEIs' strategic plans demand various monitoring measures which rely on organized information systems.

Despite the needs and legal requirements, very little attention appears to have been paid to the development of an integrated higher education management information system that would enhance evidence-based planning and decision-making at institutional and national levels. The majority of Ethiopian HEIs are known for their lack of operational direction, clearly articulated responsibilities for information management and the absence of comprehensive and integrated information systems. In addition, most do not keep consistent and comprehensive institutional data while many suffer from deficiencies in documenting their students' progress.

As evidenced in most of the quality audit reports issued by the Higher Education Relevance and Quality Agency over the past decade, determining the graduation, dropout and attrition rate of students in most universities is not easy due to the lack of coherent data. Data from different sections in the same institution is often not available or may fail to corroborate information from a different section. Engagement in the publication and wider dissemination of available data is also very rare. This has created a significant challenge for those who seek to use educational data for a variety of purposes, including research on the higher education sector in general or particular HEIs.

2 Source of Data

The only organized data on education at national level is produced by the Education Management Information System (EMIS) managed by the Ministry of Education and now by MoSHE. This is available at both national and regional level and its publication – which is produced as an Education Statistics Annual Abstract – has served the sector for decades, providing basic information for internal and external users. The abstract contains summarized information on education data and statistics on subsectors like general education, technical and vocational, and higher education and data on other relevant issues acquired through regional and national channels. As acknowledged by the ministry itself in 2017, the statistics serve as a measure of the achievement of goals set by the ministry and the regional education bureaus, in addition to being used for planning, decision-making and policy formulation. The education progress indicators in the statistical publication are also used to track

Ethiopia's achievements against global goals such as Education For All and the Sustainable Development Goals reported to external bodies like UNESCO.

Since the Education Statistics Annual Abstract collects information on a voluntary basis, there is a problem of under-reporting. For instance, for many years, the data from PHEIs has been drawn from around 30% of these institutions, due to failures in reporting. The publication of the annual abstract has not been timely due to a variety of challenges confronting the unit responsible for publishing the statistics. Having developed little sophistication over the years, the EMIS remains the only available data source but it needs to address its current challenges and augment its capacity in order to offer detailed information on particular areas of interest.

3   Towards a Better System

The Ethiopian higher education system is growing at a tremendous pace with the potential to become one of the largest in Africa in the coming decade. If the sector has little knowledge of its progress and deficiencies, it will be seriously challenged in terms of clearly understanding its achievements, the challenges it faces and the mechanisms it should create to mitigate problems. Hence, the creation of an efficient and integrated higher education information management system at both institutional and national level, is urgently required. Such a system should be comprehensive enough to address requirements emanating from various stakeholders such as students, teachers, researchers, administrators, employers, policy decision-makers and others.

Considering its importance, it is imperative that the deployment of resources, skills and continuous support to facilitate the creation of such a system should be a major government concern and a priority of institutions and stakeholders. This could begin by setting clear policy directions, strategies, structures and regulatory requirements which enforce the creation of a management information system across the whole sector at institutional level. The fact that this need has not been emphasized in the new Ethiopian Education Development Roadmap (2018–30) is a serious gap that should be corrected. Against this background, one is tempted to challenge the newly created Ministry of Science and Higher Education to take the lead in meeting the urgent need for a robust management information system that will play a critical role in the accomplishment of national higher education goals.

CHAPTER 18

University Resources

Imperatives for Efficient Utilization

An earlier version of this chapter appeared in *University World News, Africa Edition*, 31 May 2019, https://www.universityworldnews.com/post.php?story=20190529075218420

The expansion and diversification of tertiary education across the globe is welcomed as a remarkable development, but an accompanying hurdle has been governments' inability to meet the financial demands that come with expansion. This can lead to a multitude of challenges and ramifications. Although diversified financing strategies have often been suggested as the panacea to address such challenges, institutions' capacity to properly utilize their existing capacities and resources is equally important. Despite the Ethiopian government's continued commitment to the growth of higher education, many local and international observers ask how a country with meagre resources and significant competing demands such as clean water, roads, etc., is able to afford and/or sustain the financing of its higher education sector and meet its quest for growth. Indeed, as far back as 2003 the World Bank aptly commented: "Matching goals with means is at the crux of the challenge facing policy-makers in Ethiopia".

Echoing this observation, Ethiopia's Education Roadmap of 2018 notes the difficulty of reaching 22% gross enrolment in higher education by 2025 and warns that this goal is unlikely to be achieved due to a lack of resources and existing financing modalities. The answer to this conundrum lies not only in improving the existing pattern of higher education financing, but also in efficient utilization of available resources, among others.

1 Efficient Use of Resources

The quest for efficiency through the proper utilization of resources should be one of the major goals of Ethiopian HEIs since it can make a significant contribution to ensuring the sustainability of the education sector. The internal efficiency required of HEIs can be augmented through a variety of strategies including, but not limited to, the right student-to-faculty and administrative staff-to-faculty ratios, reducing student attrition and dropout rates, outsourcing non-academic services, instituting efficient financial and procurement systems, and introducing a diversified means of educational delivery.

The teacher-to-student ratio in the regular undergraduate programs was very low two decades back but has shown a constant upward climb from 1:8 in 1992; to 1:12 in 2003; 1:28 in 2008–09; and 1:26.4 in 2014–15. This was the result of the government's aggressive expansion scheme. However, after having achieved the efficient ratio set by the ministry (around 1:25) the ratio dropped to 1: 20.3 in 2018 (MoE, 2018). While maintaining the desired level of efficiency is important, exploring how the system has achieved this status is also necessary at a time when a significant number of universities complain about excessive teaching loads, especially in particular fields of study.

Although student attrition rates were a major concern in the Ethiopian higher education sector prior to expansion, they appear to have declined in most universities over the past decade. While the reasons remain open to debate, significant numbers of students continue to drop out for a variety of academic and non-academic reasons. The support schemes available at most institutions are improving but they are far from being satisfactory in terms of matching the level of assistance students require to improve their performance and complete their studies.

In similar vein, the unhealthy academic staff-to-administrative staff ratio that has been characteristic of the system since the start of its expansion has not improved. In most universities, this currently stands at 1:3 (MoE, 2018), which appears to be highly inefficient. Although some universities have outsourced services such as food provision and security, student accommodation is still provided by public universities and this has implications for the number of non-academic staff members required to support such services. As a result, university leadership's focus, which should be mainly directed toacademic-related matters, is diverted to non-academic services. Furthermore, as noted in the Ethiopian Education Roadmap (2018), staff time is not properly utilized in some universities due to a lack of accountability and poor performance on the research front. While the Ethiopian system requires academics to devote 75% of their time to teaching and 25% to research, academic staff rarely engage in research. This ratio has recently changed to 60% teaching, 25% research and 15% community service but without system improvement and clear accountability mechanisms it is unlikely that this will be realized.

2 Budget and Procurement Systems

Ethiopia's education budget is structured in such a way that capital spending in higher education takes the lion's share, with only 25% of spending dedicated to the recurrent budget. Within higher education itself, more than 50% of the recurrent budget is spent in areas such as food and accommodation, which are not directly related to the academic process (World Bank, 2016). Notwithstanding other manifestations of financial inefficiency of which universities are accused, the existing procurement system is cited by many as a serious stumbling block. As noted in the Education Roadmap (2018), the procurement system in universities is highly bureaucratic, to the extent of derailing institutions' ability to fulfil their teaching, research and related functions, all of which assume "a smooth and sustainable flow of inputs".

3   Educational Delivery

Regular, classroom-based delivery is the dominant form of educational provision in Ethiopia. Despite the possible contributions that modalities such as distance education could make in reducing costs, they have not been harnessed well due to poor delivery, infrastructural deficiencies and negative attitudes. On a positive note, in addition to suggesting the opening of a national open university – a plan previously abandoned by the government – the Ethiopian Education Roadmap (2018) recommends consolidating existing universities and using non-dormitory delivery modes such as open, continuing, distance, private and online education, with strong quality assurance and enactment mechanisms.

4   Looking Ahead

Ethiopia's dual challenge of further expanding its higher education sector and meeting the corresponding goal of providing quality education to its growing number of higher education students cannot be met without broadening its financial base and augmenting the efficiency of its HEIs. For this reason, efforts to create a strong financing system in the higher education sector should not only aim to diversify the means of financing but also properly utilize the resources universities have at their disposal. While the directions set by the Education Roadmap (2018) hold promise for the future, translating them into reality requires strong conviction on the part of both the government and individual institutions to set clear directions, lines of responsibility and accountability that will increase efficiency at all levels of the system.

CHAPTER 19

Unlocking the Potential of ICT in Higher Education

An earlier version of this chapter appeared in *University World News, Africa Edition*, 13 February 2020, https://www.universityworldnews.com/post.php?story=20200210064903949

The Ethiopian government's recent move towards liberalizing the telecommunications market may contribute to improved information and communications technology (ICT) infrastructure and the creation of a digital society – with a range of positive implications for the higher education sector. In its revised National ICT Policy and Strategy of 2016, the Ethiopian government established ICT as a key driver and facilitator in transforming the country into a knowledge-based economy and information society – a fundamental requirement to meet the country's aspiration to become a middle-income country and to achieve improved public service delivery and greater government openness. Despite these aspirations, the sector has suffered a wide array of bottlenecks that include poor infrastructure, low levels of Internet penetration, a poor communications network, a lack of organized data and information resources, and a shortage of the requisite human resources.

Despite various efforts to promote the development and application of ICT, Ethiopia continues to lag behind its neighbors. A 2016 World Bank report that assessed the country's potential for an electronics and ICT manufacturing industry indicated that Internet use and/or access in Ethiopia stood at 15%, compared to 26% in Kenya and 28% in Sudan. The mobile phone (2G/3G/4G) penetration rate was 44%, while the figure for Kenya and Sudan was 100.8% and 73.4%, respectively. Access to mobile broadband (3G) in Ethiopia stood at 8.8%, compared with 38% in Kenya and 15.6% in Sudan. Government efforts to address these deficiencies include the recent decision to privatize the telecommunications sector. Until now, Ethiopia was one of the three countries on the continent (with Eritrea and Djibouti) whose telecommunications sector was fully owned by the government.

1 ICT in Universities

Ethiopia's ICT Policy and Strategy recognizes the crucial role of ICT in enhancing the educational system and promoting access to and the quality of education. Next to infrastructure and the legal and regulatory environment, the development of human capital provided through education is identified as one of the three foundational essentials that underpin all other aspects of the policy and the sector. In addition to giving due emphasis to the role of human resources the policy envisages the need to improve digital skills, development and exploitation of ICT across all types of institutions, updating and developing ICT curricula, creating the necessary infrastructure and interconnectivity for and among institutions, and making available training and learning opportunities that include tele-education and virtual learning.

The two outstanding areas of intervention that are being implemented within the education sector include SchoolNet – the secondary school network – and the Ethiopian Education and Research Network (EthERNet), which is the network of tertiary education institutions. The EthERNet is regarded as one of the pillars of the ICT development plans and has been established with the major objective of creating interconnectivity among the country's academic and research institutions and enhancing Ethiopia's presence on the global Internet. In line with this initiative, in September 2019, the Ministry of Science and Higher Education put into effect a new national open access policy which requires universities to deposit their publicly-funded research outputs in the National Academic Digital Repository of Ethiopia which is backed by the ministry. In addition to encouraging open access to publications and data, the new policy incorporates "openness" as one of the criteria to be used for assessment and evaluation of research proposals undertaken at national level. Beyond strengthening the quality of Ethiopian research, this initiative is expected to have significant impact in increasing the visibility of Ethiopian research within national and international research circles. Over and above the promise held by this national platform, individual universities have also been involved in automating a variety of their academic and non-academic services and utilizing ICT for academic purposes. While Bahir Dar and Mekelle universities are known for similar endeavors, Jimma University has been considered as a leading example in terms of exploiting ICT as a principal vehicle to facilitate teaching and learning within the Ethiopian higher education sector.

Government plans are underway to extend such experiences across the sector. Under its broader goal of enhancing the relevance and quality of higher education, the Education Sector Development Program, ESDP V (the implementation period of which is ending in 2020), envisages providing ICT and internet connections to all public universities. Specific targets include enabling all university students to access digital libraries and increasing the percentage of smart (ICT-supported) classrooms to 25%. Ethiopia's Education Development Roadmap (2018–30) similarly identifies ICT as one of the major areas where the education sector has to undertake significant shifts in the years to come. However, considerable challenges still hinder the achievement of these ambitious goals.

2   Challenges in the Higher Education Sector

Despite its potential, research and anecdotal evidence suggest that neither the infrastructure nor the culture of utilizing ICT is at a level sufficient to enhance higher education in Ethiopia. Limited research on ICT in Ethiopian higher education indicates that ICT utilization is significantly lower for activities such as teaching and learning, communicating with students and colleagues, and monitoring and evaluating students' progress. While the use of the Internet is much better among university staff and students who utilize it to access information and educational resources, technologies such as video conferencing, multimedia and e-learning are rarely used for the purpose of teaching and/or learning and information sharing.

A cursory glance at most of the quality audit reports by the Higher Education Relevance and Quality Agency on Ethiopian HEIs similarly shows that there are universities where the penetration and use of ICT is still minimal, where the network infrastructure, connectivity and use of IT as a learning resource and teaching tool is limited, and where functions such as financial management, student enrolment, academic records and personnel records are still undertaken using the traditional paper form. The few local studies on the subject further indicate that ICT integration efforts within the higher education sector continue to be hampered by factors such as the lack of an ICT policy for pedagogical practices, a poor ICT governance structure, resistance and fear of technology, lack of training and experience-sharing among teachers and students, poor ICT skills, and a lack of incentives, technical and pedagogical support, and support from top management.

3   Planning for the Future

The foregoing discussion suggests that, despite the policy directions set at a national level, university graduates' readiness to meet the demands of the 21st century economy is constrained by a multitude of factors that affect the promotion of ICT within the education sector. It is hoped that the government's move towards a liberalized telecommunications market will contribute to improved infrastructure (one of the pillars of Ethiopia's ICT policy) and the creation of a digital society. Together with a variety of initiatives within the higher education sector, this can have positive implications for the realization of ICT's potential in enhancing higher education. The responsibility to galvanize efforts in this direction extends from promoting technology-mediated learning that allows for improved learning and additional access to higher education, to making available the human resources that will be required at the national level and across all sectors.

PART 4

Private Higher Education and Privatization

CHAPTER 20

Emerging Contours of African Private Higher Education

An earlier version of this chapter appeared in *Inside Higher Education*, 26 November 2017 (with Damtew Teferra), https://www.insidehighered.com/blogs/world-view/emerging-contours-african-private-higher-education

Since the 1970s, developing regions have exhibited massive growth in tertiary higher education in general and PHE in particular. Yet, the higher education sector remains small especially in sub-Saharan Africa where GER hovers at around 10%. This is mainly because African higher education has remained essentially a public enterprise – a symbol of post-independence self-reliance which left little room for PHEIs until the 1990s.

Private higher education has become one of the fastest growing segments of the higher education sector with the number of PHEIs continuously on the rise. Privatization policies, massive demand for higher education and other global developments account for the continued surge in private provision. Ethiopia alone currently boasts more than 300 private institutions, while Ghana, South Africa and Uganda have a significant number – in virtually all cases more than public ones. In 2009, there were an estimated 468 private and 200 public universities in Africa, though this may have been a huge underestimation. Africa has reached a level where access to higher education in its various guises would not be possible without the active involvement of private institutions. This is mainly due to the increasingly significant roles these institutions are playing in continental provision of higher education.

1   Veiled Advances

Notwithstanding the differences between public and private HEIs in terms of goals and objectives, African PHEIs have created opportunities for access and become alternatives to the public sector. It is inconceivable to imagine higher education in many African countries today without the involvement of PHEIs that currently claim 20% of enrollment. They are vital to the continent's economies and nation building as they offer employment-oriented courses and entrepreneurial skills relevant to the job market. They also help to conserve

Africa's scarce foreign exchange by creating alternative opportunities to study at home. Private higher education institutions also promote competitiveness due to their dynamic and entrepreneurial features. In 1990, public providers in South Africa offered only five Master of Business Administration (MBA) programs, serving around 1,000 students, but due to competition from private institutions, the number of providers grew to 40 and MBA enrollment rose to 15,000 within a decade. Ethiopian pubic institutions introduced distance education much later than their private counterparts and ultimately emulated the most successful private providers in their catch-up strategies. In Mozambique, the emergence of PHEIs has led to the opening of self-financing and fee-paying programs that have resulted in curricular innovation and organizational changes that make institutions more responsive to market demands.

Successful PHEIs also provide administrative features that may not be available in the public sector. While public institutions are often criticized as rigid and bureaucratic, successful PHEIs are credited for their dynamism, efficiency and flexibility in addressing student needs. For instance, unlike their public counterparts, most Kenyan PHEIs have been credited for creating a conducive environment for dialogue with students and staff. Private higher education institutions have increasingly become parents' choice for their stability compared to the infamous and incessant strikes that are common among public institutions. The existence of the private sector promotes inter-sectoral competition as well as cooperation that enhance dynamism and efficiency across the whole system.

Conventional wisdom has it that public institutions usually cater to the disadvantaged and under-represented. In fact, PHEIs also benefit the disadvantaged. In Ethiopia, more than 50% of PHE students are female while this figure stands at only around 35% in public institutions. In Uganda, PHEIs enroll an equal percentage of female and male students, while female students make up around 40% of the student population at public universities. Tanzanian PHEIs are making a significant contribution to addressing the equity imbalance that the public sector has not been able to rectify. In Ethiopia, private institutions provide annual scholarships to thousands of students who are unable to pay for tuition while public universities make no such provision. Tanzanian PHEIs have expanded opportunities by opening branches in areas where access to higher education has been particularly low. Ethiopian PHEIs also claim more extensive distance education centers than their public counterparts.

2 Emerging Features

Although Africa is dominated by demand-absorbing PHEIs, it now hosts institutions that are achieving a status that might be considered "semi-elite". These institutions offer quality programs, research endeavors, and innovative delivery – defying the generally unfavorable characterization of PHEIs on the continent. The commercial/religious and/or market-friendly orientation of private institutions is slowly changing as many PHEIs are diversifying their programs. For instance, the disproportionate focus on religious studies of Kenyan PHEIs has changed since the year 2000 through deliberate effort. The Agha Khan and Kiriri Women's Universities in Kenya have distinguished themselves by developing programs with international flavor. In some countries the reputation of some "semi-elite" PHEIs is such that admission is increasingly difficult to achieve. Admission to some, such as Kenya's United States International University, are so rigorous that it takes months before results are announced. In Nigeria, some PHEIs have earned parental respect and have become the preferred option over public institutions.

Some PHEIs pursue foreign partnerships to enhance quality and attract students from a wide range of countries. The well-equipped Institut International de Management in Benin maintains strong affiliations with established institutions in Europe and the United States. The American University of Cairo is well regarded in Egypt as an elite national institution. In Ethiopia, St. Mary's University has aligned its efforts with the Association of African Universities (AAU) and hosts an annual international conference dedicated to PHEIs in close cooperation with the African Union Commission, AAU, and UNESCO, among others. Its 15th Annual Conference on the theme Ensuring Quality through Public-Private Partnership/Regional Integration further testifies to PHEIs' expanding role on the continent.

3   Conclusion

As the issue of quality continues to challenge public universities, private institutions are slowly gaining higher status in the African higher education ecosystem and increasingly fulfilling a role that was once fully ascribed to public institutions. Private higher education institutions are providing the critical support African governments seek to respond to the demands of the time characterized by mounting needs for high level training and education. Emerging trends indicate the growth of PHEIs that are comparable to, and at times better than public ones – both in their orientation and delivery of higher education. Arguments about PHEIs not providing quality education, often resulting from the opportunistic behavior of some profit-seeking providers, are no longer the authentic narrative. Thus, the role of African PHEIs should be seen as just as critical and vital as their counterparts in the public sector.

CHAPTER 21

Unusual in Growth and Composition
Ethiopian Private Higher Education

An earlier version of this chapter appeared in *International Higher Education*, 90, 19–20 (with Daniel Levy), http://dx.doi/org/10.6017/ihe.2017.90.9791

With more than 110,000 students (MoE, 2016), Ethiopia's PHE sector is the largest or second largest in sub-Saharan Africa. This large private presence exists despite Ethiopia being a rather late starter of PHE and despite some restrictive regulation. Partly due to lack of knowledge of other countries, it is common for expert and public opinion in a given country to hold an exaggerated view of how atypical their systems are. A reasonable conclusion from scrutinizing Ethiopian PHE is that in fundamental ways, it is indeed significantly atypical for sub-Saharan Africa. After acknowledging several not insignificant commonalities, we hone in on the more striking differences. Though large in absolute private enrolment, Ethiopia's 14–17% private share is typical of sub-Saharan Africa. Furthermore, the types of Ethiopian PHE are those found throughout the region. By far the largest chunk is non-elite which is a mix of demand-absorbing and more effective job-market orientation.

1 Semi-Elite and Religious Institutions

Semi-elite and religious institutions are also visible. The few semi-elite universities compete with the good public universities, especially in teaching and other fields, and benefit from disorder in their public counterparts. Furthermore, as elsewhere in the region, the overwhelming majority of fields of study in PHE are market-oriented, with some recent diversification into other fields. Women account for a larger share of the private than the public sector. Myriad forms of community engagement are apparent. In both Ethiopia and the region, while total enrolment growth has been very rapid in the private sector, it has also been rapid in the public sector, so that the private share has recently slipped. Notwithstanding such similarities, atypical characteristics are more remarkable. One set of unusual characteristics concerns growth and regulation; another concerns the private sector's internal composition.

2　Atypical Growth and Regulation

As African PHE emerged comparatively late in terms of global PHE and from a low gross enrolment ratio, or GER, so Ethiopian PHE was late (1998) for even the African context and started from a typically low 0.8 GER. Much of the reason for Ethiopia's late entry into PHE lay in the decades of repressive Marxist rule that followed the end of the long reign of Emperor Haile Selassie in 1974 and banned all forms of private ownership. Yet today only Uganda matches Ethiopia in private enrolment.

Compared to most of the region, where the unplanned emergence and rapid growth of PHE caught governments by surprise, the fast growth of PHE was planned and promoted by Ethiopia's post-Marxist government. Indeed, the regulatory framework preceded the PHE sector's emergence – and was mostly enabling (as opposed to restrictive) regulation. While it is common for African countries to promulgate 'delayed regulation' when they become aware of the academic and other weaknesses of easily proliferating private institutions, and common to impose some rules on the private sector that are not imposed on the public sector, in notable ways, Ethiopia has gone to a regulatory extreme.

Without legal warrant, the government blocks private programs in law and teacher education. After PHE had played a pioneering role in Ethiopian distance education, it was temporarily banned from that realm as well. And while religious institutions often start within African private sectors and thrive there, in Ethiopia the religious degrees offered by religious PHE are accepted only within religious society. They are not recognized by the state, a restrictive policy with job market ramifications; to gain wider acceptance, programs would have to be secular and gain national accreditation.

3　Atypical Composition of Subsectors

It is not by chance, then, that the religious subsector holds a markedly lower share of PHE than it does on most of the continent. Nor is it by chance that Ethiopia's religious subsector is mostly non-elite. Much of it was not created afresh but, rather, emerged from pre-existing schools at lower levels. In contrast, in many African countries, religious institutions are among the strongest academic forces. Many former colonies had strong Catholic or Protestant roots to build on in higher education, whereas Ethiopia was never colonized.

So, if religious PHE is unusually small in Ethiopian PHE, what is unusually large? The answer is for-profit PHE that accounts for the overwhelming majority of this sector. This is not just a difference between Ethiopian and most African PHE, but a stunning difference. Not all African countries allow a for-profit presence and often the appearance of profit relates to legally non-profit institutions finding ways to skirt regulatory restrictions.

Moreover, in countries with legal for-profits, the for-profits sit alongside an array of non-profits. Not so in Ethiopia. It appears that the only non-profit Ethiopian HEIs outside the (small) religious subsector are a few PHEIs owned by non-governmental organizations. Among the for-profits, the bulk are private limited corporations, mostly family-owned. For-profits are allowed at all tertiary education levels.

4   Continuity vs Change Going Forward

Thus, in the face of huge growth in demand for higher education in Ethiopia, a mix of enabling and restrictive policy has enabled PHE to play a major role that is, however, limited in key respects. How will policy evolve as the country now faces not only continued growth, but projected acceleration?

If, as predicted, total enrolment will nearly double over the next five years, with the private sector expected to receive an increasing share of this growth, policy choices about how supportively or restrictively to handle PHE will assume increasing importance. Bolstered by its relative success despite restrictive regulations, the private sector is confident that it could perform a larger role into the future for a greater share of Ethiopia's enrolment, were government to provide stable and less antagonistic policy. Not all government policy-makers share that view.

CHAPTER 22

Family Owned PHEIs in Africa

An earlier version of this chapter appeared in *International Higher Education*, 95, 23–24, https://doi.org/10.6017/ihe.2018.95.10727

The increasing emergence of PHEIs in Africa over the past two decades includes a largely uninvestigated species of institutions owned by individuals or families. Little has been written about these types of private institutions at either the global or the regional level. This article broadly explores family-owned institutions in Africa where the literature on PHE itself remains meager and poorly organized.

1 Degree of Presence

The number of family-owned institutions in Africa is currently increasing despite the overwhelming presence of religious PHEIs in many countries on the continent. This new development may be partly attributed to the rise of the for-profit sector over the past two decades. The presence of family-owned institutions can be influenced by the dominant type of private institutions operating in a given country. Their availability in countries such as Congo, Kenya, Liberia, Nigeria, Tanzania, and Zimbabwe, which are dominated by religious PHEIs, is still limited but growing. Indeed, the categories of "religious" and "family-owned" are not mutually exclusive, as some families or individuals are involved in the establishment and/or ownership of religious (and other nonprofit) PHEIs. Yet, it is especially in countries such as Benin, Botswana, Ghana, Egypt, Ethiopia, Mozambique, Senegal, South Africa, Sudan, and Uganda, where the for-profit sector is gaining ground against religious PHEIs, that the family-owned phenomenon is especially strong.

Where for-profit private institutions are legally allowed, they may provide ample opportunities for individual/family ownership to thrive. Ethiopia represents an extreme case, as the bulk of PHEIs (more than 90% of 130 accredited institutions) are owned by families and individual proprietors with profit motives. In contrast, in many countries, family-owned institutions might not exceed 3–5% of PHEIs.

2   Nature of Institutions

Most family-owned institutions in Africa exist as non-university or professional schools with vocational orientations. Non-university PHEIs are more common in Botswana, Lesotho, South Africa, and Tunisia than in Ivory Coast, Kenya, Nigeria, Tanzania, and Uganda, where private universities are available. In most cases, family-owned PHEIs with business orientations are demand absorbing, for-profit institutions. Most are small in size and offer programs designed to respond to market demands. Aside from their proprietors' initial investment, they are heavily dependent on student fees, with little or no external support or income-generating activities. This can influence the way they are structured and managed. Whereas academically excellent private institutions in Africa are most often religious, the majority of family-owned institutions are teaching institutions with little involvement in research and graduate studies. However, there are exceptions, as in the case of Morocco where government policy encourages PHEIs to assume elite status. Though quite few, there are also family-owned institutions in Ghana and Ethiopia that have succeeded in achieving a high level of credibility in terms of program quality.

3   Strengths and Deficiencies

Wider acceptance of family-owned PHEIs is determined by their capacity to reconcile the elements of profitability with the academic orientations required at the tertiary education level. Notwithstanding challenges, achieving this balance is not always impossible, as the success of some institutions on the continent shows. Successful family-owned PHEIs are generally nimbler than other HEIs. Little deterred by the bureaucracy and red tape that commonly afflicts public HEIs, successful family-owned institutions are characterized by their dynamism, innovativeness, efficiency, and flexibility, which are critical to institutional success. Due to their interest in ensuring their social and economic viability, successful family-owned institutions minimize institutional spending, promote strategic planning and marketing, maintain contact with employers, offer job-placement services, student counseling and support, and promote increased staff accountability. They can have a strong commitment to community outreach programs, which includes providing free professional services, contributions to charity, participation in local projects, and social initiatives like environmental protection, feeding the homeless, and assisting the community through capacity building training and donations.

Although some family-owned institutions are set up by proprietors with altruistic motives, a significant percentage are driven by owners whose primary goals are financial. Such institutions can have family members that assume key positions with little training and experience. Institutional activities can be seriously jeopardized when the preparation, vision, and behavior of proprietors are not in tune with institutional needs and goals. Similar influences may be found in all forms of PHEIs as compared to their public counterparts, but they are magnified in poorly run family-owned PHEIs. One of the major reasons for the closure of many such institutions in various parts of Africa has been their owners' excessive profit drive, compromising the provision of quality higher education. Where there is little self-control, the power that proprietors wield in terms of the daily operations and future direction of the institutions is also a serious drawback to their social and academic legitimacy – which is critical to their wider acceptance. Proprietors who perceive their institutions primarily as business entities can use their key positions to dictate institutional direction and operations. Examples of this abound in many African countries. The overbearing influence of proprietors is usually exhibited in unbridled expansion, little attention to long-term commitment, diverting earned profit to nonacademic purposes, arbitrary appointment of staff and managers, interference in academic affairs, and imposing authoritarian governance systems. Major decisions on important institutional issues may not be openly shared and discussed.

Proprietors who act without due process of law and procedures infringe on the participation, authority, and decision-making powers of their chancellors and/or staff, in addition to eroding employee confidence and disrespecting individual rights and/or academic freedom. In Ethiopia, the influence of such proprietors is so pervasive that it usually determines the success or failure of their institutions. Similar observations abound across the continent and sometimes cast doubt on the wisdom of allowing such institutions to operate without legal restrictions in matters that are critical to institutional operations. In conclusion, while the increasing involvement of family-owned PHEIs in the African higher education context requires better understanding of their nature, operations, and potential, their emergence and the corresponding growth of the for-profit PHE sector appears likely to continue. Their wider acceptance, however, hinges on the manner in which these institutions operate and/or the extent to which they are able to resist the whims and shortsightedness of profit-mongering proprietors.

CHAPTER 23

African Private Higher Education
Progressive Policies and Ambivalent Stances

An earlier version of this chapter appeared in *International Higher Education*, 2(93), 19–21 (with Damtew Teferra), https://doi.org/10.6017/ihe.0.93.10418

The rise of PHE in Africa has mainly been driven by factors such as the public sector's inability to meet growing demand, strain on public finance that called for alternative sources of funding, and consequent economic policies that led to structural reforms. By global standards, the growth of the PHE sector in Africa remains low – currently hovering at around 20% of overall tertiary enrollment. However, the sector's importance is strongly felt in terms of addressing the deficiencies of the public sector, creating job opportunities, enhancing managerial efficiencies, and infusing an entrepreneurial culture into the traditionally conservative higher education arena.

The significant role governments play through appropriate legislation and policies remains one of the most critical levers to lend credence to, and advance the growth of the PHE sector. However, arguments against PHE have been equally strong due to a host of controversies surrounding the use of taxpayers' money on private institutions. We argue that while direct support to PHE could be difficult and in most cases controversial, an indirect form of support to PHEIs, even in resource-depleted contexts like Africa, could help the sector to thrive. As the regional experiences discussed here indicate, this type of support, some of which we consider progressive, could take various forms.

1 Loans and Scholarships

Loans to students and/or institutions are common forms of support to PHEIs, although instituting efficient mechanisms in Africa has not been particularly easy. In Kenya, students from chartered private universities benefit from loans disbursed by the Higher Education Loans Board. In Ghana, the Student Loan Trust Fund provides loans to students enrolled at accredited institutions – including PHEIs. Lesotho's interest-free Loan Bursary Fund is open to all students who have obtained admission to HEIs. Botswana provides student loans and scholarships to privately enrolled students. In Nigeria, PHE students excluded from the public higher education tax fund can access loans operated by the Nigerian Education Bank. Banks in Namibia avail collateral-based loans for higher education at commercial rates. Mozambique's Provincial Scholarship Fund is dedicated to poor students enrolled in public and PHEIs.

However, in Ethiopia, Malawi, Mauritius, Uganda, and Zimbabwe, government-sponsored student loans are either nonexistent or exclude students from PHEIs, although recently, the Ethiopian Ministry of Education started supporting academic staff at PHEIs for studies at public institutions by granting tuition remission. Loans made available to institutions – at concessional interest rates – are critical in many ways. The Tanzanian Education Authority encourages the provision of loans and grants to PHEIs to meet the cost of construction and rehabilitation of educational facilities, purchase educational equipment, and develop their human resources. In Mozambique, PHEIs are entitled to benefit from the Quality Enhancement and Innovation Fund, which is dedicated to strengthening institutional capacity. In the Ethiopian context, however, special loan arrangements that are common in sectors such as manufacturing and export trade are not yet available to the PHE sector.

2   Auxiliary Enterprises and Taxation

In Kenya and Tanzania, governments do not provide direct subsidies to PHEIs; however, they encourage the private sector to invest in such institutions. Private higher education institutions in Kenya are encouraged to set up auxiliary enterprises that engage in activities such as agriculture, cafeterias, bookstores, clinics, laundry, carpentry, and leasing of conference facilities. In Tunisia, government incentives for PHEIs include grants that cover up to 25% of their total establishment costs and 25% of faculty salaries for a period of ten years. Ethiopia has recently announced competitive research funding for HEIs, but it is not clear whether private institutions will be part of this scheme.

Favorable taxation measures have usually been a common means of spurring PHE growth. Ethiopian investment law exempts duty taxes on building materials used for educational institutions. It also allows exemption from income tax for the first three years; however, this has had limited effect due to the brevity of the gestation period for such an investment to take off. The Ghanaian government recently announced that it will scrap the 25% corporate tax imposed on private universities to enhance their roles in national development.

3   Provision of Land

Governments can also assist PHEIs by providing land free or at discounted prices or rent. This is crucial, especially where the cost of land is exorbitant and PHEIs are spending an inordinate amount of funds for rented facilities. In Uganda, the government allegedly donated 300 acres of land to Mbale University to assist in generating additional income through rentals. The Tunisian experience involves selling parcels of land to PHEIs for one dinar – as a symbolic gesture of support to the sector. Ethiopia has also granted plots of land to many PHEIs as an investment incentive.

4   Leveling the Regulatory Field

Leveling the playing field for both private and public providers of higher education is a progressive policy track pursued by governments. In Egypt, the National Authority for Quality Assurance and Accreditation of Education serves as an independent accreditation body for all types and levels of education. The same is true of Ghana's National Accreditation Board, Kenya's Commission for Higher Education, and Uganda's Council for Higher Education, which regulate both private and public HEIs. The Council on Higher Education of Lesotho regulates both public and private institutions, despite differences in their establishment. However, accreditation requirements in Ethiopia continue to only be applicable to PHEIs.

5   Conclusion

Private higher education institutions will grow and may even thrive in the African higher education landscape as global and regional thirst for higher education continues to surge. It is thus high time to change the discourse on PHEIs in line with emerging realities, and to harness their potential through favorable and progressive policies. Progressive government policies can be instrumental in fostering PHEIs as effective partners in national and regional endeavors for social and economic development. Of course, government policy pledges need to be honored to translate intentions into realities – an area where African countries are often cited as falling short. All the same, African PHEIs will find it hard to respond to wider societal expectations without substantial support, both in the form of policies and real action. Similarly, progressive policies to advance PHEIs should be meticulously implemented, without hampering the competitive spirit that drives private business.

CHAPTER 24

Overcoming the Public-Private Divide in HE Law

An earlier version of this chapter appeared in *University World News, Africa Edition*, 16 November 2018, https://www.universityworldnews.com/post.php?story=20181114065437666

The public-private distinction has been a major area of interest in the broader realms of business, law, public administration and, lately, in the evolving literature on higher education. However, the growth of privatization within the public sector has increasingly challenged the wisdom of drawing such a clear distinction between the two spheres. One frame of reference used in debates about the public-private distinction within higher education is what the legislation of a country, or higher education law in particular, says on the subject.

1 Roles and Responsibilities

Despite differences in their size, staff composition, funding sources, research traditions and capacities, Ethiopian higher education law ascribes similar roles and functions to public and private HEIs based on the broader missions of higher education – teaching and learning, research, and community service. All HEIs are expected to be led by values such as the pursuit of truth and freedom of expression, successful execution of mission, competitiveness in scholarship and cooperation with other institutions, institutional autonomy with accountability, participatory governance and the rule of law. Equally, all institutions are expected to uphold and promote justice and fairness and adhere to a culture of fighting corruption, quality, efficient delivery of services, economical use of resources and effective maintenance of assets, and the culture of recognition of merit, democracy and multiculturalism.

In addition, government expectations related to setting up internal quality assurance systems, academic and counselling services, and research and research directions are shouldered by both public and private institutions. This also applies to the broader frameworks for curriculum design, delivery and assessment, program development, research and research funding. Although the mandate for developing curricula is left to individual institutions, the overall curricular design, delivery, and assessment of learning outcomes in all institutions must be geared towards enabling the learner "to acquire pertinent scientific knowledge, independent thinking skills, communication skills and professional values that together prepare him/her to become a competent professional". More importantly, every institution is expected to develop a suitable framework that provides for purposeful curricular development and implementation by academic units.

While particulars of the organization, management, responsibilities and procedures required to conduct research are left to the discretion of each institution, the establishment of an overall framework relating to core research areas and themes is equally dictated to both types of HEIs. Furthermore, the need for an institutionalized system of research and joint research projects with other national and international institutions or research centers are broadly defined as expectations that need to be met by both private and public institutions. Both types of institutions are expected to undertake and encourage relevant study, research, and community service in national and local priority areas and disseminate the findings as appropriate. They should also be accountable in terms of reporting and publishing details of their educational achievements and financial performance.

2   Disparities

Despite the expectations of the law that apply equally to private and public institutions, there are areas of divergence. Institutions are treated differently in areas such as student admissions, institutional designation, accreditation, funding, and employment. All of these are observable differences that call for attention. While both types of HEIs are required to comply strictly with directives issued by the Ministry of Education regarding admissions of students, special treatment is accorded to the public sector relating to the way in which students are chosen for admission. Students are assigned to public universities on the basis of their grade points in the senior secondary school-leaving exam. Private institutions most often accommodate students who do not obtain placement at public institutions.

According to the Higher Education Proclamation of 2009/2019, a public institution can admit adults under special admission if procedures for the same are issued pursuant to the establishment of regulations of the institution, and if such decisions are passed by the institution's senate. This provision is not, as a matter of right, given to private institutions due to a restriction set by the law. Notwithstanding the accountability expected of both sectors, the accreditation requirement in Ethiopia is imposed exclusively on PHEIs. Both the ministry and the Higher Education Relevance and Quality Agency are mandated to take steps against institutions that transgress requirements related to only running programs that are accredited. The public sector is currently free of this regulatory burden.

Public institutions mainly receive their funding from the government while the bulk of private institutions' income is drawn from student tuition and fees. Private institutions have no access to public resources whatsoever. While there is a cost-sharing scheme for those attending public institutions, no similar system (for example, student loans) exists for students in the private sector. Despite the need to augment the staff profile in the private sector, the law mandates public institutions with better postgraduate program resources to assist their peers in the public sector to upgrade their staff. The Ministry of Education has changed this practice lately by offering assistance to private institutions that want to train their staff at public institutions. However, another similar strategy – joint employment of professionals from industry, business, research establishments – is again permitted for public institutions only.

3   Unrealistic Demands

The higher education law in Ethiopia expects private institutions to discharge similar roles to those of public institutions. However, neither the specific provisions of the law nor the general incentives that the government provides to private investors help these institutions to respond satisfactorily to the expectations. Unrealistic demands can derail PHEIs from fulfilling the roles ascribed equally to the most resourced and subsidized public institutions. In addition to promoting a competitive regulatory approach above a cooperative one, the practice has the potential to hinder Ethiopia's efforts to expand higher education through both public and private means. Unless the dichotomous treatment of public and private institutions is properly addressed through legislative arrangements, it will continue to have serious ramifications for the success of the fledgling PHE sector that is already known for its small size, restrained working conditions and a variety of capacity and ethical challenges.

CHAPTER 25

Perils of Unregulated Privatization in Public Universities

An earlier version of this chapter appeared in *University World News, Africa Edition*, 1 June 2018, https://www.universityworldnews.com/post.php?story=20180529101444550

While the PHE sector in Ethiopia continues to be demonized for its commercial motives, the issue of partial privatization of the public sector has, in general, not received the scholarly attention it deserves. The increasing evidence that is now available about the growing privatization tendencies in Ethiopia's public higher education sector demands a closer understanding of its features and implications. Ethiopia illustrates both of the common routes to partial privatization of public universities. The first is the importing of management ideas and practices from the business world in order to make the public sector more businesslike, while the second is about increased effort to raise private (non-governmental) income. The latter is probably the most impactful of the privatization measures.

In Ethiopia, higher education was for far too long totally free of charge. Neither tuition fees nor fees for services such as food and lodging were required from students. However, the past two decades have seen a fundamental policy shift in the government position from exclusive funding of university education towards exploiting private means to support public missions. Privatization tendencies have been motivated in particular by the general economic policies of the incumbent government and its 1994 Education and Training Policy (ETP) that allowed increased cost-sharing beyond secondary education and encouraged institutions to generate their own income. Echoing the ETP's directions, the Higher Education Proclamation (FDRE, 2009) underscored the need to diversify public university income through tuition, research, innovation, consultancy, donations and other activities. Public institutions are encouraged to outsource some of their services and set up an income fund and/or enterprise that functions independently as a business entity. An expansion in higher student numbers and demand for higher education led to the introduction of cost-sharing in the public sector in 2003–04. Although the government's capacity to collect the range of fees from graduates remains a challenge, it nonetheless plans to boost the current cost-sharing scheme from 15%

to 25% by 2019–20, so as to be able to cover as much as 20% of the total cost of the higher education sector by 2020.

1   Manifestations of Privatization

Ethiopia's public universities are encouraged to broaden and diversify their income through multiple means. For example, universities have been encouraged to outsource some of their services such as cafeterias, dormitories, ICT services, libraries, laboratories and health centers. While modest attempts have been made in this direction, achievements have been far below expectations. New plans are under way to develop a national strategy that indicates how non-academic services should be administered.

Providing research and consultancy services is another area where institutions are encouraged to generate additional income. Achievements in this area are again very poor. The reasons are identified as poor funding, excessive teaching loads, lack of policy direction, and the lack of incentive schemes. The only income-generating scheme that seems to be successful and is growing is the sale of educational services, aided by student demand for public institutions and the strategy's comparative easiness to manage. This is occurring in the context of a variety of challenges and regulatory loopholes. To cater for the growing market of fee-paying programs at public universities (currently covering around 44% of overall enrolment), some public universities, primarily located in the regional states, have opened branches outside of their geographical limits – usually in the capital city of Addis Ababa – where they run evening, weekend (a modality not recognized by law) and postgraduate programs. These programs are made available through branch campuses run by the mother institution itself, and/or joint ventures forged between private and public institutions.

2   Public Protection of Private Revenue-Raising?

Aware of the potential dangers excessive commercial tendencies might entail, Ethiopia's Higher Education Proclamation requires public institutions to ensure that income-generating activities do not erode the mission, and legal and ethical standards of universities. To this end, public institutions have been required to issue detailed regulations of such activities, and to use the income earned primarily for the purposes of delivering better academic services and enriching teaching and learning. However, since no national framework or guidelines have been developed to clearly delineate responsibilities and boundaries, the move appears to be driven more by the whims and actions of individual institutions. Hence, the aggressive privatization currently being pursued is resulting in mission drift, reduced staff research time, faculty absence from their main duties while covering responsibilities at revenue-generating branch campuses, avoidance of the accreditation process by private businesses, utilization of public sector credibility for private gain, and giving of undue advantage to those who cut corners over the most regulated private institutions.

Concern over revenue-raising led to the intervention of the Ministry of Education in 2015 at a time when the presence in the capital city of branches of public institutions from the regions exposed some dubious practices. Programs were accused of being run without meeting the accreditation requirements of the national agency for quality assurance, and at the expense of the developmental needs of the regions where the universities were primarily located. After the ministry ordered all regional public institutions to close their operations in the capital, things seemed to be improving. However, while some institutions complied, others did not and with few or no enforcement mechanisms on the part of government, the practice has continued. The problem is assuming a new dimension lately in that even new public universities, with little or no preparation, are competing in the business of tapping the lucrative educational market outside of their geographical remit.

3 Conclusion

Public universities in Ethiopia are exercising new forms of privatization through extended efforts directed at increasing their sources of revenue. However, an obsessive drive towards privatization in the absence of regulation can be expected to have serious consequences. Privatization can shift institutions' focus from their core educational mission towards excessive efforts at revenue generation that may threaten the traditional goals of universities. The new focus on privatization can also push institutions in directions that may clash with national goals such as access, equity, regional development and quality. Striking a delicate balance between the traditional roles of Ethiopian public universities and the new drive towards privatization requires meaningful public-policy dialogue, clear guidelines and operational routes. It is unlikely that the looming dangers of privatization can be prevented without substantive interventions from the government, which has the responsibility to provide overall guidance and direction.

CHAPTER 26

Improving the Knowledge Base on Private Higher Education

An earlier version of this chapter appeared in *University World News, Africa Edition*, 25 June 2020, https://www.universityworldnews.com/post.php?story=20200623155030832

Over the past four decades, PHE and privatization of higher education have grown to become two of the most outstanding offshoots of the higher education sector worldwide. There are now very few countries where the private sector is not part of a national higher education system. Privatization of the public higher education sector has similarly become a common feature of many higher education systems, influenced by increased demand for higher education, governments' financial constraints, and new policies that promote privatization across all sectors of the economy. Not only has PHE succeeded in becoming the fastest-growing segment of higher education with the number of PHEIs outpacing that of the public sector in many countries, but it has also grown to enroll one in every three tertiary education students at the global level.

1 Research on PHE

Private higher education continues to evolve as an area of policy and practice. The sheer size and diversity of PHEIs, the variety of levels and programs offered and the millions of students and faculty involved offer a huge research field that awaits proper mining. Under normal circumstances, the emergence of such a sector should entail a commensurate increase in its knowledge base. However, despite the private sector's substantial role in higher education worldwide, an environmental scan of the current state of affairs suggests that scholarship on the sector is limited and leaves much to be desired, perhaps with the exception of the US, where there is comparatively better research output.

The limited work available on PHE, especially in the developing world, is in most cases patchy, anecdotal and devoid of a high level of comprehensiveness and analysis. Despite huge potential to draw on theories and methodologies from a variety of relevant disciplines, there is still a limited number of publications and no specialized journals on this subject. Conferences, networks, centers, institutes, study programs, associations and funding schemes dedicated to PHE are also rare or non-existent. A significant number of organizations with international stature and a keen interest in higher education are reluctant to promote scholarship on PHE, or even shy away from doing so. As a result, deficiencies in knowledge generation, policy development and knowledge dissemination abound. Indeed, the phenomenon of PHE could have benefitted from a range of theoretical and methodological treatments that help other segments of higher education to grow at a fast pace. In this regard, the limited research output on PHE has not only affected our understanding of the unfolding realities of the sector, but continues to influence the positions and policy directions relating to it.

Professor Daniel Levy's apt observations about the sector nearly two decades ago (2002, p. 2) remain relevant today:

> While interest and debate surround the roles that private higher education plays, analysis lags far behind. Promoters routinely glorify roles, which critics demonise. Policy-makers tend to adopt simple views of what private higher education does, or what they want it to do, while participants tend to generalise from their own institution. Public discussion thus revolves around oversimplified and misleading declarations. When it comes to private higher education and the roles it plays, the gap is large between self-serving or ill-informed views and more complex reality.

The few exceptions are the pioneering work of Levy and the Program for Research on Higher Education (PROPHE), without whose contributions little could have been learnt about the sector. Financed by the Ford Foundation, PROPHE was created in 2000 at the University at Albany, State University of New York. Since its inception, it has done much to build the global knowledge base on PHE through a network of scholars in many countries, and various publications that include working papers, short articles and individual contributions in referred international journals. This 'tribe' remains the leading group that currently advances knowledge of PHE at the global level. Other efforts may be prevalent across the globe but remain fragmented and resource-strained.

An exceptional initiative within Africa is that at St. Mary's University in Ethiopia which has held an annual conference exclusively dedicated to PHE since 2003. In addition to publishing the information on its website, since 2010, the university has joined hands with the Association of African Universities and other partners like the African Union Commission, the International Network for Higher Education in Africa and Ethiopian Airlines to elevate the conference to an international level in order to contribute to the building of a wider research base on the subject. Similar regional efforts can catalyze the knowledge base of PHE, serving as a source of readily available knowledge that can attract experienced and novice researchers alike to a yet fertile research area.

2 Reason for Research Gaps

While the void in the PHE knowledge base can be partly explained by researchers' huge focus on the towering public – as compared to the miniature private – sector, conservative research traditions within mainstream higher education, a lack of interest from funders and the poor research traditions of PHEIs have contributed to the meager research focus and output. Many PHEIs do not undertake research but focus heavily on teaching. Few elite and semi-elite institutions seem to be contributing to building knowledge on PHE, both in the form of funding the project and actively pursuing research tasks. Moreover, a significant number of PHEIs, especially in the developing world, are weak in terms of properly documenting data on their operations, or they conceal, under-report or exaggerate available data, which impedes the research process.

A PHE sector that is content with this serious gap can never claim a better place in the wider higher education milieu which has an expansive accumulation of organized knowledge and data on many new areas of investigation. Where researcher engagement is non-existent and information about the sector is lacking, it would be naïve to expect a balanced assessment and understanding of a sector that is widely viewed with suspicion, mistrust and negativity. Hence, there is an unequivocal need to produce much more knowledge about and greater understanding of PHE through sustained empirical engagements and organized efforts.

3 The Need for More Scholarship

Despite its unprecedented growth in the past four decades, PHE has a long way to go before entrenching itself as a legitimate and popular field of scholarly enquiry. It is important that PHEIs take responsibility to address the challenges of building a knowledge base on PHE as this is a critical route that can offer better insights into the sector, encourage evidence-based decisions and viable policy directions, and help the sector to be viewed with confidence rather than suspicion and distrust.

Attempts to build improved understanding and scholarship about the sector cannot, however, be exclusively relegated to private institutions. The field has to be part of the wider teachings, curricular content and research engagements of tertiary institutions and other organizations with the objective of understanding the nature and challenges of private investment in higher education, which has now become a permanent part of the higher education system of many countries. Individual institutions, think tanks, non-governmental organizations, multidisciplinary researchers, graduate students, etc., should equally be attracted to PHE as a field of enquiry if its future directions are to be guided more intensely by knowledge and improved understanding than personal wishes, whims and purely commercial intents.

PART 5

Quality Assurance in Higher Education

CHAPTER 27

Towards a Diversified System of Quality Assurance

An earlier version of this chapter appeared in *University World News, Africa Edition*, 30 November 2018, https://www.universityworldnews.com/post.php?story=20181128093820l

The establishment of quality assurance agencies in many parts of the world is viewed as a means to address the attendant challenges of 'massifying' systems of higher education. However, the past few decades reveal that addressing the issue of quality requires more than setting up national agencies since the continued growth and complexity of an expanding higher education system can overwhelm and eventually render a fledgling system ineffective.

The Ethiopian Higher Education Relevance and Quality Agency (HERQA) was formally inaugurated as a sector wide agency in 2003 – coinciding with the onset of the aggressive expansion drive in the higher education sector. Its establishment was primarily driven by the increasing expansion of the public sector and the mushrooming of PHEIs. Set up as a semi-autonomous agency accountable to the Ministry of Education, HERQA was given the responsibilities of a national quality watchdog, with specific mandates to grant accreditation to PHEIs, conduct external quality audits on both public and private HEIs, offer equivalence of foreign credentials, and facilitate the development of HEIs' internal quality assurance systems.

The agency has accomplished a variety of tasks since its inception. In addition to promoting the concepts of quality across the sector, it has been instrumental in the deployment of various guidelines and procedures that respond to its accreditation, quality audit and benchmarking processes. Its direct influence in terms of offering quality-related short-term trainings and indirect influences through its regulatory frameworks are substantial additions to a changing higher education system fraught with challenges.

1   Strains in the System

Despite its contributions, HERQA has now reached a stage where its capacity, efficiency and integrity are tested to the limits. From an initial limited number of institutions, the Ethiopian higher education sector has grown to accommodate more than 350 public and private HEIs countrywide, creating an excessive workload, leading to bureaucratic delays to institutions seeking HERQA's speedy and efficient services. The agency's capacity and support activities have dwindled substantially over the years, falling short of addressing the sector's growing challenges. Notwithstanding the availability of dedicated and ethical experts who strive to discharge their responsibilities, the number, quality, experience and ethical standards of the existing staff are currently far below the professional requirements. Consequently, the agency has not been able to monitor diploma mills or control a litany of rising fraudulent activities. It has therefore found it difficult to meet the expectations of the government, institutions, students and Ethiopian society. Most stakeholders agree that there is now a sense of urgency to reverse this trend and revitalize the positive gains of the system.

Experience has shown that the major areas the agency needs to reform pertain to system and structural efficiency, institutional capacity, autonomy, resource deployment, and over-reliance on a limited mode of operation. Given the huge responsibilities HERQA is assuming, the current organizational structure demands some change and its existing budget also requires improvement commensurate with the huge operations the agency is undertaking. Poor infrastructure and underutilization of ICT have made the agency's tasks archaic and cumbersome. These areas and the poor data management system need significant improvement.

While the agency is assumed to have relative autonomy in terms of possible interference in its accreditation decisions, all matters relating to the employment and administration of staff are governed by Ethiopian civil law which offers little flexibility in adjusting existing recruitment and payment modalities. For instance, as a result of its low salary scale and per diems, HERQA has found it difficult to recruit suitable staff and prevent the staggering turnover rate, which has become a serious challenge and the source of inefficient practices.

2   Towards a More Diversified System

If anything has been learnt about quality assurance since 2003, one major lesson should be the challenges of delegating all national responsibilities to a single quality assurance agency. The Ethiopian experience calls for fundamental change. The challenges can be met by addressing HERQA's internal deficiencies and creating a mechanism whereby a set of diversified procedures and actors are aligned in the creation of a robust quality assurance system. At the internal level, the agency's organizational structure and governance system should be framed in such a way that it promotes excellence, integrity and credibility, and commands respect like any professional institution. In addition to increasing financial and material resources which allow meaningful delivery, there must be enabling arrangements that would equally permit the recruitment of professional staff on the basis of capacity, interest and integrity. Given the current size and demands of the sector, it is also important to introduce alternative and complementary mechanisms to handle some of the current responsibilities. Tasks entrusted to the agency like granting the equivalence of credentials and keeping HEIs' data could be transferred to other organs such as the Ministry of Higher Education and Science. This would allow the agency to focus on its core tasks.

In terms of diversifying the system, introducing a range of additional mechanisms of external quality assurance and relevant stakeholders can assist in strengthening the system. Employers' involvement in verifying credentials during employment could deter most of the illegal admissions at HEIs for which the agency is constantly blamed. Strengthening professional associations or introducing subject assessment schemes by external bodies could, in the long run, also help relieve the agency of program accreditation, an increasing burden. The introduction of the qualification framework being developed at national level may make its own contribution in terms of changing from the current input-focused to an output-based system. In the long term, the external quality assurance system may also consider instituting complementary agencies with different roles at national or regional level. While the major agency can have the responsibility of supervising and developing the overall quality assurance system, subsidiary or regional agencies can take on the role of program accreditation. The practice in some countries of granting a self-accrediting status to credible institutions with solid internal quality assurance systems is another useful lesson.

The task of ensuring quality at an external level demands ample resources, huge commitment and integrated tools and mechanisms. Ethiopia's quest for quality cannot be achieved with the meagre resources provided and with excessive dependence on the outcomes of HERQA alone. Strengthening HERQA's overall capacities and complementing its efforts through diversified modes of operation could ensure that the major objectives of quality assurance and responding to the evolving challenges of the higher education sector are met.

CHAPTER 28

Beyond the Establishment of Quality Assurance Agencies

An earlier version of this chapter appeared in *University World News, Africa Edition*, 22 June 2018, https://www.universityworldnews.com/post.php?story=20180622090453178

The multitude of concerns that accompany the increasing expansion of higher education continue to speed up the establishment of quality assurance agencies (QAAs) in many parts of the world, especially since the 1980s. These undertakings have been widely hailed as a success in their own right – as if the act of establishment alone could offer the spell to solve problems in a given higher education set-up. Calls for the establishment of QAAs and similar schemes continue unabated and while their presence provides a structural response aimed at addressing pertinent issues of quality, what is equally, if not more, important is the manner in which such agencies are organized and operate. Among others, the mandates of QAAs over public and private institutions, the mechanisms they use to ensure quality, the role they assume in exercising a controlling or enhancing function, and the ethical standards in place are all important caveats that need to be closely examined together with their specific operational features.

The public higher education sector in Ethiopia has existed for seven decades and continues to muster huge dominance and impact. There are currently more than 50 public universities in Ethiopia. According to recent figures from the Ministry of Education (2018), total enrolment in undergraduate and postgraduate programs (government and non-government) has reached 860,378, of which the majority (85%) is in government institutions. While education receives 25% of the national budget, higher education takes the highest share of the budget (45.9%), with general education at 47.3%. Private higher education institutions have only been operating since the end of the 1990s, and despite their sheer number, which is nearly 300, they remain limited in their enrolment size and influence. While public universities are fully financed by the government, the majority of PHEIs are self-financing and receive little or no direct help from the government.

1   HERQA – Mandates and Tools

HERQA was established in 2003 in the wake of a public higher education system characterized by aggressive expansion and the mushrooming of newly established PHEIs that needed to be regulated. The agency assumes a range of powers and duties relating to accreditation; evaluating institutions' relevance and quality enhancement systems; preparing requirements and directives to determine institutional status; advising the Ministry of Education in respect of a merger, division, closure or change of name of institutions; ensuring the relevance and quality standards set at foreign institutions or their branches operating in Ethiopia; and disseminating the status and determining the equivalence of qualifications issued by foreign institutions.

Over the past 15 years, the agency has employed a variety of tools to expedite its mandates and responsibilities which include accreditation, surprise visits and quality audits. While the first two mechanisms are exclusively enforced on PHEIs, only the third scheme is being used to influence the quality of education within the public sector. As set by Ethiopia's Higher Education Proclamation (2009/2019), accreditation requirements need to be met before institutions launch any academic program. Requirements focus on checking institutional performance in areas such as facilities and resources, curricula, staff qualification, internal structures and systems, etc.

Despite constituting a key element of quality assurance and the major task of the agency, accreditation does not apply to public institutions that accommodate 85% of higher education enrolment in the country. This means that public institutions can launch any program of their choice (including masters and PhDs) without requesting the permission of the agency. This has led to a situation where both undergraduate and graduate programs are mushrooming within the public domain without necessarily fulfilling minimum national standards. Holding both private and public providers of higher education to account through QA frameworks like accreditation is a policy track pursued by many governments, including those in Africa. Countries such as Egypt, Ghana, Uganda and Lesotho provide useful lessons for current QA practice in Ethiopia, which remains an exception in this regard.

Another important tool that could have been profitably used is the quality audit exercise which now serves as a voluntary stand-alone quality enhancement tool. The quality audit exercise is a relatively comprehensive undertaking that involves both public and private institutions and embodies process and output elements that are lacking in the input-based accreditation system. Its outcomes are communicated to institutions in the expectation that this will lead to the development of an enhancement plan that will be used as part of future institutional undertakings. As it now stands, the quality audit exercise does not have any link with accreditation. Nor does it involve mechanisms to enforce suggested follow-up measures that need to be taken by institutions after the findings of the quality audit are publicized. In terms of consequences or actions, measures that are common in many other countries such as linking quality audit results with strategic plan agreements or funding, do not exist in the Ethiopian public system. Hence, despite the huge amount of resources deployed, the quality audit exercise can only be useful for institutions that have a high level of commitment, motivation and readiness to benefit from the process.

2   Need for Change

While HERQA has the right tools at its disposal, the manner in which these tools are being used exhibits deficiencies and anomalies, requiring further improvements and change. The need for the establishment of HERQA, the financial and human resources dedicated to it, and the specific demands of an infant public higher education system do not justify the agency's overwhelming focus on only accrediting PHEIs; nor does the manner in which the outcomes of the quality audit exercise are solely left to the discretion of individual institutions. Leaving the public sector unaccountable, and underutilizing the benefits of the quality audit exercise will not only dent HERQA's image but can have serious consequences in terms of the national quest for quality education. The negative effect of these practices on institutions that produce graduates who are expected to have an impact on Ethiopia's current and future development makes the call for change a matter of urgency. This demands an overhaul of the way in which HERQA's tools are used and the immediate extension of its supervisory power over the public sector.

CHAPTER 29

Internal Quality Assurance
Key to Maintaining Quality

An earlier version of this chapter appeared in *University World News, Global Edition*, 15 February 2019, https://www.universityworldnews.com/post.php?story=20190117083946556

The establishment of an internal quality assurance system in an HEI is often regarded as the most critical element in creating a sustainable framework to maintain quality. Whereas external evaluations and publishable outcomes mainly respond to accountability issues, internal quality enhancement demands the establishment of a continuous and sustainable quality improvement scheme at the institutional level and at the level of academic disciplines. In addition to encouraging institutional change, the creation of an institution-wide quality management system could be regarded as a precursor to what are nationally constructed as external quality assurance mechanisms like accreditation and quality audits.

The introduction of a formal institutional quality audit system is a relatively new phenomenon in Ethiopia. However, this does not necessarily mean that HEIs never had mechanisms to assure the quality of their own provisions. In fact, prior to the move towards a more formalized system, most institutions were known for using mechanisms such as elitist student selection, rigorous evaluation and assessment, and periodic curriculum review for the purpose of assuring institutional quality. Such systems, however, had their own limitations including their restricted use for the purposes of self-reflection and institutional improvement. The move towards a more formalized system of quality assurance was thus justified by the deficiencies of the traditional quality assurance mechanisms, whose validity in the face of a 'massified' system was found questionable, both from the perspective of the government and the increasing complexities of the system itself. In this regard, the Ethiopian government has taken important steps not only in creating a formal framework of external quality assurance but also in broadly dictating the features of an internal quality assurance system at the level of institutions.

1   Legislative Framework

In terms of legislation, Ethiopia's second Higher Education Proclamation (2009) was the first legal framework to set out specific provisions on HEIs' internal quality systems. The proclamation underscores the need to establish an internal quality assurance framework, the elements that constitute the system, the responsibilities of individual HEIs, and the role of external bodies like HERQA and the Ministry of Education (now the Ministry of Science and Higher Education) in enhancing changes towards a strengthened internal quality management system. Such an institutional system of quality assurance was stipulated to pervade "all processes of importance to the quality of study programmes" (Article 22.3) and "provide for clear and comprehensive measures of quality covering professional development of academic staff, course content, teaching-learning processes, student evaluation, assessment and grading systems" (Article 22.2).

In responding to these requirements, HEIs have been expected to undertake periodic internal quality audits and follow up, and rectify internal deficiencies, document all interventions undertaken and report the same to HERQA, besides developing their own quality standards. In addition, HEIs should comply with recommendations made by HERQA regarding quality enhancement tasks they need to undertake after passing through the external quality assurance process. Such recommendations may include, for instance, mandatory on-job and tailor-made training that academic staff require to address deficiencies related to a lack of pedagogical knowledge on teaching and assessment.

Having been mandated by the 2009 higher education law, HERQA's quality audit practices involve the dual purpose of gauging the existing level of institutional capacity and the internal quality assurance systems of both public and private HEIs. These needs have been addressed from two major angles. The first relates to establishing formal quality management systems and units within institutions. HERQA requires that this should be ascertained through such elements as a quality audit structure at institutional level, a written policy on quality audit, a comprehensive data collection system, and a feedback and monitoring system aimed at continuous improvement. The second aspect pertains to ensuring the availability of an institutional quality care mechanism. This is more about promoting quality – supporting the provision of quality and the means to enhance quality – including features such as a quality care policy, and units dedicated to staff development and resource mobilization. In order to enhance this process, HERQA has developed guidelines on how institutions can conduct internal evaluation, prepare their own self-evaluation document (SED), and training on how the SED is prepared and/or any relevant technical assistance institutions may require. This has most often been done on a request basis.

2 The Status Quo

Notwithstanding their nascent stage of development, there are encouraging signs at both public and private institutions of the strides they are making towards the establishment of internal quality assurance systems. These initial efforts include the establishment of internal quality assurance units, the development of policies and guidelines, the designation of pertinent committees at various levels of institutions, and some practical tasks undertaken towards ensuring institutional quality. Efforts related to the latter have been especially manifested in the undertaking of internal quality assessments, program and course audits, curriculum review and pedagogic training for academic staff. However, it is not yet clear how these efforts are systematically contributing to improved internal capacity in the realms of teaching-learning, planning and decision-making processes and the overall student learning experience as opposed to the seemingly cosmetic changes occurring at the level of structure and policy design.

3 The Way Forward

While the development of internal quality assurance systems is gaining momentum across the Ethiopian higher education sector, the current state of affairs – in both public and private institutions – leaves much to be desired, as evidenced by the scores of quality audit reports produced by HERQA and some local research conducted in this area. Some of the deficiencies of the internal quality assurance system in Ethiopian HEIs may be acceptable given their overall recent history, but institutions' ambivalence in terms of promoting and strengthening the quality agenda requires urgent attention.

Local studies suggest that the lack of visionary leadership, poorly-articulated procedures to monitor internal operations, limited resource support, and resistance are some of the major factors that account for the gaps. The general observation appears to indicate that the internal quality assurance efforts undertaken by HEIs are not currently having far reaching effects due to a raft of structural and practical deficiencies that continue to hamper their efficiency and success. The few available local studies on the subject suggest that deficiencies such as a lack of leadership support, lack of resources, exclusive focus on the academic wing as opposed to the research and administrative functions of universities, overburdened quality audit staff with limited skills and a high staff turnover rate continue to have negative effects on the success of the evolving internal quality assurance system. It is incumbent upon institutional leaders and all relevant stakeholders to focus their attention and deploy appropriate resources to strengthening the internal quality assurance mechanisms of public and private HEIs, with a view to enhancing institutional change and meeting emerging challenges in a sustainable manner.

CHAPTER 30

From Gate Keepers to Gate Crashers
Corruption among University Faculty

An earlier version of this chapter appeared in *Inside Higher Education*, 31 March 2019, https://www.insidehighered.com/blogs/world-view/gatekeepers-gatecrashers

The scourge of corruption around the world remains a source of serious political and social concern. In Africa, where corruption is rampant, it is estimated to cost as much as 25% of the continent's annual GDP. Corruption knows no boundaries, although its type and range may differ from one context to another. The education sector has always been vulnerable to the practices and ethics that occur outside academe, but the sector has increasingly indulged in its own rampant corruption. Despite the dearth of research on various manifestations of academic corruption in Ethiopia, a handful of research projects conducted at a few public universities and mounting anecdotal evidence show that academic corruption is on the rise and is becoming a source of concern in a sector whose public credibility depends on integrity and ethical practice.

1   Manifestations of Faculty Corruption

While rampant academic corruption among students has been written about and appears in various guises, an alarming new development is university faculty and staff's involvement in various degrees of corrupt activity. A high level of teacher absenteeism is a common practice across the higher education sector. Where institutional control is weak, permanent faculty in HEIs moonlight in the private sector or in other public or private universities where teaching services are needed at the expense of their responsibilities to their mother institutions. Even more concerning are reports of instructors accused of demonstrating preferential and discriminatory treatment based on personal and family relations, ethnicity, religion, political affiliation when evaluating students. This is done through practices such as "exam leaking" or providing an inflated grade to a "favored" student. Requesting sexual favors from female students in exchange for grades is another practice that, sadly, still occurs. While staff of public institutions may be guilty of these activities, a significant number of private higher institutions are accused of offering inflated grades to their students to keep them in the pipeline until completion of their studies.

Another unethical practice is the ghostwriting of term papers and theses in which staff are involved. The number of assignments that have been "outsourced" and subsequently submitted by students may be difficult to verify but the proliferation of this practice is suggested by the number of advertisements near campuses that offer services for the production of different kinds of papers and theses for a fee. While the motivations need to be further studied, young university staff teaching at various HEIs are often inclined to participate in the ghostwriting of papers.

Faculty are being promoted to professorships when their publication history includes substandard work or publication in predatory journals that are known for publishing articles in return for a fee and with limited, if any, peer review. A recent study at a public university found that a significant number of faculty promotions were awarded to professors who had created a publication record by following this route. Anecdotal evidence further indicates that this promotion strategy is especially common in HEIs where it is known that articles presented as promotion qualifications are not checked. In similar vein, a few PHEIs are suspected of granting academic promotions based on substandard work in order to improve the overall profile of their faculty.

A big part of the problem in combating academic corruption is the lack of ethical responsibility at the individual level. This can be compounded by some university staff and authorities who collude to avoid incrimination when accused of corrupt practices. The spread of unethical practices reflects the lack of explicit regulations that clearly define behaviors that are corrupt and unacceptable. The problem is further aggravated by the lack of mechanisms to enforce existing regulations when faculty members are suspected of illicit acts. Most universities have legislation that outlines staff's responsibility in many areas but does not always incorporate some of the new and more 'innovative' approaches to cheating. Even when universities decide to take serious action, their decisions can be overridden by civil service law that constrains their authority to respond appropriately. However, some institutions have strict mechanisms and regulations against malpractice and seem to be handling the issue with greater efficiency, rigor and consistency.

2 Combating Academic Corruption

For countries like Ethiopia that identify higher education as their primary means of economic development and poverty reduction, there can be no more serious goal than fighting the impact of academic corruption. Although corruption needs to be attacked broadly at the national level, strategic efforts must also be made within the education sector. An important example of progress is the government's crackdown on forged degrees used by thousands of civil servants to secure positions and promotions. There is no reason why the same practice should not be repeated at universities with more careful evaluation of the publications submitted for academic promotion since there is a limited number of faculty and a more attentive examination should be an easy task.

Universities are supposed to be places where the future generation is prepared with knowledge and skills but also high ethical standards. University faculty and administration assume a critical role in promoting this ideal and must guard against corruption that inevitably undermines the success of individual students as well as the reputation of HEIs. The highest ethical standards should be expected of faculty and staff so that they are in an unassailable position to hold students accountable for their actions. Concerted action by relevant ministries, HEIs and other relevant stakeholders has so far been lacking but is urgently needed to combat the effects of academic corruption. Continuous monitoring and the creation of mechanisms to avoid possible loopholes should be instituted in order to prevent dishonest practices from persisting. While the development of comprehensive rules and regulations at national and institutional level is indispensable, strict enforcement remains the major challenge. This underscores the need to share information across institutions, develop enforceable practices, make a multi-level commitment to weed out existing maladies and prevent their future occurrence in a sector where integrity and honesty determine its success.

CHAPTER 31

The Scourge of Unscrupulous Private HE Institutions

An earlier version of this chapter appeared in *University World News, Africa Edition*, 2 December 2017, https://www.universityworldnews.com/post.php?story=2017120206012731

The past three decades have witnessed the global proliferation of PHEIs at tremendous speed. This sector currently accounts for a substantial percentage of higher education enrolment across the world, ranging from 20% in sub-Saharan Africa to more than 80% in East Asia. In Ethiopia, it contributes around 17% of national enrolment. Ethiopian PHEIs need to be accredited before commencing operation, although there are institutions that deliver programs under the pretense that they are accredited. Any credential obtained without accreditation is considered to be unlawful, and hence without value.

While a few PHEIs have achieved a good public image and semi-elite status, with recognition given to their programs, research endeavors and public engagement, the initial legitimacy obtained through accreditation is often abused by unscrupulous institutions that take advantage of growing demand for higher education and the government's finite monitoring capacity. The number of such providers is increasing, posing a serious threat to the entire system. The behavior and negative impact of shoddy institutions in Ethiopia can be gauged from repeated statements by regulators such as the Ministry of Education and the Higher Education Relevance and Quality Agency, media outlets, public and personal experiences, and a few studies on the subject.

1 Characteristics of Shoddy Operators

Shoddy providers are usually known for their myopic vision and limited appetite for long-range planning. Institutional planning and internal monitoring are considered expensive and a waste of time. Such institutions are infamous for their emphasis on short-term pecuniary gains and the lack of capital and energy invested in institutional growth. Shoddy providers are widely associated with poor preparation, delivery and output. They make little or no preparation before launching their programs. Curricula are directly copied from others and frequently lack rigor and self-initiated reviews. The will to develop programs in a manner that promotes an institutional identity is rare. The program delivery of such providers is poor due to substandard facilities, under-qualified staff and poor management. Since improvements require serious commitment, these institutions reflect little change even after years of operation. Substandard facilities and less qualified and experienced staff mean less investment and poor delivery, but undoubtedly more profit.

Unscrupulous PHEIs are adept at stage performances during accreditation visits in order to secure initial permission to operate. They may falsify documents or present resources borrowed or transferred from other sites in order to meet accreditation requirements. Aware of the power of accreditors, they have also been known to seek out godfathers placed in the higher echelons of government to give them the required backing and protection. A few have developed an 'untouchable' status due to this illegal backing. Where regulations are lax or non-existent, rogue providers are quick to disrespect admission requirements, curriculum arrangements, exam regulations and assessment practices. The files of illegally registered students are guarded against regulators so that no evidence is traced about institutions' illicit practices. Staff are coddled or bribed to keep the secrets of these institutions.

The assessment system in these institutions is designed in a manner that does not scare off potential candidates. Grades are often inflated when compared with public or some of the more serious private institutions. Managers unashamedly coax course instructors to offer 'acceptable' grades to ensure student retention. When instructors fail to comply, managers sometimes alter the grades themselves. In this way the institutions create expectations among students that enrolment will guarantee graduation.

2 Limited Regulatory Impact

Despite continued efforts, regulatory bodies' power over these providers has been too limited to protect the system. Rogue providers have not only managed to consistently elude regulators, but the way in which they behave continues to mar the legitimacy of the PHE sector as a whole. At times their actions invite sudden reaction from government, as was the case in 2010 when PHEIs were barred from offering teacher education and law courses – a ban which remains in place today – and in 2012, when a moratorium was placed on distance education programs, which affected both public and private institutions. With few exceptions, employers are increasingly losing interest in employing graduates from PHEIs despite the fact that the law does not allow such discrimination.

The impact of such institutions is so pervasive that other private providers may seek to emulate their practices for fear of losing their market share.

Public reaction towards shoddy providers has been mixed for a variety of reasons. A significant number of students who enroll in such institutions do so for the certificates that will bring them additional benefits in terms of employment, self-esteem and social acceptance. This has made them consenting accomplices. The limitations on the government authorities' ability to enforce rules continues to encourage illegal institutions and students to take their chances. Using the size of their student populations as their line of defense, rogue providers capitalize on the "excessive damage" any government action might do when their illegal acts are exposed. There have been instances where the government avoided taking serious action for fear that it would cause uproar among the public and in political circles. There are currently tens of thousands of students who feel protected in this way and continue to pursue their education at these institutions. Another challenge has been the lack of proper support for law-abiding PHEIs that continue to face the double challenge of meeting the stringent legal requirements of the system and resisting the influence of shoddy providers.

3   Required Interventions

Critical interventions are needed to counteract the effects of the burgeoning number of illegal providers. A robust and well-resourced regulatory system with ethical personnel is key. This demands meaningful and continuous support by the government. Regulators should also learn how to work with employers, professional associations and other relevant stakeholders who should be encouraged to bar the use of illicit credentials for employment, promotion or recognition of any sort. Students who wish to join such institutions should be forewarned about the distinction between the short-term gains of a dubious qualification versus the long term dangers of earning a certificate that may have no value. A mechanism should also be designed to provide extensive support to law-abiding PHEIs. In turn, these institutions should collaborate with appropriate organs to resist the influence of illegal providers. Concerted and organized efforts are required to curtail the influence of rogue providers and enable the PHE to gain more credibility.

CHAPTER 32

Academic Credential Fraud

In Search of Lasting Solutions

An earlier version of this chapter appeared in *University World News, Africa Edition*, 15 December 2017, https://www.universityworldnews.com/post.php?story=20171214061717655

The expansion of higher education in Ethiopia has, where employment opportunities are available, increased demand for better qualifications in addition to the variety of opportunities it has created. Positions that previously needed nothing more than basic literacy now require improved qualifications that sometimes demand that people go back to school. The consternation created due to growing demand for additional qualifications has led to a situation where those who cannot catch up are tempted to seek short-cut mechanisms to obtain degrees to protect their income and employment status. Nowhere is this pressure felt more in Ethiopia than in the civil service which has more than 1.5 million employees.

The sector has been embroiled in a variety of crises relating to illicit credentials, prompting nation-wide efforts to address the situation which may serve as lessons for other countries facing similar challenges. Much was known in the public arena about the rampant market for illicit credentials long before the government took action. When it did, the Ethiopian civil service, bedeviled by the mushrooming of false credentials for employment and promotion purposes, was engulfed in a wave of government crackdowns. The government claims the crackdown was prompted by inefficiencies within the civil service and the huge amount of money it spends to pay thousands of employees who earn benefits through false credentials. Whatever the truth, many have welcomed the move and stated that it is long overdue. The past 12 months in particular have witnessed arduous checking by government of the veracity of credentials submitted for promotion and employment. This verification has been done in cooperation with the educational institutions from which the degrees were supposed to have been obtained.

1 Offers of Clemency and Reverberations

In a bid to facilitate the crackdown, open promises have been made to employees holding false credentials to confess their transgressions and save themselves from dismissal, civil suits and criminal charges. This seems to have worked as a significant number of civil servants have already admitted their wrongdoing. Local newspaper *Addis Zemen* (20 October 2017) revealed that around 7,000 civil servants from the Oromia region alone – one of nine such regions in the country – have admitted to having used false credentials to obtain undeserved benefits. The most dominant counterfeit documents were found to be degrees obtained from recently established private colleges and those bearing the names of public universities. The same region is still reviewing over 3,000 reported cases of dubious credentials said to be held by civil servants. In similar vein, over 500 civil servants in the Amhara region, and 40 government employees in the Gambela region have admitted to flouting the law. The list of those exposed in all these regions includes individuals who assume various administrative and official positions within the system. These revelations have directed the spotlight on the remaining parts of the country and the federal civil service where the government is planning to expand its crackdown. As reported in the capital city's newspaper *Addis Lisan* (17 November 2017), the Addis Ababa City Administration Office of Public Service and Human Resource Development announced that those with false credentials had a month in which to admit their wrongdoing, after which the office would be taking the necessary administrative and legal measures. The city employs more than 100,000 civil servants. The federal civil service looks set to embark upon a similar purge.

The measures have sent strong reverberations across the nation. Employers have begun to take extra care in screening the credentials submitted for employment and/or promotion. Close cooperation is being forged between civil service offices and individual HEIs and the Higher Education Relevance and Quality Agency, HERQA, which maintains a database of graduates from private institutions. Those who have been following the legal route to earn genuine credentials have also felt vindicated after having lost hope in the system. Despite the message that such violations will not be tolerated, some doubt that the new moves will stand the test of time. They believe that optimism is misplaced as the measures taken thus far are narrowly focused and the government needs to broaden its net to address the full extent of the problem. While it is argued that the focus of the current crackdown has been on counterfeit documents fabricated by individuals, this excludes the verification of degrees issued by institutions that continue to register thousands of students who do not meet the admission requirements set by the Ministry of Education. As experience over the past decade-and-a-half has shown, there are students who attend programs for which they are not qualified in the first place. This has become a major breeding ground for illicit degrees and a huge income earner for institutions that have little regard for the law. Given this situation, observers argue that this is also a major route to issue illegal degrees and calls for no less attention.

2   Broader Participation Needed

Although HERQA has been entrusted with the task of regulating illegal activities undertaken by HEIs, its limited capacity and the sophisticated nature of the transgressions have meant that it is no longer tenable to impose such a huge responsibility on a single organization. It is this situation that enables institutions that are hell-bent on breaking the law to continue to outmaneuver the agency. It is also why efforts made in this direction are piecemeal and not fully effective. I would argue that the situation calls for the participation of other parties that have a stake in guarding the system from fraudulent activities.

Among other things, the new crackdown has highlighted the key gatekeeping role of employers and the government in terms of stemming the negative effects of false credentials. Simple verification of credentials at the point of entry or during promotion could save a lot of trouble and damage that is not easy to manage at a later date. The government's resolve in addressing the challenge is also the key lever of success. If meaningful and lasting solutions are to be found against illicit credentials, the government's control mechanisms should be on par with the sophisticated manner in which the credentials are obtained. This may include verifying credentials obtained through illegal admission to educational institutions that defy national regulations. However, the best place to check this remains the public sector where such transgressions can easily be traced.

PART 6

Internationalization of Higher Education

CHAPTER 33

Disparities and Parallels in Internationalization
The Ethiopian Experience

An earlier version of this chapter appeared in *International Higher Education*, 2018(92), 17–19 (with Damtew Teferra), http://dx.doi.org/10.6017/ihe.2018.92.10218

Interest and involvement in the internationalization of higher education are unavoidably on the rise across both the developed and developing worlds. In both contexts, institutions are increasingly enticed to conform to this emerging trend. However, differences abound due to the influence of contextual factors such as prevailing needs, capacity, resources, institutional status, and ambitions. We examine the manners in which internationalization is realized in developed and developing countries by exploring such factors as motives, approaches, policies, strategies, and the nature of institutional relationships in the Ethiopian context. We believe that such an exercise is instrumental to plan and develop frameworks that are relevant to Ethiopian higher education, instead of opting for wholesale adoption from elsewhere.

Higher education in Ethiopia began in 1950 with the establishment of the University College of Addis Ababa. The sector remained elitist in its orientation until the end of the 1990s – with two universities, a student population of about 38,000, and a gross enrollment ratio (GER) of 0.8%, which was very low even by African standards. Over the past two decades, the sector has achieved phenomenal growth. The number of public institutions has reached 51 and there are more than 260 private institutions – four of which hold university status. The sector accommodates over 860,000 students – 85% in the public sector – and has a GER of around 12%. This fast-changing landscape has increasingly brought internationalization to the fore as a major mechanism to address the numerous challenges associated with fast "massifying" systems. With regard to motives, Ethiopian HEIs' engagement in internationalization has mainly been driven by emerging needs.

The aggressive expansion of the sector has raised formidable challenges in terms of the availability of qualified staff and research output. Currently, only 15% of staff in the higher education sector hold PhDs despite government's plan to raise this to 30% by 2019–2020. Research output has also been somewhat low due to, among other factors, a poor research tradition, excessive teaching loads, skills deficiencies and, of course, funding constraints. Ethiopian universities are aware of the importance of internationalization in terms of the perceived benefits of improving teaching and learning, student and teacher development, and standards and quality. Their dominant forms of engagement primarily relate to teaching and research collaborations and international research projects. The government envisages enhancing such collaborations and international exchanges in the interests of advancing the effectiveness of teaching and learning and the quality of academic programs and research. In internationalizing, universities assign the highest priority to PhD and masters programs, in that order. In terms of academic disciplines, engineering and health sciences take the lead. This appears logical, given the serious shortages of highly qualified personnel at these levels and in these disciplines. As a corollary, the dominant rationales identified for Ethiopian HEI s, as in most other African countries, relate more to academic than to economic, political, and/or cultural rationales.

Issues of international student recruitment and using internationalization as a source of prestige, which appear to be dominant features of HEI s in the North and are increasingly emerging in developing economies, are not yet the focus of Ethiopian institutions. Institutions recognize the importance of national policies in shaping institutional policies on internationalization, but, no such policies existed until very recently. The lack of a comprehensive policy on internationalization was acknowledged by the Education Sector Development Program V, which envisaged the preparation and approval of a national policy and institutional collaboration strategy on internationalization in the period 2016–2020. Establishing a national unit or body to promote, monitor, and evaluate the internationalization of Ethiopian higher education, as well as developing and implementing a strategy to attract foreign students, are included in the plan. However, this has yet to materialize.

The lack of strategic engagement in promoting internationalization is widely discernible across universities. Most of the institutions that have initiated and managed partnerships with foreign institutions have not handled their engagements in an organized and systematic manner due to a lack of resources and clear direction. At the larger universities, initiatives are managed at different levels without being communicated to the higher echelons of the institution or the office in charge. Equally serious is the paucity of data on many aspects of internationalization, further compounded by weak knowledge management systems that impinge on information flows at various levels. Institutions attribute these weaknesses to the excessive burden of mundane but critical issues, such as student accommodation, catering, and leisure, diverting their attention from more strategic tasks. Most relationships established by Ethiopian universities are largely North–South rather than South–South, with Europe the preferred continent for collaborations – distantly followed by North America. These lopsided partnerships are mainly attributed to disparities in financial resources and capacity. In most cases, local institutions are mere 'recipients' and the elements of reciprocity are not evident. There have also been instances of Northern partners seeking to achieve their own objectives without much regard for the needs and aspirations of their local partners and, at times, their own funders.

A peculiar and instructive feature of internationalization in Ethiopia is the presence of regulatory regimes and frameworks that are not always available elsewhere, even in developed countries. Academic recognition and equivalence arrangements for foreign qualifications were for a long time the task of the Ministry of Education (MoE) and recognition of foreign credentials within the civil service had to pass the ministry's scrutiny. This role, and the additional responsibility of granting accreditation to cross-border higher education providers, have been transferred to the Higher Education Relevance and Quality Agency (HERQA) that was established in 2003. The agency uses its double mandate to keep dubious credentials and unscrupulous providers at bay.

The above analysis demonstrates the need to understand global trends, national frameworks, and institutional contexts when navigating the internationalization terrain and setting one's own agenda. While the trend in Ethiopia in terms of improved awareness and readiness for internationalization is upbeat, there is an urgent need to address existing deficiencies with regard to issues of policy, strategic direction, systems, and frameworks. Given the multitude of challenges they confront, HEIs in Ethiopia, and many others in similar nascent systems elsewhere, will probably continue to struggle with the complexities of internationalization for many years to come.

CHAPTER 34

Medical Education and the Ethiopian Exodus of Talent

An earlier version of this chapter appeared in *Inside Higher Education*, 15 July 2019, https://www.insidehighered.com/blogs/world-view/medical-education-and-ethiopian-exodus-talent

On May 3, 2019, the Prime Minister of Ethiopia held a meeting with 3,000 health professionals from across the country to discuss the state of health services and the challenges facing health workers. Although the Prime Minister declared that the meeting was "key for policymaking", health professionals appeared to be dissatisfied with the way he addressed their predicament. Despite the concessions and the many promises made, a wave of strikes continued across the country. While the solution to this particular turmoil was the government's immediate concern, there is general recognition that the sector's challenges extend far beyond the standoff and call for structural and systemic change. The government has vowed to make additional effort and changes with the involvement of relevant stakeholders at national and regional level. One challenge that needs to be addressed is on-going migration of health professionals, especially physicians.

1 Healthcare and Medical Education in Ethiopia

Sub-Saharan Africa is known as the region with the lowest density of healthcare workers. According to the World Health Organization, Ethiopia has a health workforce ratio of 0.7 against the recommended ratio of 2.3 per 1,000 people that is considered to be imperative for health coverage and to make meaningful health interventions. The country's physician-to-population ratio of 1:21,000 is also one of the lowest in sub-Saharan Africa. Since 1994, the government's health development programs have had an important impact on the sector's growth. According to the Ministry of Health (2016), there has been a significant increase in the number of health posts, health centers, hospitals and personnel including officers, nurses, midwives and health extension workers. The number of schools and colleges providing health education training has increased; the graduation output of public and private schools including HEIS has also grown more than 16-fold since 1999/2000. According to the Ministry of Education (2018), currently, more than 80,000 undergraduate students are pursuing studies in medicine and health sciences in public and private HEIs.

Despite efforts to improve the healthcare system that have produced quantitative gains, many challenges remain. The system still lacks infrastructure and resources, and suffers from poor quality education and internal quality assurance systems. Performance assessment deficits and challenges relating to staff retention, skills distribution, and regional disparities that result in staff's reluctance to work in rural areas and little inclination to specialize in disciplines where there are skill shortages, are further hindrances. In responding to these multi-faceted challenges, the Ministry of Health has devised several strategies including its popular "flood and retain initiative" designed to increase the number of available health workers at all levels. While these have brought about some improvement, it has not been possible to solve the various challenges of the sector in a fundamental way, including the migration of physicians who continue to leave the public sector and Ethiopia for greener pastures in the country and elsewhere.

2   Immigration Plans and Patterns

Sub-Saharan Africa has the highest levels of health worker migration in the world and Ethiopia is one of the countries with the highest emigration of physicians in the region. According to Berhan (2008), Ethiopia trained 4,629 physicians (including 1,153 specialists) between 1987 and 2006 but the public sector managed to retain only 20%, or 932 professionals in the same period. Though limited, other studies of the brain drain and medical students' emigration aspirations reflect an alarming situation. Deressa and Azazh's study (2012) in Addis Ababa University found that around 53% of medical students hoped to emigrate upon graduating, particularly to the United States and Europe. The desire to migrate was higher among fourth-year and internship students than those in their first and second years of study, stronger among male than female students, and particularly strong among those with clinical experience compared to those in the pre-clinical stage.

Johansson's (2014) study in Jimma University and St. Paul's Millennium Medical College in Addis Ababa revealed that 59.4% of medical students planned to work abroad in five years' time and as many as 73.4% indicated their intention to go abroad in 10 years. The only exceptions were female candidates and trainees who had altruistic motives to serve the community and showed less inclination to leave their country immediately after graduation. It should be noted that mobility is also a common phenomenon among a significant number of health professionals who seek to move from rural to urban areas and from the public sector to better-paying jobs in the private sector. Compared to other professional areas, medical personnel appear to be the most susceptible to the desire to emigrate due to increasing demand for health professionals in countries in the developed world that offer better pay and living conditions and a better working environment.

3 Addressing the Challenges

Educating medical doctors is an expensive enterprise for any developing country. According to one conservative estimate, nearly 30,000 USD is lost for every medical school graduate who emigrates. The decision or intention to emigrate is a complex issue that can be influenced by a plethora of factors. The health professionals that met with the Prime Minister not only called for improved financial rewards for health professionals, but for better quality education, career satisfaction, retention incentives, career advancement opportunities, and health facilities as well as for administrative inefficiencies and corrupt practices in the system to be addressed.

While there is an urgent need to overhaul the system and address the various challenges, this will not be an easy task in a country that confronts a multitude of other societal challenges and serious resource limitations. In terms of priorities, the country cannot afford to continue to educate, and then lose its medical professionals in whom significant public funds have been invested and whose contribution is critical in improving the health system. Hence, efficient mechanisms should be formulated to prevent the emigration of health professionals and tap the expertise of those who have already left.

CHAPTER 35

Foreign HE Outposts

Navigating Risks and Opportunities

An earlier version of this chapter appeared in *University World News, Africa Edition*, 5 April 2019, https://www.universityworldnews.com/post.php?story=20190401132944553

Institutional and program mobility from the developed to the developing world is a phenomenon that continues to attract research interest within the broader field of higher education internationalization, while the movement of programs and institutions within the developing world itself is little studied. More research in this area could assist our understanding of the evolving features of internationalization. This article briefly examines internationalization in East Africa through an exploration of outposts of Ethiopian public and private HEIs that have made inroads in Somalia through program mobility. Somalia lost much of its political, economic and social fabric after the civil war at the end of the 1980s and the disintegration of its central government. The country's education sector has been one of the major casualties of state failure.

1   Unprecedented Growth

The relative peace that prevailed in the country in the past decade-and-a-half has seen the unprecedented growth of HEIs in South-Central Somalia, Puntland, and Somaliland. According to one news report, from 50 universities in 2013, Somalia is now home to more than 100. The number of institutions in the capital city alone is said to be well over 60. According to the Heritage Institute for Policy Studies (2013), the biggest share of the higher education growth in Somalia is taken by PHEIs including those established by Somali nationals and those that have moved from neighboring countries such as Kenya, Uganda and Ethiopia.

Half a dozen private and three public Ethiopian HEIs are currently operating in Somalia, most of which are based in Addis Ababa. These institutions operate on a franchise basis with Somali partner institutions that assume responsibility to deliver programs, while the mother institution's major role pertains to standards, quality control and certification. Ethiopian institutions are recognized and accredited in their own country but are required to register with the Somaliland Higher Education Commission which has not yet started fully-fledged local accreditation due to legislative and capacity gaps. Although most of the programs offered by Ethiopian institutions in Somalia are accredited in Ethiopia through the national Higher Education Relevance and Quality Agency, some have not yet received such recognition, but are being delivered in Somalia.

Since its heyday in the 1960s, the quality of the Ethiopian higher education sector's offerings has deteriorated, mainly due to neglect of the sector during the 1970s and 1980s and the effects of the expansion drive over the past two decades that has resulted in a shortage of resources, qualified staff and delivery systems. One could thus ask how it is possible for Ethiopian institutions to successfully export their programs outside their territory. Among other reasons, high demand for tertiary education in Somalia has created opportunities for providers from neighboring countries to operate without necessarily carrying the quality label. Another possible explanation is the overall preference for foreign institutions which is said to be common among Somali students.

From an institutional point of view, opening a foreign post comes with a raft of opportunities and challenges. On the 'opportunity' side, in addition to financial gain, institutions can promote people-to-people relations and acquire wide academic and managerial experience from such operations. Challenges usually arise from cultural differences, student expectations and local resources – including human resources – that may not be available. A foreign institution's success is usually determined by its ability to capitalize on the benefits and navigate the challenges. Assistance of local partners in this regard is crucial.

2   Quality Concerns

Despite the opportunities created by local and foreign HEIs and anticipated institutional differences, there is little empirical evidence on the standard of education provided by HEIs in Somalia. However, grave concerns continue to be raised about the general quality of education. Most institutions are said to be deficient in terms of infrastructure and facilities, staff qualifications, and library and laboratory resources. No effective national or institutional quality assurance mechanisms appear to have been put in place to regulate or enhance the quality of local providers. A Somali education authority observed that existing HEIs admit more than 50,000 students each year, but the country's high schools only produce 30,000 school leavers, suggesting the possibility of fraudulent activities – relaxed admission requirements and enrolment of ill-qualified students – in the enrolment practices of some institutions. Another concern relates to the neophytic stage of the country's national quality assurance system. Although established in 2011 with responsibility for accreditation and quality assurance, the commission has not yet been able to enforce its mandate due to the lack of legislation. In order to commence activities, tertiary education providers from neighboring countries need only register with the Somaliland Commission for Higher Education.

3 The Way Ahead

Somalia is a classic example of how state failure or the lack of a regulatory framework can lead to a rapid rise in private providers to fulfil demand for higher education. From an Ethiopian perspective, the ability of the country's HEIs to export their programs outside the national territory is a new and exciting development within the country's higher education system. It aligns well with the government's strategy of internationalization which encourages HEIs to exploit demand for tertiary education in neighboring countries. It is also suggestive of a similar strategy that could fulfil educational needs within and outside of the region, especially in the Middle East where thousands of Ethiopians live and work without access to educational opportunities that could benefit them when they return to their country.

It should be noted, however, that while the lax legal requirements in Somalia can enhance the mobility of strong foreign institutions, the legal vacuum might also encourage illegal providers and certificate shops to proliferate, endangering the overall course of the higher education sector in the country and the sustainability of these new developments. If Somalia is to benefit from the current positive trend, it needs to coordinate its quality assurance efforts with responsible agencies in neighboring countries like Ethiopia that have established their own system to regulate cross-border higher education. Another viable option is for Somalia to develop a robust national quality assurance system of its own that addresses the country's efforts to grow higher education provision without compromising on quality. Equally important is what foreign institutions should do with regard to their operations. Although Ethiopian institutions should not deny themselves the benefits of the initial phase of a relaxed regulatory environment, they should ensure the sustainability of their operations through continuous capacity development and internal quality assurance systems that will guarantee them success not only in the short term, but also in the years ahead when they will inevitably be subjected to more stringent national regulatory processes.

CHAPTER 36

Foreign Qualification and Credential Evaluation

An earlier version of this chapter appeared in *University World News, Africa Edition*, 11 June 2020, https://www.universityworldnews.com/post.php?story=20200609072715341

The benefits of foreign qualification recognition arrangements for students, institutions and employers, and their value for employment, mobility, professional licensing and further studies cannot be overemphasized. Failure to recognize foreign credentials could lead to a variety of unintended consequences for graduates, their institutions and the labor market. Among other things, it can hamper the full utilization of skilled labor within the broader labor market and at a national level. Despite the increasing mobility of students across the globe and the attention it receives, there is limited research and information on how the recognition of qualifications is undertaken in different regions and the implications this holds in terms of student destiny, employability and institutional reputability. The practice of credential evaluation appears to be gaining some currency as a means to facilitate acceptance of foreign qualifications obtained through transnational education and student mobility.

1 Lack of a Structured Response

Available information suggests that there are wide variations among countries as regards recognition of foreign qualifications. To some extent, this speaks of the lack of a structured response to increasing demands for recognition of foreign qualifications across many regions and countries. In some countries, evaluation and recognition of foreign credentials are carried out by individual institutions or independent credential examiners. In others, government or specific agencies or offices have this responsibility. Although it is difficult to gauge the extent of their utilization, initiatives such as the UNESCO Regional Conventions on the Recognition of Studies, Diplomas and Degrees in Higher Education, and instruments such as the UNESCO Council of Europe's "Recommendation on criteria and procedures for the assessment of foreign qualifications" have been recommended as possible mechanisms for credential recognition for countries that wish to use them. Mutual recognition agreements or the establishment of joint or multinational quality assurance and accreditation systems have also been suggested to facilitate legal recognition of academic qualifications between countries. Initiatives by professional bodies working towards agreed international standards for professional recognition are posited as equally important instruments that could be used for a similar purpose.

2 The Practice in Ethiopia

Ethiopia's participation in outbound student mobility is limited compared to many countries in sub-Saharan Africa. However, there have been mechanisms for recognizing foreign credentials due to their importance for employment, professional licensing and further education. For many years, the Ethiopian Ministry of Education has been working through Ethiopian embassies and other means to collect information about foreign institutions' educational provision and accreditation status in order to grant credential equivalence for foreign educated Ethiopians. This has allowed Ethiopian graduates from foreign institutions to be accorded the same status and benefits as those with local qualifications. After new stipulations were set out in the Higher Education Proclamation of 2009, the role of developing guidelines and determining the equivalence of foreign higher education qualifications was transferred to the Higher Education Relevance and Quality Agency (HERQA). According to information obtained from the agency, from 2010 to 2014, 4,379 applications were made for recognition of qualifications obtained abroad. Out of these, 340 were rejected while the remainder were approved. Recent developments indicate that more than 1,500 applications are made annually for recognition of foreign qualifications.

3 Guidelines and Procedures

HERQA claims to not have clear, fully-fledged guidelines to verify foreign credentials but has set the principles on which such guidelines should be based. As noted by Teshome (2015), these are informed by the following:
– A comparative approach
– Access to the evaluation service
– Evaluation without prejudice
– Fair, transparent, coherent and reliable criteria
– Professional integrity
– Flexibility

- First come, first served
- Public accountability
- Self-initiation
- Client satisfaction
- Commitment to excellence

The process of credential evaluation at HERQA focuses on analyzing the nature of foreign degrees and providing Ethiopian equivalents, which requires access to reliable information and expertise. Both may not be easy for a nascent and under-resourced organization like HERQA, but the agency continues to discharge its responsibilities by setting out its own working modalities which are continuously updated. Recently, the agency has set up a separate functional unit to handle this specific responsibility. Among others, HERQA considers the following major criteria for the assessment of foreign qualifications:
- The education system of the country where the applicant studied;
- Entry or graduation requirements graduates had to meet;
- The status of the institution which the applicant attended;
- The content of the program of study; and
- The assessment modalities of the foreign institution.

Information gathered on each of these areas is verified and measured against Ethiopian standards before the recognition of a foreign qualification is granted to an applicant.

4   Challenges and the Way Forward

The recognition of foreign credentials and the creation of mechanisms that facilitate the process can pose a variety of challenges. Verification of foreign qualifications requires time and rigor which may frustrate those who need the service urgently. The process includes bureaucratic and tedious tasks such as checking the veracity of the applicant's academic history, the period of study, the authenticity of the institution and authentication of the certificates and diplomas offered. These tasks require the browsing of university websites and approaching embassies, ministries of foreign affairs and other sources for information, verification and authentication of institutional status and academic credentials.

The lack of a centralized database on foreign institutions, differences in admission requirements, programs, levels of education and the assessment mechanisms used by different universities, and the lack of a national qualifications framework are challenges that continue to confront HERQA. Where there is insufficient information and limited comparability between foreign and local standards, the recognition process could be seriously hampered. The globalization of skilled labor markets and growing student and professional mobility has resulted in a significant increase in demand for academic and professional recognition of foreign qualifications. However, serious challenges are presented by gaps in policies and practices for the provision of such recognition across the globe. These challenges call for the coordinated efforts of all stakeholders. While the development of systems that cater to such needs is a matter of urgency, clear guidelines and transparent processes by which the recognition of foreign qualifications is awarded remain critical.

The role of individual institutions in the recognition of foreign credentials should also not be underestimated. Institutions can provide substantial assistance by offering information that facilitates the procedures to earn an equivalency. For example, details about the student, the institution, entrance requirements, the period of study, study content, and grading schemes can readily be provided by proactive institutions that cater to the needs of their students. Providing such information to foreign-educated citizens before they return to their countries can save graduates from facing unnecessary challenges upon returning home. Last but not least, countries, regions and institutions should forge close cooperation and design tangible mechanisms for the mutual recognition of foreign credentials.

CHAPTER 37

Cross-Border Higher Education
Regulating the Benefits and Risks

An earlier version of this chapter appeared in *University World News, Africa Edition*, 21 September 2018, https://www.universityworldnews.com/post.php?story=20180919080813145

Cross-border higher education assists in broadening access, meeting demand for foreign qualifications, reducing the number of students travelling abroad (containing brain drain), and addressing local deficiencies by improving universities' academic and research performance. It also involves some risks, including competing with domestic institutions; a possible influx of low-quality foreign providers; and increased inequality in access to higher education. These and other related risks generate significant mistrust of cross-border education in many countries. One means of addressing this is the introduction of a regulatory framework that governs its provision.

Until now, the most common manifestation of cross-border higher education in Ethiopia was the movement of students to foreign countries, a trend driven by the absence of or limited capacity of local HEIs. While this is still the case to a large extent, unmet demand for postgraduate education, financial opportunities for educational providers and new regulations for providers have changed the terrain. Currently, half a dozen foreign institutions operate in Ethiopia, having forged partnerships with local private institutions. All cross-border providers operate on the basis of program mobility, with the exception of the University of South Africa (UNISA) which has opened a branch campus in Addis Ababa. The functional scheme for the remaining institutions is commonly known as a franchise – an arrangement whereby the local partner provides all the services but the degree is issued in the name of the foreign institution. Providers currently enroll a few thousand students at Masters level where demand for higher level studies is strong. The University of South Africa is the only institution that enrolls students at PhD level. The most popular programs are in business-related fields offered through a combination of distance and online modes with face-to-face tutorial support. The role of the local partner institution is restricted to major functions such as registration, distribution of printed materials, tutorials, and collection and remittance of payments.

1 Regulatory Frameworks

The potential dangers associated with rogue providers in many contexts is a source of concern as regards the registration and quality assurance of cross-border provision, and for those countries without regulations, the guidelines developed by UNESCO (2005) are suggested as a non-binding standard. While some countries that export higher education have binding guidelines for their providers operating offshore, similar to some recipient countries which are institutionalizing mechanisms for registration and assuring the quality of foreign providers operating within their borders, the overall availability and enforcement of laws governing cross-border higher education leaves much to be desired in many countries. Research indicates that existing national frameworks of quality assurance, accreditation and recognition of qualifications are, in many instances, not sufficiently geared towards addressing cross-border provision. Despite these global trends, Ethiopia provides positive experiences in the regulation of cross-border higher education.

Ethiopia's regulation has been effected through a two-pronged approach: authentication of credentials and accreditation of foreign providers. Previously, the Ministry of Education oversaw the granting of academic recognition and equivalence arrangements for foreign qualifications based on information on the accreditation status of foreign institutions in their respective countries (through Ethiopian embassies, among others). This enabled Ethiopian graduates from foreign institutions to secure comparable status and benefits accorded to local qualifications. In 2009, this role was transferred to the Higher Education Relevance and Quality Agency (HERQA), which now has the responsibilities of granting accreditation to cross-border providers and collecting and disseminating information about the status, standards, and programs of study offered by foreign institutions. HERQA also ensures that foreign institutions in Ethiopia are accredited in their country of origin and that they comply with local relevance and quality standards.

As a relatively new initiative within the Ethiopian higher education sector, cross-border higher education caused misgivings from the outset. In a position paper, HERQA (2008) noted the modality as an area of concern for HEIs, students, accreditation bodies, employers, and the government. This led to the development of "Guidelines for the Accreditation of Cross-border Higher Education in Ethiopia" (HERQA, 2011), which outline the need and conditions for quality assurance and accreditation of cross-border providers. The proposed legal framework assumes that cross-border provision should contribute to the broader economic, social and cultural wellbeing of Ethiopia, and strengthen the country's higher education capacity as a member of the international community. Cross-border higher education should not only instill in learners the critical thinking that underpins responsible citizenship at the local, national and global goal levels, but also expand opportunities for international mobility of faculty, researchers and students.

The framework emphasizes accountability to the public, students and government, and transparency in providing clear and full information to learners and external stakeholders on the education they offer. The guidelines prescribe that foreign institutions should be accredited in their country of origin before applying for accreditation in Ethiopia. They should also form partnerships with local institutions, after which they must go through the process of accreditation that applies to local programs (HERQA, 2011). However, public (as opposed to private) institutions that run cross-border higher education are still outside of HERQA's remit. As a result, little is known about their operations.

2 Emerging Issues and the Future

Given the limited capacity of local institutions, cross-border higher education provision has immense potential to address the deficiencies of local universities and institutions, especially in terms of postgraduate programs where there is still an observable local gap. Cross-border higher education can supplement the system by creating additional access to international training without forcing learners to travel outside their country. While the development of cross-border higher education regulations has assisted in preventing the illegal encroachment of foreign providers that are regarded as a serious threat in many contexts, issues remain that could impinge on the success of this modality in the future. One is related to the high tuition fees charged by cross-border higher education providers compared to local institutions. With increasing growth of local postgraduate programs, this might restrict the number of students able to benefit from the opportunities provided. Cross-border institutions that operate outside the remit of HERQA are another area of concern.

In view of continuing demand for and the distinct nature of cross-border higher education, more needs to be done to put in place balanced quality assurance schemes within the system. In this regard, the development of comprehensive regulations that can accommodate possible challenges in the area, extending the agency's supervisory role over cross-border operators that operate in partnership with public institutions, augmenting the internal capacity of the regulatory agency, and forging improved cooperation with foreign quality assurance and accreditation bodies that can supplement existing efforts, are important considerations for the future.

CHAPTER 38

The Challenges of Attracting and Retaining Foreign Faculty

An earlier version of this chapter appeared in *International Higher Education*, *2019*(95), 15–16, https://ejournals.bc.edu/index.php/ihe/article/view/11191/9441

The value of international faculty in terms of infusing talent and diversity and improving the status of any higher education system, is widely acknowledged. Despite the similarity of interest in attracting such faculty, the purposes for which international faculty are hired differ from one context to the other. This is reflected in the operational tasks of attracting, recruiting, hiring and retaining them. While Ethiopia has never been colonized, the history of its modern education reflects heavy, systemic dependence on foreign personnel.

1   History of Dependence on Foreign Staff

The indelible marks of foreign expatriates are noticeable in areas such as the establishment of schools, the design of policies and curricula and their employment as advisers, officials, principals and teachers in the various levels of the education system. When Ethiopia's first Western modern institution, Menelik II School opened in 1908, it relied on Egyptian Copts. The principal and the teachers in the Teferi Mekonen School, which was established in 1925 were also international faculty mainly from French Lebanon, while the position of administrator was held by Hakim Workneh Eshete, a foreign-educated Ethiopian.

Ethiopia's modest attempt to kick start its modern education system before the beginning of the Italo-Ethiopian war in 1935 was supported by a few hundred teachers, including foreign faculty. Before the war, French was the dominant foreign language in schools. After the Italian occupation (1935–41), which annihilated a large number of local intelligentsia or forced them to migrate, Ethiopia again relied on foreign professionals to rebuild its modern education system from scratch. As a result of the Allied Forces' assistance in liberating Ethiopia in 1941, the period from 1942 until 1952 was dominated by the significant presence and influence of the British in the education sector and other government ministries. British experts and teachers were replaced by

Americans in the second half of the 1950s, due to Ethiopia's strengthened links with the United States through the Point Four Program of Technical Assistance (later renamed the Agency for International Development). In the next two decades, the United States had a huge influence in many sectors, including education, where it was involved in reorganizing the Ministry of Education, supplying person power, materials and textbooks and setting up the first HEIs in the country.

When the University College of Addis Ababa (UCAA, the first HEI in the country) was established in 1950, the teachers and its president were Jesuit Canadians. Indeed, UCAA had no Ethiopian faculty during the first four years of its existence. The same was true of the handful of colleges that were founded from 1950 to 1960. The number and nationalities of international faculty recruited in these HEIs were influenced by how they were established, the nationalities of their leaders and each institution's employment policies. Although there was some change toward the end of the Imperial government as a result of the deliberate 'Ethiopianisation' policy it pursued, the Haile Selassie I University (HSIU, now Addis Ababa University) remained dominated by international faculty. In 1973, 54% of HSIU staff were foreigners. The balance between international and local staff in Ethiopian HEIs changed significantly after the 1974 revolution, which drove many foreign staff out of the country due to the country's adoption of a socialist policy and its subsequent relations with Eastern bloc countries. The huge gap created by the departure of Western expats was filled by staff recruited from socialist countries, but dependence on foreign faculty continued for as long as a decade after the socialist government assumed power. Of a total of 934 university staff in 1982–83, some 335 (36%) were foreigners, with the dominance of international faculty in senior academic positions much more pronounced.

The need for, and influence of, international faculty at the lower levels of education in Ethiopia is currently over, but their importance for capacity building in teaching/learning and research in the higher education sector continues to be acknowledged, particularly given the sector's dramatic expansion over the past two decades. Currently, around 8% of the 40,000 workforce in Ethiopian HEIs are international staff, with most working in fields of study where local staff are scarce.

A significant number of international faculty are currently recruited from India, Nigeria and the Philippines in particular, and from Europe, and other countries. Recruitment of foreign faculty follows a variety of patterns, including universities' direct involvement in recruitment and/or the intermediation of recruiting agencies, which have recently sprouted to capitalize on this new business area. In its fifth Education Sector Development Plan (2015–16 to

2019–20), the government expressed an interest in increasing the proportion of foreign faculty to 10%. However, this could be challenged by new developments within the sector.

2   Impending Challenges

Issues of salary, taxes and staff quality (among many others) appear to be factors that affect the process of attracting, recruiting and retaining international faculty in Ethiopian HEIs. Although there may be differences based on nationality, the average expatriate serving in a public institution earns on average US$2,500–US$3,000 per month. This is a huge sum compared to local faculty's meager salaries and benefits. Yet, foreign faculty contend that this salary is much lower than they would receive in other countries with a similar economy. Aside from the possible rivalry generated by the salary difference, the pay scale continues to affect institutions' capacity to attract and recruit the best talent.

The issue of taxes has lately become another source of discontent among foreign faculty, influencing their motivation to remain in their positions. The introduction of a new tax on their basic salary is causing a significant number of international faculty (especially Indians, who are the majority) to return to their home countries. International faculty also face a heavy challenge in terms of being accepted by students and the local academic community, particularly when their performance fails to meet expectations.

Until such time as Ethiopia's efforts to expand its postgraduate programs, especially at the PhD level, and to ensure the return of the numerous candidates currently training abroad, are able to meet the sector's needs, there will be a need for expat faculty. The serious challenges noted above call for steadfast national policy and sound institutional management.

CHAPTER 39

Internationalization Now a Deliberate Undertaking

An earlier version of this chapter appeared in *University World News, Africa Edition*, 8 October 2020, https://www.universityworldnews.com/post.php?story=20171214061717655

The launch of an international higher education (IHE) policy by the Ethiopian Ministry of Science and Higher Education (MoSHE) is expected to support focused internationalization efforts in the next few years. This is part of reforms that aim to transform the sector. Individual institutions are encouraged to engage and urgently design internationalization policies and strategies in line with the broader directions set in the national policy. Ethiopia's IHE policy can be regarded as a remarkable development that will encourage informed and planned moves in all spheres of the internationalization arena. It could also serve as a model for other developing countries. For too long, internationalization efforts have been fragmented and occurred in the absence of clear national and institutional directions.

Notwithstanding its limitations and paradoxes, internationalization continues to be a central aspect of higher education that many countries across the globe cannot afford to ignore. Many systems and institutions thus recognize its critical impact in shaping their missions, strategic planning and operational practices and entertain it as both a concept and an operational agenda. Successful internationalization efforts are most often accompanied by carefully crafted policies and strategies at national, sectoral and institutional levels. However, contrary to what is often thought, the internationalization of higher education as a coordinated engagement embodying policies, strategies and organized practices is a phenomenon that has only recently started to spread across the globe. It is more pronounced in developing countries. Despite increasing interest in becoming part of the global movement towards the internationalization of higher education, few of these countries have been guided by policies and strategies developed at national and institutional level.

1   Past and Present

International higher education in Ethiopia has a long history. Its growth and development have been similar to internationalization patterns globally and particularly in developing countries. The roots of internationalization in Ethiopia can be traced to the arrival of missionaries in the 19th century. Having identified education as a useful tool, missionaries in Ethiopia were actively involved in opening schools and sending promising students abroad half a century before the first modern school was established in 1908. The foreign powers' influence on the modern education system continued with the opening of schools that incorporated various features of internationalization.

Ethiopian HEIs have also been involved in internationalization activities since their establishment. Over the years, there has been an increasing recognition of its value in promoting teaching and research collaboration, mobilization of international resources, enhanced academic quality and standards, and lately, as a source of additional institutional income. The establishment and administration of Ethiopian HEIs over the past seven decades exhibit various features of internationalization including the hiring of international faculty, the adoption of a foreign language (English) as the medium of instruction, the use of foreign educational materials, engagement in international research projects and collaboration with foreign institutions. Indeed, IHE has been used as a capacity building tool in the various realms of the Ethiopian higher education system. This longstanding practice has been augmented by the expansion and increasing complexity of the higher education sector since the end of the 1990s. International higher education activities such as academic mobility and research collaboration are steadily becoming major manifestations of the system. Ethiopia's higher education and research institutions have been at the forefront of institutional capacity building efforts through various forms of internationalization.

2   Internationalization Joins the Mainstream Policy Development Process

The MoSHE's decision to develop a national policy on IHE is part of the higher education reform it is undertaking with a view to transforming the sector. In addition to shifting the process of internationalization from unintentional to a deliberate undertaking, the policy aims to enhance Ethiopia's efforts to become a middle-income country through rapid industrialization, technological development, innovation, and entrepreneurship. This will require capacity building efforts of international standard and the production of a well-trained, well-equipped workforce that will cater to the country's ever-increasing needs. The aspirations articulated in the new policy are mainly drawn from existing national and sectoral policies such as Ethiopia's Growth and Transformation

Plan II (2016), its Education Sector Development Program V (2015), the Higher Education Proclamation (2019) and MoSHE's 10-Year Strategic Plan (2020–2030), but they also seek to position the Ethiopian higher education system as a microcosm of global higher education. To this effect, the policy's vision is "to see the Ethiopian higher education sector meet its full potential to serve the national interest, and become a regionally and globally competitive system through a high quality and multidimensional approach to internationalisation".

The policy offers a broader framework in which the internationalization of higher education will be planned, supported, directed, and achieved in Ethiopia. It identifies the principles and rationales on which internationalization efforts are based. This is an indication that the framework aims to position the Ethiopian higher education to gradually move towards a formal endorsement of IHE in a more coordinated manner. The policy aims not only to set a national framework to enhance current undertakings but also to mainstream internationalization across the higher education sector by creating the necessary synergy between institutional, national, regional and global strategies and procedures. It provides the wider context for operational direction by identifying critical policy issues and practices that need to be considered at these levels. Accordingly, HEIs are expected to design institutional policies and operational frameworks in order to actively engage in and benefit from various modes of internationalization activities. It is expected that plans and activities that advance the internationalization of higher education in Ethiopia will be designed and executed along the broad lines set out in the policy document. However, this requires that institutions give priority to doing so designing their own policies and strategies.

Another encouraging move has been the establishment of a consortium of directors of internationalization offices at public universities. Accountable to the ministry, it aims to share experiences and align efforts to achieve the goals of internationalization. If pursued with sufficient focus and coherent operational plans at all levels, the current move to adopt IHE as a strategic direction could provide solutions to maximize the benefits of internationalization and harness new opportunities. Such efforts will not only transform the hitherto poorly coordinated and fragmented activities into a coherent structure, but will also elevate the internationalization of the Ethiopian higher education sector to a more strategic position in years to come. In conclusion, it should be noted that the success of the plans and expected outcomes of the policy framework is dependent on what can be practically implemented at national and institutional levels.

PART 7

Research and Outreach

∴

CHAPTER 40

Towards a More Productive and Aligned Research System

An earlier version of this chapter appeared in *University World News, Africa Edition*, 17 October 2019, https://www.universityworldnews.com/post.php?story=20191014092037354

There is a clear need to augment research output in Ethiopia through the active participation of the major actors in the broader research framework. Equally important is the establishment of an effective and well-coordinated system that will build better research capacity and facilitate improved output at a national level. Ethiopia is making much of effort to improve its research performance and output. As key centers of knowledge generation, HEIs are being urged to improve their research output – with positive results. For example, as reported in Ethiopia's Science and Technology Report of 2014, findings from Elsevier indicated that in 2013 more than 4,000 scientific articles were published by Addis Ababa University faculty. Information from Elsevier's SciVal further reveals that Ethiopia has the potential to increase its research output by around 28% in just a year.

As elsewhere, HEIs in Ethiopia are not the only institutions which conduct research. In addition to universities, government research institutes; national laboratories; donors; intellectual property offices; science and technology parks; manufacturing and service enterprises; national quality infrastructure agencies; technical and vocational education and training institutions and industry have all been identified as major actors in the country's broader research framework. While the current growth of the higher education sector is expected to augment national research output, little is known about the nature of research conducted outside of academia. Ethiopia's overall performance in research productivity has also rarely been examined in terms of various actors' role and participation within the existing national research framework and their productivity, all of which vary widely.

1 National R&D Activities

According to Ethiopia's 2014 Science and Technology Indicators Report, only 8% of business entities engage in research and development (R&D) activities. In similar vein, 53% of Ethiopian private nonprofit educational institutions never undertake research: 26% outsource their R&D and only the remaining 21% conduct in-house R&D. As regards government organizations, 95.4% are engaged in R&D activities, with only 4.6% not involved. On the other hand, 66% of public HEIs reported that they engage in R&D, 1% said they outsource their research activities, and the remaining 33% indicated that they do not engage in R&D. These findings indicate that, whereas government organizations and HEIs are responsible for the lion's share of R&D activities, the least active sectors are business and private non-profit institutions. This situation is obviously contributing to Ethiopia's poor performance in overall research output, innovation and competitiveness at the global level, which is reflected in the quality of its research institutions, company spending on R&D and university-industry collaboration in R&D activities.

The 2018 Global Competitiveness Report published by the World Economic Forum ranked Ethiopia 122 out of 140 countries in the world. Ethiopia's score, which is 44.45 points out of 100, is lower than the regional median of 45.2, and other African countries such as Ghana (51.33), Kenya (53.67), Uganda (46.80), Rwanda (50.94), and Tanzania (47.21). If Ethiopia's overall performance is to change significantly, the national research framework needs to be revised to better align the various research actors.

2 The Need for Alignment

While current undertakings to augment Ethiopia's research productivity should be strengthened across all sectors, it is critical to create a well-coordinated and aligned national research system. This would promote improved coordination of research activities at the national level; identification and exchange of research information; cooperation and interaction among researchers from disciplinary and institutional backgrounds; improved monitoring and evaluation of performance, scientific productivity and competitiveness, and excellence.

Establishing such a framework requires responses to a variety of questions such as: How will integration and cooperation among different actors be achieved? Who should lead the framework? How will allocation and utilization of resources be handled? How will assistance and support be coordinated? How will the process be monitored and evaluated? As yet, there appears to be no national framework to respond to these questions and enhance the various actors' activities in a manner that would contribute positively to the country's overall research output and reduce unnecessary duplication of research and infrastructure investment. The only exceptions in this regard are the role and responsibilities the law ascribes to the Ethiopian Ministry of Innovation and Technology which might assume the coordination of national research programs and the establishment, coordination and support of councils that facilitate coordination of research work. However, the ministry does not yet appear to have taken this role to heart.

3 Universities and Links with Other Actors

While the business and nonprofit sectors' research performance is in need of serious improvement, the distinction, links and alignment between the two best-performing actors in the Ethiopian national research framework – universities and government research institutions – is especially important in improving current research output and the country's competitiveness. In most contexts, universities are considered the most effective institutions to conduct research, disseminate knowledge across the research community, and link the national research and innovation system to the outside world. Universities also hold a unique position as a major source of researchers and scholars and thus assume an important place in the overall research framework of a given country. The facilities available at universities and doctoral students' involvement in research not only provide universities with capable researchers, but also help to reduce the cost of research.

It is often argued that, within a broader national research framework, universities can be successful where little or no competition arises from non-university research organizations or where strong ties exist between the universities and such organizations. While some countries integrate or merge government research institutes/organizations and top universities for the purpose of strengthening their research output, the tendency in other countries is towards establishing universities as the principal or leading entities around which research activities coalesce. Where this is lacking – as in the case of Ethiopia – it can drain resources, limit capacity for cooperation and interdisciplinary work, weaken the research talent pool, and affect the broader research and innovation system's output.

4 Towards a Coordinated System

There is a clear need to augment the research output in Ethiopia through the major actors' active participation within the broader research framework. Equally important is the establishment of an effective, well-coordinated system that will build improved research capacity and facilitate improved output at a national level. Hence, in addition to enhancing the individual performance of the different actors, serious thought should be given to the establishment of a national framework that will direct and coordinate different stakeholders' research efforts across the nation. Success in this regard could accelerate the positive achievements in research productivity witnessed over the past decade and help the country to improve its regional position in the global competition of knowledge production and utilization.

CHAPTER 41

Catalyzing R&D

The Need for More Government Funding

An earlier version of this chapter appeared in *University World News, Africa Edition*, 31 October 2019, https://www.universityworldnews.com/post.php?story=20191028062534176

The research output of many countries is significantly affected by the amount of money dedicated to research and development (R&D). While increased investment does not always guarantee excellence, research shows that there is a strong correlation between the level of research excellence a country attains and the amount of money it dedicates to research and development. The 'critical mass' of overall R&D expenditure required to achieve research excellence is usually set at above 1.5% of GDP. Notwithstanding recent efforts and promises to change the situation, Africa's participation in global knowledge generation remains negligible compared with the rest of the world. Figures from the World Bank show that the continent produces less than 1% of global scientific knowledge, despite being inhabited by 16% of the global population. According to UNESCO Institute of Statistics (UIS), Africa's funding of R&D in 2019 was estimated at 0.42% of GDP, which is far below the global average of 1.7% and the lowest in the world.

Despite rhetoric about improving the continent's capacity and contribution, a limited number of African countries have demonstrated improved investment in R&D. In 2016, the African Union Executive Council set a target of 1% of GDP to be invested in R&D in all member countries in order to improve innovation, productivity and economic growth. Although improvements are being witnessed across the continent, data from the UIS show that only South Africa, Kenya and Senegal are close to meeting this target, with about 0.8% of their GDP dedicated to R&D.

1 Research Challenges in Ethiopia

Among the variety of factors contributing to Ethiopia's low research performance, the major ones have been identified as limited funding and the system's limited capacity to produce qualified researchers at national and institutional levels. With regard to the latter, Ethiopia's performance in PhD training has improved over the past decade. Enrolment of PhD candidates rose from 789 in 2010–11 to 3,994 in 2017–18. The number of graduates also increased from 21 in 2010–11 to 237 in 2017–18 (MoE, 2018), with consistent variations over the years. While the steady increase in the number of PhD graduates has positive implications for increasing research output, commensurate improvement has not been observed in research funding.

Ethiopia's Science and Technology Policy of 1993 can be considered as the first expression of the government's commitment to spend about 1.5% of the country's GDP on R&D, although this has never been achieved. Indeed, to the dismay of many, the level of investment in R&D decreased significantly from 0.61% in 2013 to 0.23% in 2017. This hampers the achievement of the country's ambitious plan to improve its research and innovation system.

2 Plans and Ambitions

Ethiopia's five-year Education Sector Development Plan issued in 2015 states that the higher education sub-sector will seek government approval for an improved budget allocation model for universities. The purpose is to provide "greater autonomy to each institution, allowing a more responsive research agenda and increasing the share of funds allocated to research to be in line with international standards". The sectoral plan further outlines the need for the introduction of a performance-based research system that links the delivery of quality research to the delivery of funding, and the establishment of a research funding body that operates on the principles of competition, relevance and positive action.

While these plans appear to be in line with Ethiopia's ambition to improve its research output, they have not yet been realized. Moreover, little concrete attention has been paid to the issue of funding. Indeed, a close reading of the document suggests that, in addition to failing to meet its envisaged goals, the government lacks commitment to fundi R&D activities, with most of the funding assumed to come from the efforts of individual institutions. A similar expectation is reflected in the Higher Education Proclamation which encourages institutions to establish research and innovation funds and to allocate sufficient funds for research focusing on technology transfer and innovation.

According to the 2015 fifth Education Sector Plan, plans are in place to increase the percentage of research funds from HEIs' annual recurrent total budget from the current 1–2% to 5%. Similarly, the percentage of research funds secured from industry and international sources is planned to increase to 50%. Although encouraging HEIs to generate funds for research purposes is a necessary step, especially in view of competing demands that constrain the government, without government's active involvement, it will be difficult to achieve these targets. To begin with, university-industry relationships in Ethiopia are highly constrained due to a variety of challenges that emanate from both parties. Unlike most developed countries where R&D funding is substantially drawn from the private sector, Ethiopia's private sector is currently too weak to serve as a major source of such financing.

3   Reliance on Donors

According to the 2024 Science, Technology, and Innovation Strategy of Africa (STISA, 2024), the continent not only invests the least in R&D, but more than half of the investment is obtained from abroad. Most of the research funds for projects and PhD programs at public Ethiopian universities such as Addis Ababa University – the country's flagship university – are obtained from international partners such as the Swedish International Development Cooperation Agency (SIDA-SAREC), the Netherlands Organization for International Cooperation in Higher Education (NUFFIC), the British Council, European Union, World Bank, UNESCO, Department for International Development (DfID) and the United Nations Development Programme (UNDP).

It should be noted that overreliance on external sources can have negative consequences on important issues such as setting priorities and sustainability which are critical to the success of the national research endeavor. Likewise, institutions' research output and training highly skilled researchers through PhD programs may not always be dictated by national ambitions and institutional needs since they can be influenced by international partners' desires and capacity. In view of these challenges, it is hardly possible to achieve government plans and ambitions for the country's research universities based on a strategy that is defined by limited funding from local sources.

4   Government Funding

There are encouraging moves within the higher education sector in terms of policies, structures, institutions and institutional activities that could propel Ethiopia's current research output to the next level in the future. However, these efforts will not have meaningful results unless institutions and the private sector increase their expenditure on R&D and the government raises public expenditure dedicated to the same purpose. In the absence of strong commitment from the government to increase its current level of funding and to initiate diversified forms of domestic funding for R&D, not only will the country fail to meet its ambitions but the positive gains made in research output and especially in building critical human resources will not be utilized in a meaningful way.

CHAPTER 42

The Meager Output of Ethiopian PhDs

An earlier version of this chapter appeared in *Inside Higher Education*, 22 April 2018, https://www.insidehighered.com/blogs/world-view/meager-output-ethiopian-phds

The motivation for increasing the availability of doctoral studies is multidimensional. Individual goals aside, the justification for the huge investment countries make in doctoral education is improving teaching, increasing research output, and contributing to scientific development through innovation. The increasing presence of PhD holders in universities and research institutes reflect the demand for the active participation of highly trained staff. Despite the growing global emphasis on PhD education, information with regard to PhD graduates' output remains relatively limited, especially in the developing world where, despite a seemingly endless quest for more PhDs, little research has been conducted on how doctoral candidates perform against expectations.

Doctoral study is expected to offer a range of personal and strategic institutional advantages. A PhD can provide access to academic and non-academic jobs with many opportunities for meaningful contributions. Doctoral programs facilitate the production of academics and technocrats who can engage in various institutional activities and responsibilities. Doctoral education's contribution to research output is also widely acknowledged. It is partly for this reason that doctoral training is regarded as essential to an academic career and the cultivation of future researchers and professors. Doctoral studies also serve as a pipeline for a workforce that will drive innovation and facilitate participation in the global knowledge economy. As a highly-trained group of people, PhD holders are considered critical in the advancement and diffusion of knowledge and technology. This has motivated many countries to develop policies that enhance the massive expansion of PhD programs. Notable examples from the developing world are Korea, Thailand, Malaysia, Singapore, Mexico, Brazil, India, and China which has now surpassed the US in annual production of PhD graduates. Given the above general assumptions, what is the trajectory of PhD training and to what extent do PhD holders in Ethiopia deliver in the real world of work?

1 The PhD Profile

Ethiopia has produced a growing number of PhDs to respond to the demands of its planned development, not least of which is its rapidly expanding higher education sector. Although government set a target of 30% of the 40,000 university staff having a PhD, the level currently stands at around 15%. A plan formulated by the Ministry of Education in 2008 promotes training at this level both within Ethiopia and abroad. From a low of 21 in 2010/11, local universities now award hundreds of PhDs every year. More than 3,000 students are currently pursuing doctoral studies at local universities. These numbers compare favorably with the production of PhD graduates in eight flagship universities in sub-Saharan Africa revealed in a study conducted by the Higher Education Research and Advocacy Network in Africa (2014). While the exact number of people studying abroad is not known, the trend in Ethiopia is indicative of a strong inclination towards significantly increasing the number of PhD holders in the future.

Despite this encouraging trend, little is known of the performance of Ethiopian PhD holders. The career tracking survey conducted by the Ethiopian Ministry of Science and Technology in 2017 of 908 Ethiopian PhD holders revealed some interesting facts. Among the PhD holders who participated in the study, 24.3% completed their studies in Ethiopian universities and the rest were trained abroad. The primary funding was fellowships or scholarships from foreign sources while the rest were funded by the Ethiopian government. The majority (26.2%) studied natural sciences, followed by agricultural sciences (21.4%), social sciences (18%), engineering and technology (18%), medical and health sciences (6.9%), and humanities (8.7%). Nearly 80% of the PhD holders worked in higher education while the rest were distributed among government offices (11.3%), private non-profit organizations (5.6%), and business enterprises (2.1%). The unemployment rate among the PhD holders was 3% – not a negligible number.

2 Output

Seventy-seven percent of the survey participants indicated that their work involved research or experimental work while the remaining 23% noted that their job did not involve these activities. However, 30% of those surveyed did not publish any articles during the period of study, 2013–2015, and 60% had fewer than ten publications. Doctoral graduates also underperform in terms of innovation and knowledge creation. The study revealed that only 15% applied for patents, mainly between one and five applications. Only 13% were successful in obtaining patents. In similar vein, 95% of the patents obtained did not result in commercial products, processes, or a license. Only 2.6% managed to start one company and a meager 0.4% started two companies. A variety of reasons were suggested to explain poor performance in research and innovation. The PhD holders cited working conditions (26.2%), low remuneration (21%), limited job opportunities in research, the lack of a research career structure (19%), and a lack of interest (2.9%) as key factors. Only a few expressed satisfaction with their job and working conditions.

3 The Way Forward

Ethiopia's plan to become a middle-income country by 2025 hinges on its ability to produce a highly trained workforce that can respond to the country's complex needs. In line with the envisaged developmental needs, Ethiopian universities are currently tasked with increasing postgraduate opportunities, especially doctoral studies. In addition to improving the qualifications of academic staff, the government intends to set up research-intensive universities with postgraduate students representing 20% of enrollment and with 50% holding earned doctorates. Plans are also underway to establish research centers that will be joint ventures between universities and industry. These and other similar initiatives require the continued availability of PhD holders in the system.

However, national plans and pertinent sectoral or institutional needs cannot be met by merely increasing the number of PhD holders. Maximizing the benefits of PhD holders, demands that output be monitored and that working environments facilitate their contribution to institutional and national goals. Producing more PhD holders without due consideration to their productivity and working conditions will simply be an exercise in futility.

CHAPTER 43

Increasing the Visibility of Local Journals

An earlier version of this chapter appeared in *University World News, Africa Edition*, 8 February 2019, https://www.universityworldnews.com/post.php?story=20190117083946556

In 2017, the Ethiopian Academy of Sciences (EAS) published an important survey that disclosed for the first time the nature, current status and challenges of Ethiopian academic journals that publish local articles. Among other things, the EAS' empirical findings identified various challenges confronting journal publication in Ethiopia such as a lack of funding, shortage of submissions, poor online visibility, lack of rigor and quality, absence of international indexing, and frequent interruption (36% of the 72 Ethiopia-based journals suffer from publication interruptions extending from five to 10 years). While some of these challenges are difficult to surmount given publishers' financial austerity and related factors, others like online visibility can be managed by means of limited additional effort and using accessible open platforms at institutional, national, regional, continental or international level.

1   Institutional and National Platforms

According to the EAS report, most Ethiopian journals (45 in number) are published by public universities, followed by national professional associations (19 journals), PHEIs (four), government research institutes (three) and religious institutions (one). However, only one or two of the existing 51 public universities and 300 PHEIs have their own institutional repositories. Acquisition of such repositories should not have been a difficult task, given the limited challenges in setting up such a platform and considering its huge importance in alleviating existing gaps in the documentation and information dissemination practices of most HEIs. Notwithstanding the lack of institutional repositories, only a very limited number of the journals (five) have their own dedicated websites, while 32 rely on the websites of their publishing institutions to promote their articles.

Over the past few years, a national platform known as the Ethiopian Journals Online (EJOL) has been launched, although its usage remains at a rudimentary stage. The EJOL is hosted by Addis Ababa University libraries with the objective of improving the visibility and accessibility of Ethiopian journals and freely delivering content to all institutions. The site was first launched in 2014 with six journals; after four years it only hosted 22 journals with 145 issues and 804 articles. The fact that only a quarter of the available journals in the country use the EJOL platform is a clear indication of the huge gap in exploiting such an invaluable avenue. A quick glance at this open platform reveals that a significant number of the journal issues posted by institutions are also not updated on time.

Another useful platform that awaits full utilization by local journals is the Ethiopian Education and Research Network (EthERNet), which is currently operational. Founded in 2009 under the Ethiopian Ministry of Education (now under the recently restructured Ministry of Science and Higher Education), the EthERNet was established with the purpose of supporting HEIs to share information and resources, disseminate their work and make their output available to the global academic and research community. However, this platform is also little exploited in promoting the visibility of local journals, mainly due to the low level of engagement by journal publishing institutions.

2 Continental and International Platforms

Ethiopia's performance in terms of the visibility of its local publications at continental and international levels still leaves much to be desired. A prominent platform available to African journals which Ethiopian journals could benefit from is the African Journals Online (AJOL) launched in 2000. The AJOL project was initiated by the International Network for the Availability of Scientific Publications, a charitable organization based in Oxford, United Kingdom. To promote its mission of supporting African research in general and research output in particular, the AJOL provides an online system to access African-published, open and subscription-based, peer-reviewed scholarly journals free of charge, and provides an article download service for users.

Over the past two decades, the number of participating journals and researchers that use the AJOL platform has grown, although the website is still far from claiming to be a platform for all peer-reviewed journals on the continent. In 2019, the AJOL hosted 523 journals from 32 countries covering a wide array of academic disciplines. It accommodated 256 Open Access journals, 167,510 abstracts, and 161,715 full text articles for download, of which 103,017 were Open Access. Among the 32 countries featured on the AJOL, Ethiopia ranked third with its 30 journals, next to Nigeria (222 journals) and South Africa (96), closely followed by Kenya (29) and Ghana (28). Nonetheless, current levels of participation of Ethiopian journals could improve given the fact that only 44% of the available journals in the country use the AJOL platform. While this surpasses the number on the local platform, EJOL, weaknesses with regard to the timely posting of journal articles also abound on the AJOL platform.

3   Towards Greater Visibility

Enhancing research and research-publishing practices in Africa is widely considered as one of the most critical aspects of improving higher education on the continent. Although the use of journals that serve as core avenues of academic communication has been the major means of achieving this goal, many journals from Africa lack visibility even after being published. This continues to hamper the availability of relevant research output both to those within the continent and beyond.

Given the increasing traction the open science movement is gradually gaining across the globe, one would expect that local journals would seize new opportunities and innovative ways to promote their research output. However, current achievements indicate that the level of responses by local journals is not in tandem with evolving developments within the sector. Although long-term policy strategies and sufficient resources might be needed to bring about sustainable change, making published articles available on existing free and open platforms should not be a difficult task. While increased awareness and some technical assistance are required to create institutional repositories and ensure that such sources are shared through local platforms, additional routes that are freely available at national, continental and international level should be wisely and urgently harnessed to increase the accessibility of published journal articles. Ethiopia's efforts in this regard should thus be further augmented to promote the rising research output of its HEIs and research centers, without which increased local capacity and dissemination of research will continue to be a challenge.

CHAPTER 44

Towards a National System of Journal Accreditation

An earlier version of this chapter appeared in *University World News, Global Edition*, 3 March 2018, https://www.universityworldnews.com/post.php?story=20180303075443425

Despite the various advantages they offer in terms of production and sharing of local knowledge and augmenting visibility, publication of local journals in Ethiopia continues to suffer from a variety of challenges. Any new initiative is usually confronted by the perennial hurdles of lack of funding, expertise and structures that are critical for success.

The publication of scholarly journals in Ethiopia does not have a long history. A recent research report by the Ethiopian Academy of Sciences (2017) indicated that although local publication of scientific journals started in the 1960s, it did not show significant change until 2000, with only 24 journals launched in four decades. According to the report, improvements have been noted since 2000 when the Ethiopian higher education sector embarked on aggressive expansion, with the introduction of 48 additional journals, bringing the total number of locally published journals to around 73. The Ethiopian Academy of Sciences' research report shows that the majority of the journals in the country are published by public HEIs, national professional associations, private universities, government institutions and religious institutions, in that order. Notwithstanding the limited number of publications for a country with 37 public and more than 120 private HEIs and a teaching population of 30,000, Ethiopian journals continue to exhibit a variety of systemic and structural deficiencies.

1 Drawbacks

Most of the local journals have limited copies of the publication, and poor online visibility and international indexing. Thirty-six percent of available journals suffer from interruptions in publication extending from five to 10 years. The quality and rigor of articles considered for publication are also of a questionable standard due to a shortage of submissions. Most editors are drawn from publishing organizations and lack the requisite expertise and experience. The cosmetic inclusion of advisory board members from abroad does not seem to help much due to the fact that the roles of co-opted members have in most cases been purely nominal.

In addition to these shortcomings, Ethiopia has no tradition of evaluating the standard and quality of journals through a nationally coordinated system. This task has long been relegated to the discretion of individual publishers and/or editors. In light of this, the Ethiopian Academy of Sciences (EAS) developed a national Journal Evaluation and Accreditation framework to standardize assessment of scholarly publishing in Ethiopia. The scheme aims to institute journal accreditation through a comprehensive national quality audit system and hopes to bridge the existing gap by drawing on relevant experiences from within and outside the African continent. According to the EAS report, the main objective is not only to set uniform standards to assess the scholarly merit of research journals, but also to promote excellence in local scholarship; introduce international standards; and encourage stronger linkages between scholarly publishing, graduate research and mentorship in order to facilitate meaningful interventions at the national and institutional levels.

2   Prospects and Challenges

The introduction of a national system for the assessment and standardization of Ethiopian journals could have considerable impact on the quality of future research in the country. The new scheme holds promise. With its detailed guidelines that offer mechanisms to translate the scheme into reality, it can be considered as both a policy direction and a recipe for practical undertakings. By creating additional outlets for researchers, the scheme could also support the improvements Ethiopia has been making in terms of scientific publication at a regional level. According to the UNESCO Science Report 2010, Ethiopia ranks 6th out of 17 countries in sub-Saharan Africa.

However, the new scheme has yet to surmount some major challenges that appear to be critical to its success. The first relates to the poor tradition of research and research publication in Ethiopia. Infusing demanding standards in an environment where research articles are so limited might be interpreted as inhibiting. Although a journal accreditation system may not appear to be a priority against the backdrop of other fundamental problems, a change in this direction could motivate academics seeking publication in high standard local journals and such efforts should be rewarded by substantive and scaled-up support from the government in terms of promoting research publication at all levels. South Africa's experience of introducing a government-induced research funding framework run by the Department of Higher Education and Training is worth emulating in this regard.

Secondly, the plan needs to be endorsed and an appropriate body needs to be established to oversee the accreditation and evaluation of journals at national level and provide the necessary support. In this regard, immediate action is required from important and powerful bodies like the Ministry of Science and Higher Education to acknowledge the efforts of the EAS and endorse its proposed scheme. It is clear that without the practical involvement of the government and especially key ministries, the proposed national scheme for journal accreditation may not see the light of day. Considering the importance of the scheme, one would hope that, like many other plans with noble intentions and high relevance, it does not end up gathering dust on office shelves.

CHAPTER 45

Re-Engaging with Community Service in Universities

An earlier version of this chapter appeared in *University World News, Africa Edition*, 3 May 2019, https://www.universityworldnews.com/post.php?story=20190501082547889

The goals of higher education in Ethiopia are closely linked to national development and poverty reduction. Higher education institutions are accordingly expected to align their major activities with national needs and societal demands. The Ethiopian Higher Education Proclamation (2009) identifies the "design and provision of community and consultancy services that shall cater to the developmental needs of the country" as one of the objectives and a major responsibility of HEIs. The Education Sector Development Program V (2015) also emphasizes the need for positive community engagement through various means, including research that responds to national and institutional priorities and development plans. The document also highlights the need for community consultation and envisages the establishment of a national multi-sectoral stakeholder panel to produce a national research and community engagement framework, institutional research and community engagement strategies, and a resource mobilization and utilization system for research and community services, although these have yet to be realized.

1   Past Experience

The higher education sector in Ethiopia has wide-ranging experience in community outreach activities, the most notable perhaps being the Ethiopian University Service, a mandatory year-long national service in the 1970s which required all university students to serve in rural areas. Individual universities have also been involved in various forms of community service, although their performance varied. The early forms of such engagement at institutional level included the establishment of an extension division at the Haile Selassie I University (now Addis Ababa University) which mainly focused on adult education programs in the evenings. This offering still forms a major component of the training services provided by all Ethiopian universities. In addition to evening and distance programs, which are popular, universities have offered special training and professional assistance to their surrounding communities based on perceived needs in areas such as health, industry, agriculture, rural development, water and finance.

Although most universities continue to engage in these or similar activities, only a few have distinguished themselves as leading institutions. An outstanding example is the community-based education program pioneered by Jimma University whose motto is: "We're in the community". This approach has been emulated by many other universities. Most also include community service as a criterion for academic staff promotion. For instance, the 2013 Senate Legislation of Addis Ababa University – Ethiopia's flagship university – regards professional service to the community at local, regional and national levels as evidence of public service and professional activity. However, as revealed by the Higher Education Relevance and Quality Agency's (2008), quality audits, these popular programs are increasingly at risk of being discontinued or diluted due to the increasing number of students, high attrition rates of experienced staff, problems related to programming, shortage of transport facilities, lack of incentives, and limited budgets and time.

2 New Directive, New Directions?

A new directive by the Ministry of Science and Higher Education in 2019 aims to elevate community service in universities by means of a national harmonized system with defined elements of accountability. It clearly defines the areas in which community service might occur, dispelling previous confusion as to what areas fall under this umbrella term, and calls for structural changes to realize the plan. The directive identifies core areas of community service as training, consultancy and outreach or development service or projects, and other professional services. It proposes changing the previous allocation of staff time – 75% for teaching and 25% for research – to 60% for teaching, 25% for research and 15% for community service.

The directive also demands the creation of the formal organizational and administrative structures for efficient and effective execution of community service activities. A council led by a state minister is expected to be established at national level to oversee activities related to research, technology transfer, university-industry linkage and community service. Universities are also expected to set up an office and allocate a budget based on priority areas identified. The office is to be accountable to the vice-chancellor who is a member of the council at the ministry. A community service team comprised of members of staff and students is also to be established at each university to be involved in operational tasks. The nature of community services to be provided by institutions is to be directed through a thematic approach which requires the identification of local, regional and national priorities and is based on the relative strength and comparative advantage of individual universities. In addition to making their research and/or technological output available, HEIs are expected to explore, enhance and utilize indigenous knowledge to address community problems.

3 The Next Steps

Universities have frequently been criticized for failing to address the concerns and challenges of their societies, which look to them as important drivers of societal transformation. Despite the existence of community-oriented programs at Ethiopian universities, there has been little emphasis on the way such activities have been structured, resourced and most importantly, aligned at sectoral and national levels. The ministry's new directive is therefore an important step in bridging this gap and in translating national ideals through unfettered institutional commitments. While galvanizing the university community is an important component of this new plan, equally important is the role of the community itself.

Any university's engagement with community depends heavily on the latter's informed understanding and participation. While universities primarily exist to serve society, this does not necessarily mean that their role is to respond to every demand without scrutiny and prioritization. A community that imposes its will without understanding the university's capacity, priority and resources will always be more of a challenge than a partner. Universities therefore need to seek the participation of the community and its leaders in setting priorities and deploying resources. The ministry's new plan should also consider how the interests of the community and universities are closely and sustainably aligned in order to achieve the envisaged goals.

CHAPTER 46

University-Industry Ties
The Need for Good Management

An earlier version of this chapter appeared in *University World News, Global Edition*, 8 June 2019, https://www.universityworldnews.com/post.php?story=20190605094229995

Perceptions of universities as important drivers of economic development have enticed many governments to strengthen their focus on forging links between universities and industries to promote national competitiveness. Governments are becoming increasingly aware of the benefits of university-industry linkages for technology transfer, training, enterprise support and development, consultancy, contract and collaborative research, internship and externship. As a result, governments are encouraging HEIs to be actively involved in this engagement.

Among others, Ethiopia's Growth and Transformation Plan I (2010/11–2014/15), Education Sector Development Programs, and science and technology policies underpin the key role of universities and industries in sustaining rapid and broad-based economic growth in the country. The driving forces to realize Ethiopia's goal of becoming a middle-income country by 2025 have been identified as "innovation-friendly institutions that enable genuine science, technology and innovation development, institutions that can develop a structured system with smooth science and technology information flow, technology incubation and utilization" (Ethiopian Science and Technology Information Centre, 2014). Article 25.4 of the 2019 Higher Education Proclamation also states that "every institution shall have the responsibility to forge relations with industries for mutual benefits" and that institutional research should emphasize transfer of technology and joint research projects with industries. These policy considerations underpin the need for HEIs to forge closer links with industry and business in order to transfer knowledge produced in these areas. However, government has not achieved what it hoped for and, despite some improvements, major deficiencies remain, especially in the way university-industry linkages have been managed.

1 Managing Professional Relationships

University-industry linkages require handling at both the strategic and operational levels. While strategic management is concerned with the incorporation of university-industry relations as an explicit university-wide policy and strategic direction, operational management includes managing interfaces, finance, staff and intellectual property rights. Despite increasing interest in embarking on fruitful university-industry linkages in Ethiopia, more needs to be done to ensure professional management of relationships. This appears to be the major reason for the lack of meaningful development in this area. Universities need to create structures to bring industries on board. This could include the creation of higher positions to manage partnerships, or the establishment of specialized/dedicated offices, corporate/business liaison offices, or external structures that coordinate and manage relations with industry and business. Researchers note that such interfaces are critical in enhancing tasks such as developing networks of businesses, marketing universities' research strengths, advising on consultancy agreements and contract research, arranging collaborative research agreements, and securing sufficient specialization in support services in the management of intellectual property and business development.

Management of university-industry linkages also requires clearly defined financial management rules and procedures at institutional level. For instance, costing and pricing policies related to professional fees and rates, calculation of overheads and the distribution of generated income are important in terms of clarifying expectations and addressing friction that could arise among the parties. A personnel policy also needs to be in place to identify the tasks and roles to be performed by both managers of university-industry relations and academic staff. There is also a need to address demands related to new competencies, skills and abilities required to perform such tasks adequately. However, this area is said to be underdeveloped in many university contexts. The issue of incentives also needs to be addressed. Stakeholders need clarity on the benefits of a linkage. Another area of deficiency is management of intellectual property, where little has been achieved. Managing intellectual property that has a commercial value may require some form of patent, which is an important area of consideration in university-industry linkages. If there is no framework to deposit a patent within the framework of a university-industry relationship, universities and industries will come into conflict sooner or later.

2   Experiences and Deficiencies

The first formally recognized antecedent to many of the university-industry linkages in Ethiopia is perhaps the co-operation program initiated in 1986 between the Addis Ababa University and the Ministry of Industry. Although it achieved much in creating the required links with industries and the commensurate benefits that ensued, it was unfortunately discontinued during the change of government in 1991. In the past two decades most of the consultancy and outreach services (under which university-industry linkages were classified) have been administered under the jurisdiction of "research, extension and publication offices", most of which are mostly led at vice-president level. However, university-industry linkages have not developed sufficiently because they have received limited attention compared to other institutional activities like running evening classes and/or distance education programs, which are more popular at universities.

Notwithstanding the lack of policies to guide their operations, many of the existing institutional activities have not been well-organized and documented. The technology transfer activities and the strategic and operational arrangements required to handle such activities have been lacking in most universities. With a few exceptions, most Ethiopian universities still aspire to well-organized units or offices that provide an administrative and consultative interface between universities and industries. Many have not yet developed specific financial management rules and procedures to manage revenues generated through these linkages. Nor do they have specific regulations related to staff management, development and incentive schemes for those who wish to participate.

3   New Directions

While university-industry linkages in Ethiopia were pioneered by Addis Ababa University at the same time that such initiatives were being pioneered in Europe, the country has not made progress on par with HEIs elsewhere in the world. Despite the availability of policy directions and some institutional attempts, university-industry linkages remain at the rudimentary stage and are hindered by the lack of professional management, which appears to be negligible or very poor in Ethiopia.

In recognition of the need to enhance this line of work, the newly-formed Ministry of Science and Higher Education recently developed a Research,

Technology Transfer, University-Industry Linkage and Community Services Guideline that sets clear directions as to how university-industry linkages are to be led by addressing gaps and introducing new modalities. It sets out mechanisms to address issues such as intellectual property rights, commercialization, revenue generation and sharing, licensing and start-up companies, and setting up linkage offices and teams. This is a significant move that will help chart institutional direction in the years ahead. However, the new developments that aim to bridge previous gaps should heed past mistakes and avoid false starts through a close examination of the challenges faced by HEIs that had the will to establish a vibrant system of university-industry linkage but were constrained by structural and operational deficiencies beyond their control.

PART 8

The Link between TVET *and Higher Education*

CHAPTER 47

When TVET Fails to Provide the Answers

An earlier version of this chapter appeared in *University World News, Africa Edition*, 14 June 2019, https://www.universityworldnews.com/post.php?story=20190612074425937

The Ethiopian TVET system has well-organized components: an outcome-based system, cooperative training that involves industries and training institutions, and an assessment scheme that operates on the basis of nationally defined occupational standards. In addition to the development of a revised national TVET Strategy (2008) that accommodates most of the changes, a National TVET Council was set up to shoulder the responsibility of overseeing and coordinating the overall function and effectiveness of TVET at a national level. The TVET sector is led by a state minister accountable to the Minister of Science and Higher Education. While a Federal TVET Agency has been set up to oversee the implementation of the TVET strategy, a Federal TVET Institute has also been established to assist in the upgrading of trainers' skills.

Despite its long history, fundamental reform of this sector appears to have only occurred in the past two decades. As a result, the number of TVET institutions across the country has increased substantially. Access has improved, especially for women who now represent more than 50% of enrolment, although in fields that are considered to be traditional female domains. However, the question remains as to the extent to which these numerical and structural changes have translated into the significant quality outcomes expected of the sector.

TVET is assumed to fulfil a variety of national goals. It is conceived as a primary tool not only to facilitate technology transfer but also to produce the middle-level skilled person power Ethiopia needs to spur its industry-led growth strategy aimed at transforming it into a middle-income country. As set out in the 2008 national strategy, TVET aims to create a competent and adaptable workforce that will serve as the backbone of economic and social development. This objective is echoed in other country-wide strategies and development plans. In terms of operational plans, the policy directions further indicate that 80% of those who complete secondary education are expected to be absorbed into the TVET stream. While this target has not been met for many years, a more worrying trend relates to the output of TVET institutions.

1   Failure to Deliver

Counter to the purposes for which it was created and the many expectations it raised, TVET appears to be failing in terms of delivering on its promises. One of the most common observations is that these institutions are not addressing the demands of the economy and are producing low quality graduates. This is illustrated in the mismatch between the skills required by the job market and the training provided at TVET institutions. It has resulted in many TVET graduates being unemployed, even in areas where there is particularly high demand for skilled personnel. According to a 2013 employers' survey, despite vacancies in manufacturing firms, employers found it hard to recruit TVET candidates with the appropriate technical competencies and socio-emotional skills and behaviors such as a sound work ethic and commitment. A 2014 report by the Ethiopian Central Statistical Agency shows that despite being one of the biggest job creators in the country, the textile and garment industry remains one of the areas in which more than half of TVET graduates remain unemployed. The same appears to be true in areas like woodworking and carpentry, weaving and plumbing. This has been attributed to the lack of graduates with appropriate training and skills.

2   Foreign Investment

Inadequate training of graduates is also regarded as a major constraint to the operations of foreign employers who are encouraged to invest in the country. Many companies are not happy with the quality of graduates coming out of the various sections of the school system including TVET. This appears to be a common phenomenon especially in large foreign-owned companies, manufacturing firms (particularly in textile, garments, and food producers), and the construction and export sectors. The poor availability of skilled person power in certain sectors is forcing some companies, especially foreign ones, to import personnel – even those with low levels of skills. For instance, a small survey of Chinese investors indicated that a substantial percentage of skilled positions (67%) are taken up by Chinese employees. A related problem is employers' limited interest in using TVET institutions as sources of skilled personnel when they need to recruit qualified candidates. This is mainly due to these institutions' low status. The 2013 Ethiopia Skills Module Survey found that only 14 of 60 firms reported contacting TVET institutions to fill their vacant technical positions.

Research conducted in the local context points to a variety of factors that explain this ongoing anomaly. While some consider the need to address the mismatch between training components/curricula and employers' needs to be a key priority, others raise issues relating to the administration of occupational standards and assessment schemes. Yet others question the way TVET students are assigned to specific training programs, the quality of TVET instructors, the method of TVET delivery, and trainees' attitudes towards menial jobs. Further system-level challenges include underfunding of the TVET sector, poor management, the lack of a well-organized information system for job seekers, and poor linkages with industry which continue to hinder the sector from meeting its envisaged goals.

3 Improving TVET – A Sense of Urgency

Ethiopia places particular emphasis on TVET not only as a mechanism to create employment for its growing youth population but also as a critical lever to enhance economic growth. To this end, the government has formulated policies, strategies and structures commensurate with other countries where TVET has succeeded in meeting the aforementioned objectives. However, despite some improvement, TVET's current output falls far short of fulfilling existing policy directions and meeting the subsector's broader goals. This not only undermines policies and strategies but holds the danger of creating an unemployable work force that may be a threat to society. The factors that hamper TVET from serving as a poverty-reduction tool and a viable source of gainful and self-employment need to be urgently addressed. Fortunately, the new Ethiopian Education Development Roadmap (2018–30) proposes TVET reform in terms of policy, strategy, governance, delivery, image-building and financing, among others. While the overwhelming list of challenges is daunting, it is indisputable that the system and stakeholders in general need to urgently address them.

CHAPTER 48

Universities vs TVET

Are Attitudes the Problem?

An earlier version of this chapter appeared in *University World News, Africa Edition*, 20 March 2019, https://www.universityworldnews.com/post.php?story=20190315095852544

Technical and vocational education has become a vital component of many educational systems due to its importance in helping students to develop the technical and practical skills needed to improve their livelihoods and to be competitive in today's ever-changing world. The Ethiopian education system attaches significance to TVET as a mechanism to enhance the country's development. The main objective of the country's TVET Strategy (2008) is "to create a competent, motivated, adaptable and innovative workforce in Ethiopia contributing to poverty reduction and social and economic development through facilitating demand-driven, high quality technical and vocational education and training, relevant to all sectors of the economy, at all levels and to all people".

TVET institutions have been identified as the major means of technology adaptation and transfer which can enhance national growth in line with the country's Science, Technology and Innovation Policy (2012), the mission of which is "to create a technology framework that enables building national capabilities in technological learning, adaptation and utilization through searching for, selecting and importing effective foreign technologies in manufacturing and service-providing enterprise". Although TVET enjoys a long history in the Ethiopian education system, in the past two decades, attention has shifted to developing a strengthened vocational-oriented training system, which culminated in the development of an outcome-based system that focuses on eight priority areas: agriculture, industry, economic infrastructure, health, hotel and tourism, trade, mining, and labor and social affairs. As experiences in many contexts show, TVET's success can be determined not only by measurement against specific goals but also by a variety of factors that may include the economic benefits of the training system, the quality of the training and the higher qualification routes made available to TVET graduates. There are increasing signs that TVET in Ethiopia is challenged by deficiencies in all these areas. An equally important hurdle has been attitudes towards this level of training, which requires serious attention.

1 Educational Structure

The educational structure in Ethiopia consists of eight years of primary education followed by four years of secondary education that is divided into general and upper secondary cycles. A national examination is held at the end of the general secondary cycle (Grades 9-10) to identify students that will continue to a higher level. Those who score well are promoted to the second cycle of secondary school (Grades 11 and 12), which is regarded as preparation for college or university. Those who perform below national standards and cannot continue to upper secondary are expected to join formal TVET programs. In Ethiopia, TVET has not only been delivered through formal (school-based) means, but also through non-formal (employment-oriented short-term) and informal (on-the-job) training, whose overall integration is envisaged in the current system. The formal system is structured in such a way that 80% of students who complete Grade 10 (general secondary) are expected to join the TVET stream. However, as reported by the Ministry of Education (2018), national enrolment in TVET has not yet reached this level. Instead, there has been a decline from a total of 346,160 enrolments in 2014–15 to 302,083 in 2016–17. The failure to meet the ministry's target has been explained by a variety of factors including a lack of awareness of the benefits of the system and poor public communication about the far-reaching reforms the TVET system has undergone over the past years.

2 The Attitude Factor

Despite its potential to address the challenge of skill gaps and to reduce unemployment, students, parents and the broader community appear to show little interest in TVET as compared to university degrees. In most cases, it is regarded as the last resort for those who wish to pursue a post-secondary academic path. It is widely considered as inferior to the academically-oriented degrees offered by HEIs and as a training route suitable for those with poor academic ability. It is for this reason that most trainees perceive TVET as a second prize to university education. Such negative perceptions can affect not only the commitment of enrolled students but their plans after graduation. Recruitment and deployment of mentally prepared TVET trainees is not always an easy task due to trainees' lack of interest in pursuing blue collar jobs and in working in difficult circumstances including rural areas. Such attitudes can also prevent students at the lower levels from developing a positive interest in joining TVET institutions.

3 Plans for Improvement

TVET has been recognized as a means of enhancing Ethiopia's development in its bid to become a middle-income country by 2025 through the supply of skilled workers to various sectors of the economy. Ethiopia's efforts in this direction are evident in the various reforms it has undertaken to improve TVET delivery. Such efforts have attracted the attention of external sources such as the World Bank that released a plan in 2018 (Ligami, 2018) to finance some 17 TVET institutions as part of a project to introduce innovative solutions to Africa's development needs that included Kenya, Tanzania and Ethiopia. However, compared to efforts directed at other areas, the issue of attitudes appears to have received little attention and strategic direction.

Although Ethiopia's Science and Technology and Innovation Policy (2012) identifies the need to develop positive attitudes towards TVET programs within society, this has not been achieved. For instance, the TVET component of the fifth Education Sector Development Program (2015) focuses on three areas, namely, development and assessment of occupational standards; trainees' development and institutional capacity building; and industry extension and technology transfer services. While the importance of these components cannot be debated, neglecting the impact of attitudes and how these can be addressed can be considered a serious oversight.

Attempts to improve the status of TVET may continue to be challenged if perceptions held by students, parents and the general public are not meaningfully addressed. Only through the promotion of TVET as a key ingredient for change in national development can it become attractive to trainees and other stakeholders. Thus, active promotion of TVET is an important area of engagement. While a variety of awareness creating activities should be launched across the nation to galvanize key stakeholders, the government should also play a role in promoting the reputation of this modality through strengthened public-private partnerships, the provision of well-qualified teachers, improved financing and capacity building, quality assurance systems and other pertinent schemes, which can bring about meaningful change to the ultimate benefits of TVET and the image it deserves.

CHAPTER 49

Applied Universities

A Viable Path to Higher Education

An earlier version of this chapter appeared in *University World News, Global Edition*, 11 May 2019, https://www.universityworldnews.com/post.php?story=20190510121428558

The notion of the applied university is gaining traction in developed and developing countries alike, offering a vehicle for system differentiation and the production of high-level practical skills. The applied university goes by many names – polytechnic university, university of applied sciences, vocational university, applied technological university – according to what countries think best describes their context. For example, the German term Fachhochschule, the French haute école, the Dutch hogeschool, and the Italian scuola universitaria professionale all hint at the different emphases given by the institutions to functions such as teaching, research and professional qualifications. Despite these variations, the applied university distinguishes itself from traditional universities in its focus on practical knowledge.

Enhanced opportunities for the development of high-level practical skills that these institutions represent are especially appealing to countries and systems that seek a highly trained workforce that can contribute to national economic growth and development. The fact that applied universities are increasingly assuming status and prestige similar to that of traditional universities further augments their appeal. The availability of applied universities within a given system also promotes differentiation of a higher education system, providing more choices to students who seek a study path based on their interests and career plan.

1 The Ethiopian Experience

Ethiopia has a long history of school-based technical and vocational education. The first TVET institution was founded in 1942 as Ecole National des Artes Technique, later known as Addis Ababa Technical School. Other middle-level schools with a vocational orientation operated across the country with a particular focus on areas such as agriculture, technology and business. In the early 1960s Ethiopian high schools were structured along two streams: one purely academic and the other focusing on vocational training. In 1963, the Bahir Dar Polytechnic Institute was established as a higher education institution with vocational orientation.

Ethiopia's national education sector review that was initiated in 1973 viewed TVET as a major solution to the perennial problems of the theory-oriented education system that offered neither practical skills nor employment opportunities for thousands of school-leavers. However, despite this solid start, the next two decades were characterized by the mushrooming of academic-oriented institutions across all levels of education and the gradual dominance of an academic orientation in the higher education sector. Today, the country has 51 universities and around 300 PHEIs which together accommodate nearly a million students.

2   A Separate Stream

Growth has also occurred in the TVET stream and it is expected to grow further. However, since 2009 it is no longer part of the higher education sector. While it was expected that 80% of those who complete general education (Grades 9 and 10) would join the TVET stream, this target has not always been met and the sector currently accommodates just over 300,000 students, which is far below the government's original plan. Among the many challenges TVET graduates currently face are limited opportunities for higher education and training after completing their training through middle-level TVET programs.

In principle, the Ethiopian system allows TVET graduates to pursue further degree studies after completing their training as middle-level technicians as long as they fulfil government requirements, which includes one year work experience after graduation and passing an entry examination set by the higher education institution. However, even if they meet the criteria, candidates face the challenge of immersing themselves in a strongly theoretical degree program. Since there are no parallel TVET academic paths, students who complete the TVET stream have no choice but to join the academically-oriented university system and pursue further studies at degree level and above.

Despite the new programmatic design of Ethiopian universities, which focus heavily (70%) on programs in science and technology subjects, the majority of universities across the country are comprehensive universities and are substantially oriented towards theory. The only exceptions are perhaps the Addis Ababa and Adama Science and Technology universities that were split from the previous structure in order to gradually assume special status as science and technology universities. Having TVET graduates join comprehensive universities in some ways defeats the purpose of TVET education, which aims to produce mid-level technicians that can fill the skills gap and promote the government's plan to produce skilled human resources to contribute to the economy and national growth.

3   The Role of Applied Universities

The Ethiopian higher education sector is now bracing itself for a more differentiated system, a component of which will be the establishment of applied universities that offer high-level professional and practical degrees different from what those provided by comprehensive universities. The manner in which applied universities will be distinguished from comprehensive universities and how they will operate across the system remains unclear. Such a move will not only create additional opportunities in the higher education sector, but will also provide invaluable opportunities for further study to TVET graduates who have been forced to abandon TVET streams in search of higher-level training at comprehensive universities, or who are tempted to turn away from the education sector altogether.

CHAPTER 50

The TVET Sector's Challenge to Recruit, Retain Competent Trainers

An earlier version of this chapter appeared in *University World News, Africa Edition*, 12 November 2020, https://www.universityworldnews.com/post.php?story=20201111080728727

The professional development of trainers has been identified as a critical component in the success of TVET in Ethiopia and as a criterion for the accreditation of these institutions. Ethiopia's TVET Strategy (Ministry of Education, 2008) recognizes the indispensable role of highly competent, qualified and motivated trainers. Two types of TVET trainers have been identified in the system: institution-based and industry-based. Local studies show that many institutions suffer from a lack of competent, motivated and creative trainers of both types. It is stipulated that TVET trainers should receive special training and certification before they can work in the system. Continuous professional development opportunities are also identified in Ethiopia's TVET strategy as a means of enhancing the competencies of TVET trainers, but such opportunities are rare. Most TVET trainers also lack industry experience, despite it being set as a mandatory requirement. Additional challenges such as an unattractive work environment, high workload and poor incentives also impact the recruitment and retention of TVET trainers.

1   Trainer Qualifications

Depending on the five levels of training (I–V) identified for TVET education, trainers are expected to be qualified at three levels: levels A, B, and C, with A signaling that a trainer has the most advanced level of qualifications. Level C trainers are expected to teach at Levels I, II and III. They should be graduates of a TVET institution, having completed their education above Level III. Level IV students are expected to be taught by at least Level B trainers who must have a bachelor's degree, be assessed as competent to train at this level and have taken a B-level training methodology course. After qualifying as a Level C instructor, an individual can upgrade him/herself to a Level B trainer by enrolling for three- to four-year courses at teacher training institutes. Level

V students are supposed to be taught by Level A trainers who are expected to have a master's degree, must have been assessed as competent to train at the level, and have completed Level A teaching methodology training. Since the highest instructor level within TVET institutions is Level A, these instructors can also teach at any of the lower levels.

The TVET sector is challenged by the lack of adequate and qualified trainers. The total number of trainers in 2017–18 was 19,236, with 20% being female. Most of the trainers in the Ethiopian TVET system are Level C trainers. The Federal TVET Agency's 10-year strategic plan similarly indicates that, currently, 63.4% of TVET trainers available in the system are Level C trainers that are often cited as being deficient both in theoretical knowledge and pedagogic competence in addition to having poor mastery of English, the medium of instruction. Major skills gaps have also been identified due to their lack of practical experience in business and industry. The fact that the TVET sector is dominated by Level C trainers means they currently teach at levels they are not equipped for in terms of the national standards. Apart from their limitation in numbers, Levels A and B trainers are also found to be deficient in technical skills and fail to deliver hands-on practical training, which is identified as a key element of the TVET delivery strategy.

2 Impact on the System

The few studies in the Ethiopian context indicate that, in general, there is a shortage of compctent, industry-experienced and motivated trainers at all levels. Government observations attest to the fact that the delivery of generic courses by TVET teachers who are neither proficient nor enthusiastic about these courses has contributed to poor quality TVET. The shortage of trainers is often identified as one of the obstacles in improving the quality of TVET education and its expansion in Ethiopia. This can be attributed to a variety of factors. The Ethiopian Ministry of Education has observed that TVET is affected by factors such as sector's poor reputation, limited incentives and the trainers' excessive workload.

Low salaries and a lack of incentives and reward systems are often cited as major obstacles to attracting new trainers. The poor working environment in institutions is also identified as an inhibiting factor that restricts the recruitment and retention of skilled and experienced trainers. Trainers are overburdened with tasks that include curriculum development, the development of teaching and learning materials, coordinating training opportunities for students in industry, supporting small and medium enterprises and transferring technologies to industries. The scope of these responsibilities could contribute to trainers leaving TVET. There is also limited systematic professional development for teachers to upgrade their skills and competence on a continuous basis so that they can contribute to improving the system and the training at specified levels. In similar vein, though the system requires that trainers from companies be made available by cooperating companies, this is not the case. Studies indicate that most companies or enterprises do not have trainers who meet the requirements and there is a general shortage of industry-based trainers in the sector. These factors continue to impinge on the overall performance and effectiveness of TVET institutions.

3   What Needs to Be Done?

A variety of efforts are underway to improve the skills and competence of TVET trainers and leaders. According to a 2019 report by the Federal TVET Agency, such efforts have helped to bring the trainer: trainee ratio to 1:27. However, limitations persist with regard to the professionalization of TVET lecturers and especially in producing trainers in the required quality and quantity. Given the growing emphasis on TVET in the national system of education, more needs to be done to address the current challenges and develop an overall strategy to improve the profile and competence of TVET trainers in Ethiopia. While the need to strengthen relations between TVET institutions and industries is vital, the latter should assume the responsibility of not only providing a physical site for internship purposes but also availing the right type of industrial trainers who can enhance training. The government should also devise new and innovative mechanisms to raise awareness of TVET across society and to improve TVET trainers' working conditions. When it comes to the professionalization of TVET trainers, universities need to work closely and actively with the TVET authorities and colleges to solve the prevailing problems. The recent differentiation of the Ethiopian higher education sector into various streams of institutions and the creation of applied universities should enhance cooperation.

CHAPTER 51

Gains and Challenges for Women in the TVET Sector

An earlier version of this chapter appeared in *University World News, Africa Edition*, 15 October 2020, https://www.universityworldnews.com/post.php?story=20201014201839782

Ethiopia's interest in participating in the competitive global market economy has put TVET at the center of its education policy and strategy, but women's participation in certain areas remains of concern. As stipulated in the country's National TVET Strategy (2008), the overall objective of TVET programs has been "to create a competent, motivated, adaptable and innovative workforce that contributes to poverty reduction and social and economic development". This plan is set to be realized through "a demand-driven, high quality technical and vocational education and training, relevant to all sectors of the economy, at all levels and available to all people".

1   Women's Enrollment Patterns

While women's participation at all other levels of the education system in Ethiopia remains low, TVET is the only sector where women are equally or better represented. However, this does not necessarily mean that all forms of inequity have been addressed. According to 2018 annual statistics generated by the Ministry of Education, total enrolment in TVET was 292,378, with half (50.8%) of the students female. The average annual growth rate for female participation has shown a positive trend, exceeding the male growth rate in the period 2012–13 to 2016–17. In 2016–17, TVET female graduates accounted for 52% of all trainees. The proportion of female students is higher in private than public TVET institutions. In terms of the number of TVET institutions, there are also more private than public ones. While 57.6% of those enrolled in non-government private institutions in 2018 were female, government institutions recorded a figure of 49.4% women in the same year.

Despite the overall encouraging trend of female participation in TVET, there are areas where significant gaps still exist. One such area concerns the enrolment share of female students in the different training levels. According to the Ministry of Education (2010) the Ethiopian TVET system is structured along five levels. While Levels 1 and 2 are for trainees below Grade 10, Levels 3 and 4 are for those who have completed general education or Grade 10 and Level 5 is training at the polytechnic level. Using this classification, the largest proportion of female enrolment is currently found at the lower levels of the training strata. For instance, those registered in Level 2 programs constitute 33.7% of overall enrolment, while the share of female enrolment at Level 5 – polytechnic level – is only 1.8%. Another area of concern is the programs in which students are enrolled. According to the 2014 Ethiopian gender strategy, the concentration of females in short-term programs (that focus on traditional 'female' fields such as business, IT, and hairdressing) could be as high as 85%, as opposed to long-term ones (which focus more on science, mechanical and technological skills or on manual skills like construction and/or building).

The increasing tendency among female trainees to enroll in a very limited set of technical fields is influenced by a variety of factors such as traditional stereotypes of what jobs are appropriate for women, and family and environmental influence associated with the traditional role of women. Discrimination among instructors, employers and the community at large, and fewer prospects for employment and practical assignments discourage female students from enrolling in science, mechanical and technological courses. Women's level of participation can also be compounded by a lack of information about technical and vocational educational tracks and systemic features of the technical and vocational education system.

2   Awareness and Role Models Required

Creating equal opportunities for women requires that the sociocultural, educational and employment limitations that discourage them from pursuing TVET educational opportunities and technical careers be addressed. In order to increase enrolment, women require sufficient information about the nature of these programs and career options; they also need to regard them as an acceptable educational option. However, information gaps exist on the future trajectory of industries and emergent skills needs, the returns on investing in particular skills sets, and projections on the future returns of education and training investment.

While Ethiopia has launched strategies to create such awareness with the support of civil society organizations, the Ministry of Women and Children, Ministry of Youth and Sport, and related offices at 'woreda' (district) and regional levels, and the involvement of small and medium enterprises and agencies, and regional technical and vocational institutions, the level of success of these initiatives is unclear. The power of female role models in motivating women to pursue technical education and employment has also been a consistent theme in many countries as a mechanism to promote behavioral change. In this regard, much remains to be done in Ethiopia. Currently, 51% of students and 20% of trainers are female. Given the number of female students, more women role models are required within TVET institutions themselves.

3   The Way Forward

The foregoing suggests that while Ethiopia's promotion of female participation in TVET is commendable, a key challenge remains in promoting gender equity across all programs and levels, as these appear to be areas where their participation needs to be further augmented. Efforts should be stepped up not only to increase the participation of female trainees but also female labor participation and livelihood prospects. Reforms to improve current deficiencies in this area could include an increase in the status of TVET in general and improving female participation in this stream of training. Apart from developing a comprehensive strategy that addresses all facets of this challenge, there is also a need for increased efforts to raise awareness among the community, TVET instructors and administrators, employers, female students and their families on the importance of girls' and women's participation in levels and fields of study where it is still meager or non-existent.

PART 9

Graduate Employability

CHAPTER 52

Education and the Workplace

Addressing the Yawning Gap

An earlier version of this chapter appeared in *University World News, Global Edition*, 31 August 2018, https://www.universityworldnews.com/post.php?story=20180829082114142

Skill mismatches resulting from a gap between an individual's type or quality of training and their employment opportunities can have adverse consequences for employees, employers, organizations and the economy at large and are associated with a range of challenges including unemployment, low wages and job satisfaction, the ability to find suitable work and the economy's overall productivity and competitiveness.

The Ethiopian workforce is becoming more educated with young entrants to the labor market having more years of education than before. According to a recent World Bank study, the share of employees with post-secondary qualifications more than doubled from 9% in 2003 to 23% in 2014. One of the drivers was post-secondary education's positive impact on employment. Ethiopia's Labour Force Survey estimates that those with post-secondary education earn 106.5% (2.06 times) higher monthly earnings than those who have completed Grade 12. However, unlike in the past, graduates from post-secondary institutions are now being affected by rising unemployment. According to the Urban Employment Unemployment Survey (2015), the unemployment rate among Ethiopians with secondary education and below fell between 2003 and 2014, while it increased among TVET and university graduates. The World Bank reports that, 14% of unemployed youth in Ethiopia are currently graduates of post-secondary institutions.

1 Challenges

While the rate of higher education expansion may account for this new development, a more serious explanation is the increasing mismatch between the skills available and the requirements of the labor market. Indeed, the World Bank's Enterprise Surveys data for Ethiopia (2015) identifies poorly educated workers as one of the most common obstacles identified by business owners and top managers in 848 firms. This finding concurs with an assessment of skills and competitiveness in Ethiopia which revealed that vacancies for skilled production workers and managerial positions remain open for long periods of time, with 57% of firms identifying a lack of appropriate applicants as the key reason. In similar vein, the Ethiopia Skills Module Survey (World Bank, 2013) which involved 102 firms found that a quarter of the firms (27) reported having vacant positions as a result of a lack of skilled labor. For about 67% of those with vacant positions (18), the positions were unfilled for more than four months. Among 21 firms that provided a reason for failing to fill vacancies, 12 (57%) mentioned a lack of applicants for the unfilled vacancies, while eight (38%) cited a dearth of adequately qualified applicants. Furthermore, employers report difficulty in finding workers with the required technical skills, ethics and commitment, and computer skills – in that order. Skills concerns are especially evident among manufacturing firms (particularly textile, garment and food producers) and exporters who cite the shortage of skills as a key constraint to growth and increased productivity. Another related research report indicates that firms report that they often struggle to find the technical and soft skills they require when recruiting candidates.

While their increasing presence in Ethiopia is encouraging, large firms and companies with foreign ownership view the lack of skills as one of the major obstacles to their operation and growth. A small survey of Chinese investors – significant employers in Ethiopia – conducted by the World Bank found that 93% of professional positions and 67% of skilled production workers' positions were held by Chinese employees. Furthermore, more than 50% of the Chinese firms indicated that an inadequately educated workforce is a severe constraint to their operations (compared to 4% of domestic firms), particularly in the manufacturing and construction sectors, forcing 75% of Chinese firms to invest in training workers compared to 27% of domestic firms.

2   National Requirements

According to Ethiopia's Higher Education Proclamation, HEIs are expected to prepare knowledgeable, skilled and attitudinally mature graduates, in sufficient numbers and of the required quality within relevant fields and disciplines for the country to become internationally competitive. Similarly, the country's Education Sector Development Program (ESDP) V recognizes the importance of graduates with the appropriate skills and technical knowledge and notes that academic institutions should equip graduates with relevant industry knowledge, up-to-date specialized skills and competencies and work ready attitudes that will help them succeed in the world of work. Despite these expectations, Ethiopia's university graduates are now confronted by the twin challenges of a shortage of jobs and skills. The success of the education system in general and the relevance of attending universities for the youth in particular will be determined by whether or not these gaps are addressed.

In response to the growing challenges, the Ministry of Education has started working with public universities to provide targeted employment and skills enhancement activities by way of improving the curriculum, teacher training, university-industry linkages, career advisory services, assessment schemes, and communication and other soft skills. Shifting the focus from pure content delivery towards skills and learning outcomes may be the key to realizing these goals. However, it should be noted that for this targeted effort to succeed, similar improvements should be made in the overall quality of institutional provisions which may pertain to the student-staff ratio, infrastructure and facilities, the quality of the staff employed, student engagement and representation, and internal quality assurance, among others. The challenge remains how this can be done amidst an expansion drive that shows no sign of abating.

3   Aligning Expectations

Another important consideration is the need to align employers and HEIs' expectations. There has been a great deal of resistance on the part of HEIs to concede to demands from employers for improved skills due to the practical problems attached to the issue and the implications for the wider goals and purposes of higher education. Institutions resist subjecting themselves to industry's endless expectations of a finished product which they consider unrealistic and argue that universities should not degenerate into training institutions. While this argument may partly hold true, HEIs cannot shy away from the responsibility of reforming themselves at a time when their graduates are deemed unemployable due to a lack of the skills demanded by the labor market. On the other hand, in addition to assisting HEIs' training efforts by providing experiential opportunities for trainees and forging close relations, employers should be willing to broaden their view and take some responsibility in filling graduates' training gaps on an on-going basis rather than expecting everything to come ready-made from institutions.

CHAPTER 53

Graduate Employability

Whose Responsibility?

An earlier version of this chapter appeared in *University World News, Global Edition*, 9 February 2018, https://www.universityworldnews.com/post.php?story=20180206100000225

Through its Ministry of Education, the Ethiopian government is planning to improve the employment of university graduates over the next three years with specific targets to be met by individual institutions. University education in Ethiopia has a long history of creating easy access to life-time jobs. However, this is no longer possible due to the significant expansion of the higher education sector which now produces more than 150,000 graduates every year. The challenge of employability has now become a political lightning rod, with the government attracting criticism for driving higher education growth regardless of local needs and labor market demands. One mechanism to respond to such challenges has been the creation of a national Employment Policy (2009) as a mechanism to coordinate employment creation and labor administration across all sectors and sections of society. However, the effects of this policy are as yet unclear. Other strategies included encouraging graduates to create their own jobs, and increasing the ratio (70:30) of programs in science and technology offered at public universities versus the number in the social sciences and humanities.

However, due to the sheer numbers of graduates, these strategies are by no means adequate. Rapid population growth and a youthful population, coupled with limited growth in jobs, mean that unemployment and underemployment are serious social problems in Ethiopia. Studies also indicate that employment creation in the country continues to be affected by a variety of unaddressed challenges related to private investment, labor laws and economic development. The new plan for universities sets out to create degree-relevant employment for 80% or more of each year's graduates within 12 months. This ambitious target was drawn from the institution-specific plans of 33 public universities and assumes employment creation for a minimum of 160,000 graduates each year. While the policy and operational directives are a reflection of country-wide efforts to improve employment in general, the intention is perhaps the first organized move from a government that has directed its attention over two decades primarily to the expansion of a system that was, prior to 1990, marked by a strong elitist legacy.

1   Core Issues

The new plan identifies the core issues that influence low graduate employability as: questionable teacher quality, poor quality graduates, and weak linkages with industry. Teacher quality is regarded as the most critical factor impacting graduate preparation. Staff is believed to suffer from a lack of technical knowledge and pedagogical skills. Thus, the quality of graduates is mainly attributed to poor teacher competency as well as ineffective student learning. The latter is explained through students' lack of practical and soft skills that are critical for employability. The contents of the curricula, assessment schemes and students' poor language and communication skills have also been identified as areas for improvement. Curricula are to be reviewed to assess whether they assist graduate employability. More emphasis will be given to practical experience as part of the training modalities adopted by universities. The mismatch between the supply of graduates and labor market demands and the limited cooperation between industries and universities are also seen as major challenges. Universities are therefore expected to design strategies that strengthen these links.

The delivery plans set for universities assume that strategies need to be implemented with existing capacities and resources, and with a focus on tasks that can have the most impact over the next three years. These include improvements in student learning in the classroom, in the areas of teacher competencies, performance and motivation, linkages with industry and support for students through value-added internship experiences. For its part, the ministry is expected to develop external assessment guidelines to validate teacher assessment at each university, coordinate and administer exit examinations across prioritized fields of study, revitalize pedagogical and language improvement training in each university, and oversee the implementation of tracer studies and labor market demand forecasts that influence university policies and program offerings.

2   Matching Aspirations to Challenges

While Ethiopian universities' desire to address the challenge of graduate employability is commendable, much remains to be done in terms of realizing the goals of the delivery plans in the limited time available and taking into account resource constraints. The fact that the new plan focuses only on the next few years is an indication that it is being used as a tool to achieve government's short-term goals contained in the Education Sector Development Program V. Ideally, in addition to what it seeks to achieve in the short term, the new plan should look at how current initiatives will serve as stepping stones to more comprehensive and nationally coordinated efforts that address concerns about graduate employability. It is also difficult to imagine how the plan can be successful in the short term without the influence of what are dismissed as external factors, which include infrastructure and inputs, leadership and administration, the poor quality of university intake, and impact of the labor market. For instance, while improving teachers' knowledge and skills is seen as a priority area, there is little detail on how teachers will be able to implement modern methods of teaching and assessment in the large classes created by the unabated expansion drive that afflict every university.

The new university-industry linkage plans also rely on the capacity of the private sector to accommodate the thousands of students that graduate every year. Achieving employability at this level seems quite inconceivable. While it may be a new step in the right direction, the difficulties of apportioning the major responsibilities of the new plan to individual universities is another critical area which requires attention. I would argue that the initiative calls for the participation and coordinated efforts of all parties – at federal and regional level – that have a stake in the preparation and eventual employment of Ethiopian university graduates. It remains to be seen to what extent other stakeholders will be involved and whether they will respond favorably to the call.

CHAPTER 54

Producing Work-Ready Graduates Requires Strong Partnerships

An earlier version of this chapter appeared in *Inside Higher Education*, 3 October 2019, https://www.insidehighered.com/blogs/world-view/work-ready-graduates-require-strong-partnerships

A significant number of young people face difficulties in finding a job due to the mismatch between their education/training and labor market requirements. The specific skills and attributes identified as essential components of employability are widely defined as communication skills, critical and analytical thinking, team work, problem-solving, self-management, business and customer awareness, taking initiative, leadership and managerial abilities, systems thinking, work ethic, etc. Successful and appropriate graduate employability benefits all stakeholders – graduates, employers, HEIs, governments and the economy at large. On the other hand, failure to equip graduates with these skills can have adverse consequences for all these stakeholders since it can pose challenges with regard to unemployment, low wages and job satisfaction, the ability to find suitable work and the overall productivity and competitiveness of a given economy.

While it would be most appropriate for all stakeholders to come together to improve graduate employability, there appears to be inordinate demand on HEIs to produce graduates with the profile that industry needs without sharing responsibility for this goal. These exaggerated expectations of HEIs sometimes overlook the importance of commitment from other critical stakeholders like employers and students, resulting in their passive role which can have a detrimental effect on success. If left exclusively to HEIs, the objectives will remain difficult to achieve. A shift in attitude is thus needed to bring about changes where important stakeholders assume a variety of roles in identifying employability skills, enhancing the mobility of graduates and university faculty, and facilitating the transitional phase for new graduates.

The wider discussion on graduate employability assumes that graduates must develop skills and attributes that respond to today's fast changing work environment. Higher education institutions are usually left to define and deliver these skills and incorporate them into their programs. While the role of HEIs in preparing qualified graduates cannot be discounted, this cannot be accomplished singlehandedly without bringing employers and others on board. However, most often, the role of employers in developing such skills appears to be a missing element or a neglected issue.

It is important to note that many of the 'generic skills' required could differ from one geographic or industrial context to another. While the identification of specific employment-related skills or competencies has been pursued in many countries such as Australia, New Zealand, the United Kingdom, and the United States, the reality is different in contexts like Africa where this exercise has been non-existent, perhaps with the exception of South Africa. In the absence of frameworks, the definition of employability skills and competencies cannot be left solely to HEIs. Rather, it should be developed through the active participation of employers who should assume the role of clearly articulating what they expect from recent graduates. Continuous updating of the skills needed by graduates is also necessary through the ongoing involvement of employers who are more aware of changing demands in the work environment.

1   Enhancing Student Internships and Externships

In addition to involving employers in curriculum design, their assistance in creating opportunities for experiential learning is key. Student internships appear to be a common activity in universities across the world to expose students to the world of work. This practice demands the active involvement of employers in assigning student interns to appropriate workplaces, providing them with support, and closely monitoring their performance.

Experiential learning programs succeed not only when employers grant permission for student placements, but more importantly, when they are involved in monitoring student progress and providing constructive feedback. However, in many contexts this level of employer participation remains passive. Where it does happen, the success of externship programs in which university staff stay at industrial placements to acquire practical experience requires a similar level of willingness, assistance, follow up and feedback.

2   Facilitating the Transitional Phase of Employment

The role of industry and business during the initial phases of graduate employment is also a critical component in enhancing new graduates' employability skills. Traditionally, employers assumed the role of grooming such graduates to become productive members of a given work force. This role is gradually being eroded as employers want graduates 'ready-made' with the required skills or with a few years' work experience. Both expectations are unrealistic and can disadvantage the majority of young graduates who cannot fulfill these requirements.

Employer readiness to assume some responsibility during the early phase of young graduates' work life not only helps new graduates to develop new skills but also to develop confidence that will help them respond to the various demands of their jobs. This requires that employers devote time and resources to the task. Research in this area indicates that employers that are most successful in developing the employability skills of young graduates are those that create additional opportunities to learn – an environment less friendly to young employees can derail learning capacity, self-confidence, and output.

3   Towards a Strengthened Role for Employers

Since work readiness involves the various intellectual, social, and personal dimensions that evolve both during the university years and in the work place, cultivation of employability skills cannot be left exclusively to universities. It is true that universities have responsibility for curriculum reform that will better prepare graduates for the increasingly complex demands of the workplace. But their success depends on other stakeholders being equally committed. Benefits to employers will be determined not only by how much universities adapt, but also by their own readiness, capacity and effort to contribute. Employers cannot complain about young graduates being 'half-baked' if they themselves remain outside the education and training process. It is important to move beyond lamenting graduates' limited skills and assume a proactive role in influencing and contributing to universities' output. While universities have a major part to play in this change, active involvement of governments is critical in many environments to set policy directions, galvanize multi-stakeholder engagements and offer direct and indirect incentives to companies that get involved in these initiatives.

CHAPTER 55

Job Creation Plan

What Role for Higher Education?

An earlier version of this chapter appeared in *University World News, Africa Edition*, 21 September 2019, https://www.universityworldnews.com/post.php?story=20190919075953486

Among the most prevalent features of the Ethiopian economy are a growing population and an increasing supply of labor – seen as both opportunities and threats. According to the Central Statistical Agency of Ethiopia, the country's economically active population ballooned from 3.9 million to 9.23 million between 2003 and 2018. Youth make up a significant proportion of this number. The agency also noted that the unemployment rate for youth stood at 25.3%. With the rate of increase in the labor force calculated as 4.4% per year, it is estimated that between two to three million youth are joining the job market annually. Creating employment for such a rapidly growing labor force is admittedly a Herculean task.

In response, the Ethiopian government set up a national investment and job creation steering committee, led by the prime minister, to create jobs and improve the investment climate. Three sub-committees will deal specifically with business, job creation and investment. The committee has 27 members including the deputy prime minister, presidents of the nine regional governments, the mayors of Addis Ababa and Dire Dawa cities, 10 representatives of federal ministries, and two from the prime minister's office. Among the various ministries included is the Ministry of Science and Higher Education. According to the prime minister's office's Twitter page, the role of this committee will be ensuring the creation of sustainable and decent work by aligning policy and institutional systems. The committee will also play a leading role in attracting investment and ensuring the implementation of plans to increase job creation efforts.

1 Job Creation

The committee is thus set to coordinate the work of federal and regional entities and other stakeholders to create a conducive investment environment to accelerate job creation. The aim is to create three million jobs within the next year through a particular focus on sectors that are considered to have potential: agriculture, mining, tourism, and creative and IT industries. The Oromia region has been earmarked for 1.1 million jobs, followed by Amhara with 700,000 and Southern Nations, Nationalities and People's Region with 600,000. Thirty percent of the jobs are intended to be created during the first and second quarters of the planned year while the third and final quarters are expected to generate the remaining 70%. The committee will meet every two months to evaluate progress and follow up on issues requiring immediate action. Improvements in the investment and business climate will not only help to create jobs, but also to address past failures and weaknesses in attracting investment. The poor investment climate and regulation-related problems have often been cited as major bottlenecks in attracting foreign direct investment in Ethiopia. The new initiative aims to address these deficiencies and meet the broader goal of creating an enabling business environment in which the private sector assumes the critical role of job creation. Indeed, the government has announced plans to open up key economic sectors to private investment.

The initiative is good news, especially for the thousands of young graduates leaving school, HEIs and TVET institutions every year. While primary and secondary level graduates still dominate the active labor force in Ethiopia, the number of graduates from post-secondary institutions has increased significantly. Currently, more than 160,000 graduates from HEIs and 130,000 from TVET institutions join the labor market annually. And it is this group that is facing unemployment which, according to the World Bank, stands at 14% but could be much higher. The success of the job-creation plan depends partly on the skills each targeted sector demands. It is not yet clear what type of jobs are expected to be created and the specific skills required. Technical and vocational education and training institutions and HEIs need this information in order to assist in building the required workforce. As a member of the national steering committee, the Ministry of Science and Higher Education which coordinates TVET and higher education institutions is expected to have such information which may determine what can be done at the level of these institutions.

2 Current Shortcomings and the Need to Align Efforts

The job creation committee will be able to achieve its goals when educational institutions support its grand initiative by supplying the right number and type of quality graduates. But even before the education sector begins to work on this, it needs to address some of its critical current shortcomings. Skill shortages are increasingly becoming a concern among employers, especially foreign investors, in Ethiopia. Efforts to fill vacancies have been hampered countrywide by HEIs not producing graduates with appropriate or adequate skills. Indeed, the poor supply of appropriately-skilled labor is regarded as a major obstacle to improving the competitiveness of the country's manufacturing sector. According to the World Bank's fourth Ethiopia Economic Update (2015), skills shortages constitute a key constraint to growth and improved productivity in the manufacturing sector. Research further indicates that many foreign companies consider the lack of trained personnel as one of the many challenges they face in recruiting workers in Ethiopia.

While this national plan may be overly ambitious, government's commitment to creating jobs in Ethiopia signals its recognition that unemployment is critical and must be addressed. In order to supply an appropriately-trained workforce, all relevant stakeholders including education institutions, employers and relevant ministries should work closely together to ensure the success of the project. Higher education and TVET institutions should also familiarize themselves with the government's goals and begin thinking about how they can create the graduates that will be required. These institutions should address their shortcomings, such as paying too little attention to practical training, weak links with industry and business, poorly-qualified educators and poor teaching methods, infrastructure and facilities. They should also seek to align their earlier efforts with current demands so that nationwide efforts are geared towards a coherent end.

CHAPTER 56

Employment Gender Gap also a Higher Education Issue

An earlier version of this chapter appeared in *University World News, Africa Edition*, 3 December 2020, https://www.universityworldnews.com/post.php?story=20201130220329453

Having more women in the workplace generally benefits a nation's growth and prosperity. Although the situation has improved steadily over the past decades, the labor force gender gap is still an issue of global concern. According to a 2019 International Labor Office report, the global gap in labor participation rates between women and men was 27% in 2018. Fewer than half of all working-age women (48%) participated in the labor market compared with 75% of men. Studies in developing countries indicate that gender discrimination in society and laws, including the roles and positions of women in society, social norms, and socio-economic conditions hamper women's equal participation. Research further indicates that an underdeveloped enterprise culture, inadequate support systems for businesses and underdeveloped markets and infrastructure can also affect women's participation in employment.

1 Patterns of Employment

In Ethiopia, persistent policy directions outlaw any form of gender-based discrimination and guarantee equal rights and obligations for both sexes. In reality, however, significant gender gaps still exist in many areas, including employment patterns, labor participation and participation in business. According to the 2018 World Bank Enterprise Survey Ethiopia (WBESE), the urban unemployment rate in Ethiopia is 19.1%. The unemployment rate among women is 26.4% – more than double the rate among men (12.2%). In similar vein, the unemployment rate among young women and men is 30.9% and 19.0%, respectively. A recent study on youth self-employment in Ethiopia showed the same pattern, with the unemployment rate among women in urban areas (28.1%) almost twice that of men (14.4%). According to the study, the disparity increases as people grow older.

Few women work full time. According to the 2018 World Bank survey, only 27.8% of working women were employed in permanent, full-time positions and 27.6% as full-time production workers. The number of women in full-time non-production jobs remained at 33.9%. A 2019 International Finance Corporation (IFC) report on the same subject further indicates that women also leave the job market more rapidly than males and end up confined to the home, where they have various responsibilities.

2   Owning and Managing Businesses

In 2015, the WBESE showed that few women owned a business (36.2%) and that women owned only 16.5% of corporations. When it came to management, only 4.5% of corporations had women in top management. Other studies also show how a variety of challenges and gender-based discrimination affect women's participation in the labor market. The 2019 IFC report, for instance, shows that women struggle to raise funds, and access relevant training and education opportunities, information and market outlets. In similar vein, the 2019 Gender Diagnostic Report of Ethiopia revealed that, compared with male business managers, female business managers in general have less access to resources to grow and formalize their businesses. The 2015 World Bank Ethiopia Enterprise Survey revealed that 49% of female-managed firms identified access to finance as a major constraint, compared with only 19% of male-managed firms. As a consequence, many growth-oriented female entrepreneurs in Ethiopia are forced to continue to manage low-margin, smaller firms with lower profitability and limited potential for business growth. This does not necessarily mean that there are no women-owned firms with the potential to grow into larger enterprises.

3   Addressing Gender Gaps in Employment and the Role of HE

Apart from the political arena where there have been significant gains in the participation of Ethiopian women, wider participation in employment, as well as economic activities, is still far from satisfactory, despite some government initiatives. It is understandable that, even where there is political will, addressing gender gaps is not an easy task due to various underlying factors that fuel its existence in the first place. It is for this reason that societies should clearly understand the barriers confronting young girls and women. The little research in this area suggests that minimizing gender gaps in employment should begin by examining the specific nature of employment creation, which appears to be heavily influenced by gender dimensions. Furthermore, targeted interventions are essential to tackle the challenges women face in employment and investment. Among many possible interventions, government policy should identify specific barriers that deter women, and create more favorable conditions to allow women into the workforce and keep them there. Women should also have access to advice, counselling and mentoring services to support and sustain them, as well as encourage them to grow their businesses. While government support in these areas has to be ongoing, sustainable and targeted at enhancing women's participation in labor and investment, the role of HEIs cannot be ignored.

Women in developing countries face many complicated challenges. Adding employment challenges can exacerbate the situation and compromise possible benefits. Hence, this challenge, like all other related challenges, should be a priority. There is a variety of ways in which education and HEIs can contribute to addressing gender gaps through empowering and training women. For instance, programs offered at HEIs can be geared to improve women's technical competencies and skills, which will help them to succeed later. Another mechanism is to encourage and support women to enroll in programs which can reduce unemployment and diversify women's participation in the labor force. Traditionally, the most dominant fields of study for female students have been the social sciences and humanities while there has been underrepresentation in fields related to engineering and the sciences that offer more employment opportunities.

In addition to creating awareness of the challenges of the job market, HEIs could also offer special sessions for female students to increase awareness of the gender dimensions of job creation and placement and how they could be overcome. This should prepare women for their future and help them navigate challenges. While increasing interest in tackling the issue of employability in Ethiopian universities is a positive trend, institutions should also examine the gender dimensions of employment and seek solutions at the national and institutional level.

CHAPTER 57

Students Face Challenges on Route to Self-Employment

An earlier version of this chapter appeared in *University World News, Africa Edition*, 26 November 2020, https://www.universityworldnews.com/post.php?story=20201124222501838

Today's young graduates are confronted with the huge challenge of unemployment because of the fast-changing world of work and the limited and competitive opportunities available. While graduates are increasingly conscious of the wider range of opportunities that can open up as a result of their educational qualifications, they are equally aware that securing jobs on the basis of simply possessing academic credentials – as was the case in the old days – is extremely difficult, if not impossible. There is now an emphasis on skills training at universities, since many of the challenges young people face in finding jobs are related to the mismatch between their education or training and labor market requirements. While this is understandable, it is obvious that the transition from universities to careers is not solely dependent on the acquisition of skills defined to be important in the job market.

In addition to the need for skills training, which it is assumed will solve the huge challenges that emanate from the misalignment between educational preparation and the demands of the job market, graduates are also advised to seek different mechanisms of job acquisition, including self-employment. However, this route, which has led many developing countries to adopt programs that aim to promote self-employment and small-scale entrepreneurship, does not appear to have been properly investigated. As a result, there is limited information on its characteristics and especially its potential as a viable route to graduate employment. Hence, there is a need to understand the nature of self-employment and the challenges that hinder its success, especially for those who seek to use it as a possible route of graduate employment.

1 The Self-Employment Sector and Challenges

A significant percentage of the working population in developing countries is engaged in self-employment. In urban areas of Ethiopia, for instance, the majority of the employed are paid employees, (52.3%), who work in the formal economy and receive salaries, while 41.1% are self-employed. As in most countries in sub-Saharan Africa, self-employment opportunities in Ethiopia largely lie in small, informal firms. Embodying substantial patterns of self-employment, the informal sector contributes to 38.6% of Ethiopia's GDP, which is consistent with the figure for sub-Saharan Africa and that of low-income countries.

The self-employment sector is heterogeneous and can include those who earn very little and are less successful businesses than those led by successful entrepreneurs with promising growth potential. If properly coached and given the necessary support, there is every reason to believe that university graduates can join the latter group. The self-employment sector, in particular, holds special significance for women, who tend to have fewer opportunities in the wage sector and are better represented here.

Graduates are often encouraged not to stick to wage and salaried employment but rather pursue self-employment. There is a growing interest among graduates themselves in pursuing this route and become successful, but things may not always go according to their expectations. In fact, those who seek to be self-employed and successful often face challenges that extend from the initial stages of opening a business to obtaining the required support to run their businesses successfully.

Despite some improvements over the years, starting a business in Ethiopia is still regarded as difficult. According to the World Bank (2020), Ethiopia ranks 168th out of 190 countries in the world in terms of the ease of starting a business. This is far below the sub-Saharan African average and neighboring countries such as Rwanda and Kenya, which are ranked 35th and 129th, respectively. It is obvious that interventions such as access to financial resources can benefit the self-employment process. However, for those who seek self-employment, obtaining the required financial support remains a serious challenge. For instance, the World Bank (2020) report on 'Doing Business' in Ethiopia reveals that getting credit to start their own business is among the most serious challenges faced by prospective entrepreneurs. According to the Ethiopian Urban Employment and Unemployment Survey (2018), the majority (54%) of the unemployed in Ethiopia who would like to establish their own businesses report financial constraints as their main problem. Other studies on the subject consistently echo similar findings. Even where financial support is available in the form of access to credit, significant administrative gaps hinder the road to self-employment. Studies across the African continent indicate that most youth credit schemes suffer from weaknesses such as poor program design, implementation, loan disbursement, and loan repayment rates, a lack of monitoring skills, and inadequate financial control systems.

Another important factor that challenges those who seek self-employment is the lack of work space or land, which often determine the performance of micro and small enterprises. Still another factor that affects the success of self-employment, both at continental and national level, is the lack of relevant education and training that are critical to the success and growth rate of businesses owned by young entrepreneurs. Other factors identified include technology, infrastructure, market accessibility and government regulation. Psychosocial constraints such as the fear of failure and criticism, attitudes toward self-employment and inadequate motivation are also identified as serious problems confronting young entrepreneurs.

2 Beyond Skills Training

While the increased emphasis on skills training may be regarded as a welcome trend within academia, regarding it as a panacea for all the challenges that hamper graduate employment is naïve and simplistic. Universities may promote the value of job-related and entrepreneurial skills which graduates can use to enhance their career opportunities in the form of wage and salaried employment or self-employment. However, they also need to encourage graduates to think beyond wage and salaried employment and more toward self-employment. There have been such efforts within academia like the creation of spin-offs which encourage graduates to establish and run their own businesses.

However, equal consideration should be given to enhancing the success of self-employment schemes that are affected by a variety of challenges beyond the control of HEIs. For its part, the government should facilitate graduates' entry into business and promote initiatives that enhance mobility and employment – one of the youth-focused employment strategies of Ethiopia's National Employment Policy and Strategy (2009). Despite their limitations in handling this challenge single-handedly, HEIs should also actively engage in conducting research that seeks to understand the factors and interventions that promote or discourage the success of self-employed entrepreneurs. Such studies can contribute evidence on the relative importance of different barriers to self-employment growth and entrepreneurial success, which the government and other stakeholders can use to design appropriate interventions. Among others, this requires working closely with the government, financial institutions and funding agencies to alleviate the multitude of challenges that graduates who wish to be self-employed are facing.

CHAPTER 58

Advancing Employability through a Labor Market Information System

An earlier version of this chapter appeared in *Inside Higher Education*, 2 October 2018, https://www.insidehighered.com/blogs/world-view/advancing-employability-through-labor-market-information-system

The extant literature on responding to the challenges of graduate employability approaches the issue primarily from the perspective of graduate preparation. It is often argued that the attributes, skills and knowledge students acquire during their stay at universities have direct implications for later employment. However, the increasing incidence and duration of graduate unemployment can result from the disparity between the number of graduates educational institutions produce and the labor market's capacity to absorb them. A positive link between the two is regarded as an essential ingredient in facilitating graduate employment. Indeed, producing the right number and mix of graduates the market can accommodate remains one of the major challenges of many higher education systems, calling for mechanisms to bridge ensuing gaps. Efforts in this direction include the setting up of labor market information systems that can provide the national data required.

1   Experiences and Challenges

Ethiopia has a long history of planning the outputs of its educational system. Indeed, it introduced one of the first sectoral planning exercises in sub-Saharan Africa. As part of its national economic plan, the Ten-year Plan for the Controlled Expansion of Ethiopian Education: 1955–1965 was adopted in 1955, dictated by the principles of what one writer called, "invest for what you get in return; educate only as many as can be absorbed by the developing economy and administration; and educate only the type you need". Although the higher education sector was included in this planning trajectory until the demise of the socialist Dergue in 1991, this practice has been abandoned by the current government due to its market-oriented economic policies. The fact that this has occurred against the backdrop of a rapidly massifying system has rendered the strategy of leaving everything to the market more challenging. The country's more than 350 public and private HEIs currently churn out more than 160,000 graduates per year. With an annual enrollment capacity approaching a million, the graduation rate is expected to more than double in a few years.

One of the mechanisms by which the country has responded to the challenges of rising student numbers has been adjusting the annual student intake of public institutions into a program mix of 70/30 science and technology versus the social sciences and humanities in the hope that this will support Ethiopia's plan of becoming a middle-income country by 2025, with the corresponding job creation opportunities envisaged. Moreover, the Ministry of Education – working closely with public universities – is planning to raise the percentage of graduates employed within 12 months after graduation to 80%. Another sectoral plan which could have supplemented the national effort, but has so far received little practical attention is the establishment of a national labor information system.

A labor market information system (LMIS) offers a variety of advantages to policy makers, employers and employees, universities, training institutions, and other relevant stakeholders by facilitating the collection, analysis and dissemination of relevant information about the labor market, including skills and supply, progress in meeting employment goals, and other pertinent data. In addition to facilitating labor mobility and the hiring process, such a system can assist HEIs in aligning their programs and curricula with the requirements and absorption capacities of the labor market and influence the quality and relevance of their provisions. Despite these wider benefits, the practice of setting up an efficient LMIS remains a rare and challenging exercise across many countries, due to the high level of commitment, technical expertise, resources and sectoral coordination it demands.

2   The Way Forward

As early as 2003, recommendations were made to the Ethiopian Ministry of Education to set up a Labor Market Observatory through the Higher Education Strategy Center in order to monitor labor market demand for graduates, assess graduate job performance, and disseminate relevant findings to HEIs. The specific tasks set to be accomplished by the observatory were conducting regular, detailed surveys of the demand/supply balance for university graduates at least once every three years, collecting information on job vacancies, salary structures and unemployed graduates, tracer study comparisons of public and private university graduates, employer satisfaction with graduate employees, demand for specific skills, etc. Current developments in Ethiopia's higher education sector echo the need to examine and respond to this call.

Fortunately, the need for an LMIS appears to be gaining traction at both national and sectoral level. Government recognizes the relevance of information on labor market skills and the need for close links with existing economic planning and forecasting efforts. Although the federal Ministry of Labour and Social Affairs, and its regional counterparts – Bureaus of Labour and Social Affairs – and informal channels have so far been used to access labor information and employment services, they have not been able to provide comprehensive and efficient services due to various limitations. The Education Sector Development Program (2015/16–2019/20) also underscores the importance of the scheme in terms of influencing the relevance of courses offered at HEIs and envisages the establishment of such a system. However, little seems to have been achieved in terms of its practical realization. It is now clear that in addition to serving as a component of a stronger national database, the availability of an LMIS will make an important contribution to the Ethiopian higher education sector in terms of improved focus, efficient use of resources, and addressing the scale, causes and effects of unemployability that is becoming a serious challenge to the system. Towards that end, this is a propitious time for the government to urgently put in place such a system in the interests of aligning the outputs of Ethiopia's HEIs with the capacities and needs of the job market.

PART 10

COVID-19 and Its Impact on Higher Education

CHAPTER 59

COVID-19 Threat to Higher Education
Africa's Challenges, Responses, and Apprehensions

An earlier version of this chapter appeared in *International Higher Education*, *102* (with Damtew Teferra), https://doi.org/10.36197/IHE.2020.102.14

The onset of the coronavirus pandemic became primetime news in Africa as the plight of its international students in Wuhan, China – where it began – took center stage. At the time of the outbreak, Hubei, the province where Wuhan is located, hosted around 5,000 of the nearly 82,000 African students in China. In the early days of the crisis, concerns in the Global North focused primarily on the disruption that the pandemic would bring to student flows from China and its economic impact on their higher education systems. Efforts to prevent the spread of the virus ranged from extending or postponing academic terms to banning incoming students. Most of Africa's initial response focused on repatriating students stranded in Wuhan or providing assistance from afar. Nigeria, Senegal, South Africa, and Algeria and its North African neighbors succeeded in repatriating their students – an achievement that was much celebrated. Other countries lacking the readiness and resources to do the same had to assume a low profile against public opinion, which favored repatriation.

1   Responses

Africa has taken the coronavirus pandemic seriously only in the past few weeks, following the confirmation of its first cases. Initial responses included the closure of schools and universities beginning mid-March. Increasingly, universities across the continent are setting up institution-wide task forces to mitigate the impact of the pandemic. Some are striving to participate in high-end research toward finding a cure for the virus. Many are attempting to shift to online teaching and learning through institutional, national, continental, and international initiatives. Most plans are only in their initial stages of implementation and current efforts need to be ramped up, forging wider cooperation, and sharing experiences and resources across the continent. Two major issues that hold serious implications in the fight against the pandemic are online teaching, which is now championed as an alternative form of educational delivery, and the pandemic's economic impact on African higher education.

2   Online Delivery

According to UNESCO, 9.8 million African students experienced disruption in their studies due to the closure of HEIs, especially in the first few months of the onset of the pandemic. The danger of contamination triggered institutions to move their courses online. However, going online is not that simple on a continent where only 24% of the population has access to the Internet, and poor connectivity, exorbitant data costs, and frequent power interruptions are serious challenges.

Increasingly, universities have partnered with Internet providers and governments to overcome this critical challenge by negotiating zero-rated access to specific educational and information websites, as in the case of Rwanda, South Africa, and Tunisia. At the institutional level, a number of universities, such as the public University of KwaZulu-Natal in South Africa, and private universities such as Ashesi University in Ghana, offered data bundles to their students and staff. Going digital effectively requires substantial coordination with, and swift support from institutional and national service providers, regional entities, international partners, NGOs, the private sector, and ICT providers to rally behind such tools and platforms at little or no cost. It is imperative to seriously seek alternative means and approaches, in order not to leave behind students with little or no access to electronic communication. The painful reality of the digital divide on the continent has to be strategically and systematically managed; reaching out to millions of marginalized students must become a national priority in this time of crisis. While this is taking shape, institutions need to develop a comprehensive plan and a rigorous follow-up to ensure that academics and students make proper use of digital platforms. This task cannot be left solely to the discretion of individual actors.

3   Impact on the Economy and Higher Education

Prolonged civil wars, Africa's economic downturn in the 1970s, structural adjustment programs in the 1980s, and the debacle of the flawed rate-of-return discourse are just a few of the challenges that have impacted higher education in Africa. However, in the past decade, many economies have been booming. Half of the fastest growing economies in the world are currently located on the continent. Africa's growth performance (3.4% in 2019) was expected to increase to 3.9% in 2020. With an average of 5% of national GDP dedicated to education (one of the largest globally), the African region was beginning to witness revitalization of its higher education sector prior to the onset of the crisis.

Most of Africa's 54 countries have confirmed cases and fatalities due to COVID-19 and are passing through phases that include closing their borders, banning international flights and complete lockdowns. Economic forecasts show that Africa's economy could experience a loss of between US$90 billion and 200 billion in 2020, with GDP shrinking by three to eight points. In South Africa, growth is expected to contract by 1.5% in the first two months of the outbreak due to its effect on key economic sectors such as mining and tourism. Ethiopia's request for assistance on behalf of African nations to the G-20 for US$150 billion emergency financing, the freezing of interest rates on loans, and the cancellation of debts, is an indication of the massive threat to the continent's economies.

4 Apprehensions and Opportunities

The continent's meager institutional and national capacity, weak healthcare systems, and gregarious way of life may prove catastrophic should the virus continue to spread at the same rate and intensity as in other critically affected countries. The impact of such a calamitous scenario is easy to imagine and frightening to predict. The effects of the pandemic on Africa's nearly 2,000 HEIs cannot be overemphasized. If the crisis persists, it may seriously impact governments' commitment to higher education in the face of competing demands from the healthcare, business, and other priority sectors serving vulnerable segments of society. Furthermore, global support for higher education, research collaborations, and partnership schemes, most often directed at critical areas such as strengthening PhD programs, could be massively scaled back.

African HEIs are expected to do more, while concurrently battling on many fronts. This includes addressing the more immediate challenges arising from COVID-19, seeking improved mechanisms for online delivery, and planning to address the long-term effects of the pandemic on institutional capacity. In the aftermath of the pandemic, cost recovery through financial contributions from beneficiaries in the form of fees or loan repayments will not be easy, since economies will have seriously declined – if they indeed avoid total collapse. The expansion of public universities will be abruptly frozen. Private providers, which are dependent on tuition and fees, will also be hard hit, with many facing downsizing or even closure, as they receive little or no support from governments. On a positive note, this threat – and approaches to overcome it – may be catalytic for long-lasting changes in African higher education. Among others, diversified means of educational delivery, in particular a non-residential model, may become more mainstream, more acceptable, and more respectable.

CHAPTER 60

COVID-19 – Private Higher Education Faces Precarious Future

An earlier version of this chapter appeared in *University World News, Africa Edition*, 7 May 2020, https://www.universityworldnews.com/post.php?story=20200506081039701

When the Ethiopian government decided to close all types of educational institutions on 16 March to contain the possible impacts of COVID-19, sending nearly a million students home, the news did not come as a surprise to many of the more than 250 PHEIs that had been following global events and watching similar measures being taken by other African countries. In the immediate aftermath of the closure, the government set up a national task force that started mobilizing the public to combat the impacts of the pandemic. Most private institutions responded to the call by donating money, sanitary items, essential supplies and even their buildings to be used for quarantine and storage purposes. According to a figure obtained from the Ethiopian Private Higher Education and TVET Institutions' Association, donations worth more than ETB30 million (nearly US$1 million) were raised by private institutions for the cause. Private medical colleges also enlisted nearly 4,000 of their medical students to be deployed by the government should the situation escalate beyond the capacity of full-time professionals in hospitals and health centers to combat the pandemic.

1 Mounting Strains on Private Higher Education

The period since the onset of the COVID-19 has increasingly shown the difference in the pandemic's impact on public and private HEIs. Public institutions, whose budget is fully covered by the government, have suffered no serious setbacks in terms of running their businesses and paying employees' salaries. Their main challenge has been supporting their students online and responding to their communities' needs. However, the private sector started to feel the strain within the first few weeks. This was not unexpected, given the weak status of the sector. The vast majority of PHEIs across the country depend almost entirely on student tuition and other fees for their existence. There are very few non-profit private institutions established by religious entities and NGOs which may be able to seek support from their parent organizations. Most PHEIs run their programs in rented buildings owned by individuals and private businesses. They employ tens of thousands of people and incur substantial expenses (70% to 80%) relating to rentals and salaries. Private higher education institutions pay taxes and duties and repay loans from financial institutions at exorbitant rates – as is the case with many other private enterprises. They receive little or no direct or indirect assistance from the government. A student loan system that benefits all students, including those in the private sector, is not a policy instrument in Ethiopia as is the case in neighboring countries like Kenya and Tanzania.

The challenges of providing online education and support have also not been simple. These include poor Internet connectivity, exorbitant data costs, and a lack of appropriate technology – all of which are serious challenges to students over and above their possible lack of preparedness to pursue their studies during such an uncertain period. The pervasive lack of a well-developed learning management system has forced many institutions to revert to social media platforms like Telegram, Facebook, etc., as an immediate resort to send lessons to students. The difficulties of using these platforms have been noted when it comes to submitting assignments and institutional materials that need to be protected. Another serious challenge is the mounting number of students that do not have the opportunity or capacity to access the digital platforms created. These challenges continue to be a source of unhappiness for students and disagreement between students and institutions.

2 National Directives

Despite general directives by government to shift all forms of teaching online, the physical absence of students from campus has meant, in the case of private institutions, the absence of revenue on which the existence of most depend. At first, most private schools including HEIs were discouraged from collecting fees due to the moral implications and because of obvious limitations in their capacity to deliver teaching and learning with the same momentum and in the same way they did in the past. Statements from government officials and the public discouraged the charging of fees on the grounds that it was "not the right time" to do so. It was argued that private institutions should be showing sympathy towards society which was under strain and that institutions' running costs should in any event have declined due to the closures.

There followed a direct instruction from the Ministry of Education: private schools would be allowed to collect only 50% to 75% of monthly fees in compensation for the online services they started offering, and only in consultation with parents' committees set up at each school. This coincided with a national state of emergency that prohibited commercial and private employers, including PHEIs, from reducing their workforce or prematurely terminating employment contracts, which further compromised the position of private institutions at all levels of the education system. Private higher education institutions conceded a 25% monthly reduction of fees of their own accord. Despite the lack of official statistics, the strain of paying monthly staff salaries, rent and other expenses is already evident in the PHE sector and it is wary of mounting pressure in the future and as the academic year draws to a close.

3   Bailing out the Private Sector

While some forms of assistance have been made available to the private sector at large, given the government's capacity, there is little that the sector can expect in terms of alleviating its mounting challenges. Financial institutions that could have provided substantial assistance by reducing interest rates and offering long-term loans have not been forthcoming despite some positive gestures. The benefits extended thus far are restricted to postponing repayment periods for bank loans. The government has been encouraging landlords to reduce or waive rentals for businesses over the next few months but the number of those heeding this call is far below expectations.

Apart from its daily challenges, it is clear that the private sector will not escape the negative impacts of the pandemic. Most PHEIs are already struggling to survive the first wave; a few have started downsizing, while others are closing some branches or units and are laying off what they consider to be redundant staff. Given the strains, more challenges along this line are yet to come if the closures continue for the next few months. This will have direct implications for the students and their families that the government aims to protect. Previous experience has shown that the closure of private institutions entails a variety of challenges that include the loss of student records, difficulties in transferring to a new institution, labor tensions and other complex issues that the bankruptcy of any private business bring. The effects are not restricted to individual institutions but extend to families, regulatory agencies and government authorities that are often embroiled in endless litigation and bureaucratic engagements, which may not end to the satisfaction of individual parties whose finances and energy could be compromised.

4 Anticipating the Future

The demand for PHE is not likely to diminish post COVID-19, assuming that tuition fees at PHEIS stay the same and the individual income of employees at both public and private enterprises are not seriously affected. Furthermore, there will inevitably be strain on the public higher education sector as other sectors compete for public funding, which means an additional gap that will need to be accommodated by the private sector. However, interest in investing in such a volatile sector may not continue as it used to in the short- and medium-term. While the future may not be quite as bleak as suggested, the private sector's continuity depends heavily on what can be done today. It is understandable that government is overwhelmed by a multitude of social, political and economic pressures unleashed by COVID-19. However, unless substantial interventions are made to bail out the PHE sector and/or influence financial institutions to provide meaningful assistance at an early period of the crisis, this sector, which boasts the largest number of students in Africa, will be significantly weakened.

CHAPTER 61

The Shift to Online Learning Calls for Global Cooperation

An earlier version of this chapter appeared in *University World News, Africa Edition*, 16 April 2020 (with Damtew Teferra), https://www.universityworldnews.com/post.php?story=20200413115722610

Since the onset of the coronavirus pandemic, the closure of schools and universities has become a common phenomenon across the world. In the past few weeks alone, Africa's close to 10 million students have discontinued classes to stave off the impact of the pandemic. Invariably, institutions have been advised to shift to online modalities of educational delivery. While this may be possible in advanced countries with well-developed systems, it remains a serious challenge for many in the less-developed world with relatively meager information and communications technology (ICT) infrastructure, expertise, systems and policies. Shifting to an online modality in response to the new reality may not be easy in Africa, where inadequate ICT access, capacity and systems are evident. The limitations have different dimensions including structural, economic, social and technical.

1   Structural Dimensions

ICT has been identified as one of the major instruments to meet many of the development imperatives expressed in the Sustainable Development Goals. It also holds potential to drive development and transform Africa into a knowledge-based economy and information society. However, ICT infrastructure across the continent has been restricted due to the lack of investment, policies and systems that promote its growth. For instance, 65 million people in Ethiopia, which has the second largest population in Africa, have no electricity, which is a key component in ICT access. Even the most technologically advanced country in Africa, South Africa, has been experiencing power cuts in the form of load shedding, with serious consequences for all aspects of life. Within the education sphere, the use of technology-mediated learning that allows for improved learning and additional access to higher education has been limited across the continent.

2 Economic Dimensions

A lot is said about the encouraging changes taking place with regard to using mobile technology in Africa but access to mobile broadband and cost are still serious challenges. A mobile handset and 500MB of data cost 10% of the average monthly income in Africa, which is double the 5% threshold recommended by the UN Broadband Commission. This harsh reality will continue to affect the business of academia conducted through online platforms in a meaningful way by inhibiting students' capacity to access available resources from their own institutions or other external sources. Governments may also need to direct universities to channel their resources – for instance those dedicated to meals, accommodation and so on – to Internet and data access so that students can pursue their studies.

3 Social and Political Dimensions

Since most African governments closed universities due to the pandemic, students have returned to their parents and communities. A significant number who live in rural, remote and marginal areas lack Internet access. By and large, these students are cut off from their universities due to a lack of ICT access, compounded by high costs and poor infrastructure. No one knows for sure how universities operate in the aftermath of the pandemic. This means that a proactive political decision is needed to address some of the key challenges, one of which is the provision of subsidized and zero-rated data for students so that some semblance of learning – whether formal or informal – can continue. Delivery of educational content mounted on online platforms may engender social inequities and marginalization. Not much is known about what alternatives exist for students without Internet access but alternative solutions that do not necessarily demand an Internet connection should be sought, including the use of media such as radio, TV and other forms of offline delivery.

4 Technical Dimensions

Despite its limitations, social media for educational purposes may be an immediate alternative considered by many African institutions. However, setting up a full-fledged and effective online system for educational delivery involves much more than Internet connectivity. Such a system demands a host of technology tools, a user-friendly interface and accessibility standards. In an ideal scenario, online platforms should be developed to incorporate multiple learning modalities and activities that promote active learning and wider interaction. Among other things, an institution needs to have an organizational structure, requisite expertise and a dedicated budget to run such a system in an efficient and sustainable manner. Further, online instructors and students should be equipped with the technical skills to function in the new environment and hence require sustained support pre-, during and post-delivery. Yet, there is a scarcity of qualified human resources to support the ICT system, and high-end ICT skills are typically low in many institutions across Africa. The move to online delivery of lessons in Africa has been greeted with considerable skepticism due to these challenges and has been rejected outright in some countries like Tunisia.

5 Call for Broader Cooperation

In addition to combating the health, economic and social threats of the coronavirus, African governments need to explore mechanisms to marshal cooperative schemes, resources and expertise at national, regional and global level towards addressing the threats posed by COVID-19 to the education sector. In the months following the onset of the pandemic, we have witnessed local initiatives and high-profile international support to Africa in the fight against COVID-19. In addition to what African governments themselves and regional institutions like the African Development Bank and the African Import Bank are doing, the World Bank Group (including the International Bank for Reconstruction and Development and International Development Association), the G-20 and foundations like the Alibaba and Gates Foundations have made direct commitments to Africa to help mitigate the negative impacts of COVID-19. While the various forms of support directed towards the impending health and economic crises are critical, the need to keep the out-of-school population occupied and engaged through the 'transformation' of educational delivery modes should receive similar consideration or else, in addition to the educational losses, we run the risk of social and political upheavals.

Concurrent with the encouraging African initiatives by governments, service providers and the private sector, support from regional and international sources should focus on getting the education system on its feet by ramping up technological and resource assistance to those in need. This becomes urgent in the event that lockdowns continue for a considerable period of time. The role of technology giants, global and regional IT companies, development partners, communication platforms, software developers, elite universities and others – all of which are key in linking institutions to their students through their products and services – remains critical. In addition to playing a role in galvanizing and coordinating such assistance, African governments and the academic community expect to hear about innovative and more generous initiatives in this area in the weeks ahead.

In summary, if the current unprecedented crisis has proven anything with respect to education delivery, it would be the need for Africa to fully commit itself to building its ICT infrastructure, exploitation of ICT across all sectors and types of institutions, creating interconnectivity for and among institutions, and improving digital skills across all levels. Despite the many threats COVID-19 is posing to the continent, this could be a momentous opportunity for Africa to undertake significant steps in improving its ICT profile in collaboration with development partners and the private sector.

CHAPTER 62

Stemming the Impact of COVID-19 on Employment

An earlier version of this chapter appeared in *University World News, Africa Edition*, 23 July 2020, https://www.universityworldnews.com/post.php?story=20200720135723920

COVID-19 is having an immense effect on global economic growth. A recent report by the World Bank estimates that the global economy could contract by between 5% and 8% in 2020, pushing 71–100 million people below the international poverty line of US$1.90 per day. Data on developing countries is limited but it is anticipated that they will continue to bear the brunt of the pandemic due to the limited resilience and vulnerability of their economies. In Ethiopia, predictions by the National Planning Commission indicate possible reductions of 2.8% to 3.8% in the national economy. Independent researchers show potential reductions in GDP by at least 5.6% for 2020–21. A related problem is the impact of the pandemic on employment and income across many sectors. One of these sectors is higher education where thousands of students have been pursuing their education to earn a living and improve their way of life, apart from their contribution to national development and the economy.

1 Unemployment

As in other parts of the developing world, unemployment is a serious challenge in Ethiopia. Currently, nearly 15% of those who attend post-secondary education are unemployed. Over the years, efforts have been made to combat the increasing challenges of unemployment at all levels, including higher education. A recent effort in this regard has been the setting up of a national committee led by Ethiopia's Prime Minister Abiy Ahmed geared towards the creation of 3 million jobs per year. However, this ambitious plan appears to have been seriously jeopardized since the onset of COVID-19 with increasing threats to employment creation and the maintenance of available jobs.

A joint report by Ethiopia's Jobs Creation Commission (JCC) and the International Labour Organization (ILO) on the impact of COVID-19 on employment, predicts three possible scenarios in Ethiopia. In the first, 'low epidemic', scenario, which assumes maintaining low prevalence levels, Ethiopia will face a reduction of 1.53% of GDP per month, and a loss of 1.34 million jobs. In the second scenario of an 'epidemic of intermediate virulence', requiring the shutdown of additional sectors, more stringent limitations to personal mobility and the suspension of all economic activity outside bare necessities, it is estimated that job losses could reach 3.7 million, with the economy losing 2.59% of GDP for every month of lockdown. In the third and worst-case scenario involving a full lockdown, job losses are predicted to reach 6 million. This would require the public deficit to be raised to 3% of GDP for each month of economic closure. Appropriate targeted fiscal measures, including capital injections, need to be taken in all these scenarios in order to compensate for deficits and avert job losses and bankruptcies.

The ILO and JCC report predicts that, even in the first scenario, there could be significant revenue loss in sectors such as culture, sports, entertainment, bars, transportation of persons, personal services, tourism and export-oriented manufacturing, among others. Some of these are already experiencing damaging revenue losses. For example, Ethiopian Airlines, the largest airline in Africa, has reported a loss of US$550 million since February 2020. Floriculture and horticulture, two of the fastest growing sectors in the economy, experienced an 87% decline in prices and 63% increase in cancellation of orders in the first two months of the pandemic. The Ethiopian Hotels Association reported that the travel and tourism sectors will see a 30% reduction in growth in the 2019–20 fiscal year, with an estimated monthly loss of US$35 million in revenue, and a risk to the jobs of 15,000 employees.

Among the agriculture, mining, tourism, creative and IT industries that have been identified by the JCC as key areas for potential job creation, the only sector that appears to be relatively safe for the time being is agriculture, where Ethiopia still has a large share of its workforce. In terms of the impact of the pandemic, another joint study conducted by the World Bank and the JCC revealed that the biggest challenges faced by private firms are payment of rent, invoices, staff wages and social security contributions. Most firms suggested waiving tax payments as the most appropriate policy measure to help them keep afloat, followed by access to working capital at beneficial rates.

2   Higher Education Institutions and Employment

When it comes to higher education, there is an urgent need for wider investigation of the impact of COVID-19 on employment in order to explore possible damage to existing patterns of employment, graduate employability, and the alignment of government policy with institutional needs. Nonetheless, it can be predicted that the impact of COVID-19 will be substantial in terms of sustaining existing jobs, and for graduate employability. For the time being, the state of emergency declared in Ethiopia prohibits all types of institutions from terminating their contracts with employees. However, many institutions have stopped employing part-time workers who constitute a significant proportion of employment in the higher education sector, especially in the private sector that relies heavily on such staff. New appointments have been frozen both in public and private institutions. COVID-19 is expected to have a significant impact on the future employability of graduates across both sectors due to its possible influence on the availability of jobs and delays in graduation. Many students do not know when they will go back to their universities to complete their studies. In Ethiopia, this concerns around 160,000 students that HEIS graduate every year.

3 Responding to the Crisis

Despite its limitations, the Ethiopian government has been taking a variety of measures to contain the economic impacts of the pandemic, but it is important to examine how such measures relate to particular sectoral needs. Assistance to private enterprises thus far appears to have mainly been extended to manufacturing, hotels, horticulture, floriculture, and other industries seen as most affected by the pandemic. While the support provided to the public higher education sector can sustain its existence, current policy directions are perceived to have a limited role in terms of ensuring the sustainability of the tuition-dependent PHE sector in particular. For example, private institutions were asked to reduce their tuition fees by 25%. Undergraduate students were not allowed to progress to higher academic levels until contact time was resumed and graduations were also prohibited. The possible impact of the lockdown on new admissions and related challenges is creating serious financial stress that could lead to the closure of many institutions, especially the new ones. All these issues point to the need for close monitoring to gauge the impact on specific sectors, and continuous dialogue between government and the various sectors in order to maintain the confidence of business and education institutions in government policy aimed at sustaining employment and avoiding a long-term economic recession. However, solving the challenges of the economy remains key to solving anticipated employment problems.

In an article published in *The New York Times* in April 2020, the prime minister noted that Ethiopia will need an additional US$3 billion by the end of 2020 to address the consequences of the pandemic. A moratorium on bilateral and commercial debt payments for the rest of 2020 could save the country US$1.7

billion, while extending the moratorium until the end of 2022 would offer an additional US$3.5 billion. In addition to allowing countries to combat the negative impacts of the pandemic on the economy, such a scheme would provide the chance to reduce short- and long-term effects on employment, offer hope to the youth, and avert social unrest and instability which could be serious threats in the not-too-distant future.

CHAPTER 63

Defying the Notion of the Ivory Tower in the Aftermath of COVID-19

An earlier version of this chapter appeared in *University World News, Africa Edition*, 14 May 2020 (with Damtew Teferra), https://www.universityworldnews.com/post.php?story=20200511152721215

Universities throughout the world and those in Africa in particular have been criticized for being ivory towers: aloof, unaccountable and disengaged from the interests of their communities. African universities especially have been incessantly, unfairly and harshly attacked for not lifting the continent out of its cycle of poverty and economic deprivation – as if they were the only players in the complex web of the development universe. This allegation has been on the table for decades – without any vigorous rebuttal from institutions. Indeed, this narrative has been instrumental in shaping the discourse on African universities' contribution to the development of the continent, supporting the notion that such contribution is insignificant. This article discounts the notion of the 'Towerization' of African universities as the current pandemic is decisively exhibiting their role as frontline institutions in combating the killer disease.

1 Ivory Tower – Where Is the Evidence?

In a chapter in *Flagship Universities in Africa*, Damtew Teferra observes that the unflattering term 'ivory tower' has often been evoked to criticize (flagship) universities as much for their purported inclinations as to what matters most in the international sphere as for their presumed lack of relevance to conditions in their own backyard. Criticism of these institutions has been harsh despite their massive contributions, as measured by the graduates – including doctors, nurses, educators, engineers, architects, accountants, lawyers, and agriculturists, among others – they have produced and their impact on the everyday lives of citizens and nations despite huge challenges. The long-standing allegations, and charges, have been that the contribution of universities is lacking. Since the COVID-19 pandemic, universities have sent most of their students and staff home. However, many remain involved in a host of activities aimed at combating the disease. Here is a snapshot of direct community-related activities undertaken by universities, in addition to their role in providing life-saving medical services.

2 'Relevant' Research

African universities have been widely criticized for not undertaking (relevant) research or for focusing on 'blue-sky' research which is considered less relevant to the needs of the people. While governments have provided virtually no research grants to most African universities, they have been among the most vocal of critics. Currently, a number of universities are undertaking research on issues of COVID-19 in national contexts. Ethiopian universities are already undertaking 30 research projects – one has indicated it is engaging in over 20 such efforts. A Ghanaian university is undertaking gene sequencing. Others are involved in developing a vaccine and in antibody development, among others. All of them are visibly and directly contributing to the needs of their communities.

3 Public Awareness

Since university students have returned home following closures, institutions, in close cooperation with their respective communities and the authorities, have been making efforts to deploy them in a number of public awareness initiatives. Accordingly, students and staff have been deployed in reaching out to their communities in markets, religious institutions and other public spaces to raise public awareness of the disease. Materials that have been produced, packaged and translated at the universities are being used in these endeavors. Universities that own community radio stations have used them for this purpose.

4 Production of Consumables

University labs and teaching centers have shifted into producing essential health and sanitary items needed to prevent the spread of the pandemic. This includes using chemical laboratories to produce sanitizers and liquid soap and using fashion design labs to produce masks and medical apparel. These activities have become common in a number of universities in Africa since the outbreak of COVID-19 – largely prompted by a lack of such resources in their respective countries. Quite a number of universities in Africa, from Botswana to Gambia and from Nigeria to Namibia, are involved in these activities.

5 Design and Development of Equipment

The world has witnessed a shortage of preventive equipment and curative medicines which has sparked diplomatic wrangles between countries such as India and the United States. This has prompted many countries to produce home-made products. As a result, a number of universities have been involved in designing, developing and producing prototype headgear, ventilators, 'oxygenators' and even dedicated software.

6 Testing, Quarantine and Storage

Many African public universities have teaching hospitals which now serve at the forefront of testing and medical services to combat the pandemic. Due to their resources, universities have also been chosen as one of the best locations for the quarantine of patients. Their facilities are also being used to store necessary medical supplies.

7 Philanthropic Activities

Students and staff are also involved in a number of philanthropic activities that range from fundraising, to supporting the weak, the sick and the elderly. Volunteerism is being rekindled as students and staff engage in multiple direct community services. Furthermore, many university facilities have turned into emergency bunkers in the service of their communities.

8 From Global Competitiveness to Human Survival

Recently, higher education has been advanced as key to economic development and global competitiveness. Vigorous arguments have been advanced to support higher education to achieve these core objectives. COVID-19 has added a new frontier in the case for supporting higher education: ensuring the very survival of the human species. In the face of the mighty adversary that is devouring the confidence and capacity of powerful economic, political and medical forces, all those remarkable human advancements and achievements appear to be in great danger. The key role of universities in all aspects of human life and in combating the pandemic is now so evident as to be beyond doubt. This is in concert with the arguments already made by Teferra to situate higher education (in Africa) at the center of human development in the blueprints of development imperatives such as the Sustainable Development Goals.

9 A New Perspective Post-Pandemic

COVID-19 has made it clear, once again, that countries cannot depend on the knowledge-producing capacity of others. For that matter, putting to use knowledge produced elsewhere itself requires capacity built on the ground. The nature of the virus is such that countries are rekindling their relationships with their universities as they seek indigenous solutions to an 'exotic' problem. Ethiopia, Cameroon and South Africa, for instance, are working actively to develop capacity in indigenous knowledge and innovations. Initiatives to promote African responses to COVID-19 are now commonplace on the continent and these institutional experiences of more intimate social engagements may come in handy in a post-COVID-19 era.

Many stakeholders have disproportionately and unfairly criticized universities for what they claim is a lackluster engagement in issues of national significance. COVID-19 has helped universities to showcase what they are capable of. The skeptical public, distrustful governments and diffident development players will hopefully attain a new perspective on the 'lease' of universities post-COVID-19. Public relations is the Achilles heel of universities. They should thus seize this historic opportunity to proactively pronounce their role and vigorously and systematically communicate their raison d'être in order to assume a position in society commensurate with their contributions. Multiple strategies sanctioned by national and regional organizations, such as university, professional and civic associations, will be paramount in achieving this goal.

References

Addis Ababa University (AAU). (2013). *Senate legislation.* AAU.

African Union Commission (AUC). *Science, technology and innovation strategy for Africa 2024* (STISA 2024). https://au.int/sites/default/files/documents/37448-doc-stisa-2024_english.pdf

Berhan Y. (2008). Medical doctors profile in Ethiopia: Production, attrition and retention. *Ethiopian Medical Journal, 46*(supp 1), 1–7.

Beyene, B. M., & Tekleselassie, T. G. (2018). *The state, determinants, and consequences of skills mismatch in the Ethiopian labour market.* Working Papers 021. Ethiopian Development Research Institute.

Bunting I., Cloete N., & Van Schalkwyk, F. (2014). *An empirical overview of eight flagship Universities in Africa: 2001–2011. A report of the Higher Education Research and Advocacy Network in Africa (HERANA).* Centre for Higher Education Transformation (CHET).

Central Statistics Agency (CSA). (2005). *Ethiopia household income, consumption and expenditure survey.* CSA.

Central Statistics Agency (CSA). (2007). *Ethiopia population and housing census.* CSA.

Central Statistics Agency (CSA). (2013). *Ethiopia national labour force survey.* CSA.

Central Statistics Agency (CSA). (2014). *Statistical report on the 2013 national labour force survey.* CSA.

Central Statistics Agency (CSA). (2015). *Urban employment unemployment survey – Ethiopia.* CSA.

Central Statistics Agency, CSA. (2016). *Ethiopia welfare monitoring survey 2015–16.* CSA.

Central Statistics Agency (CSA). (2018). *Urban employment unemployment survey – Ethiopia.* CSA.

CSRP (2004). *Civil service reform program in Ethiopia.* CSRP.

Dalichow, F. (1996). Criteria and procedures for the recognition of foreign qualifications. *Higher Education in Europe, 21*(4), 26–38. doi:10.1080/0379772960210403

Deressa, W., & Azazh, A. (2012). Attitudes of undergraduate medical students of Addis Ababa University towards medical practice and migration. *BMC Medical Education, 12,* 68.

Duermeijer, C., Amir, M., & Schoombee, L. (2018, March 22). *Africa generates less than 1% of the world's research; data analytics can change that.* Elsevier. https://www.elsevier.com/connect/africa-generates-less-than-1-of-the-worlds-research-data-analytics-can-change-that

Education Strategy Center (ESC). (2018). *Ethiopian education development roadmap (2018–30): An integrated executive summary.* ESC.

Ethiopia Jobs Creation Commission (JCC). (2020). *COVID-19: Ethiopia potential impact on jobs and incomes and short term policy options.*

https://www.jobscommission.gov.et/wp-content/uploads/2020/04/Potential-impact-of-COVID19-on-Jobs-and-Income-JCC_English.pdf

Ethiopia Jobs Creation Commission (JCC), & International Labour Organisation (ILO). (2020). *Containing the Epidemic and its impact on jobs and incomes in Ethiopia rapid assessment and response plan.* https://www.ilo.org/wcmsp5/groups/public/—africa/—ro-abidjan/—sro-addis_ababa/documents/publication/wcms_747210.pdf.

Ethiopian Academy of Sciences (EAS). (2017). *National Journal evaluation and accreditation: A strategy for standardizing the assessment of performance in scholarly publishing in Ethiopia.* EAS.

Ethiopian Science and Technology Commission (ESTC). (1993). *National science and technology policy.* ESTC.

Ethiopian Science and Technology Information Center (STIC). (2014). *Science and technology indicators report 2014.* STIC.

Ethiopian Science and Technology Information Centre (ESTIC). (2014). *Science and Innovation Policy.*

Federal Democratic Republic of Ethiopia (FDRE). (1995). *Constitution of the federal democratic Republic of Ethiopia.*

Federal Democratic Republic of Ethiopia (FDRE). (2003). *Higher education cost sharing regulation No. 91/2003.* FDRE.

Federal Democratic Republic of Ethiopia (FDRE). (2004). *Refugee proclamation No 409/2004.*

Federal Democratic Republic of Ethiopia (FDRE). (2009a). *Ethiopia higher education proclamation 650/2009.* FDRE.

Federal Democratic Republic of Ethiopia (FDRE). (2009b). *The National information and communication technology policy and strategy.* Ministry of Communication and Information Technology.

Federal Democratic Republic of Ethiopia (FDRE). (2016). *National ICT policy and strategy.* Author.

Federal Democratic Republic of Ethiopia (FDRE). (2019). *Higher education proclamation 1152/2019.* FDRE.

Federal Democratic Republic of Ethiopia Ministry of Health. (2016). *National human resource for health strategic plan for Ethiopia 2010–2025.* FMOH.

Heritage Institute for Policy Studies. (2013). *The state of higher education in Somalia: Privatization, rapid growth, and the need for regulation.* Heritage Institute for Policy Studies.

Higher Education Relevance and Quality Agency (HERQA). (2008). *Position paper on cross boarder higher education.* HERQA.

Higher Education Relevance and Quality Agency (HERQA). (2011). *Guidelines for the accreditation of cross boarder higher education in Ethiopia.* HERQA.

International Labour Organisation (ILO). (2019). *World Employment and Social Outlook – Trends*. ILO.

Johansson, S. (2014). *Migration of Ethiopian Doctors A cross sectional study on attitudes among Ethiopian medical students towards studying medicine, migration and future work*. [Thesis]. Oslo University.

Kiringai, J. W., Geiger, M. T., Bezawagaw, M. G., & Jensen, L.(2016). *Ethiopia public expenditure review*. World Bank Group.

Levy, D. C. (2002). *Unanticipated development: Perspectives on private higher education's emerging role*. PROPHE Working Paper No 1.

Ligami, C. (2018, April 13). World Bank invests in vocational education in 3 countries. *University World News*. https://www.universityworldnews.com/post.php?story=20180413150958664

Ministry of Capacity Building (MCB). (2006). *Business process reengineering study, Final report*. MCB.

Ministry of Education (MoE). (2005). *Education sector development program III (2005/06–2010/11)*. MoE.

Ministry of Education (MoE). (2008a). *National technical & vocational education and training strategy*. MoE.

Ministry of Education (MoE). (2008b). *Strategy and conversion plan and postgraduate studies*. MoE.

Ministry of Education (MoE). (2008c). *TVET strategy*. MoE.

Ministry of Education (MoE). (2010). *Annual statistics bulletin 2009/10*. MoE.

Ministry of Education (MoE). (2015a). *Education statistics annual abstract 2014/15*. MoE.

Ministry of Education (MoE). (2015b). *Education sector development program IV (2015/16–2019/20)*. MoE.

Ministry of Education (MoE). (2015c). *Education sector development programme V (2015/16–2019/20)*. MoE.

Ministry of Education (MoE). (2016). *Education statistics annual abstract 2015/16*. MoE.

Ministry of Education (MoE). (2017a). *Introduction to deliverology in Ethiopia: Deliverology to ensure graduate employability 80% by 2020*. Delivery associates consultative document. MoE.

Ministry of Education (MoE). (2017b). *Annual statistics abstract 2016/17*. MoE.

Ministry of Education (MoE). (2017c). *Education statistics annual abstract 2016/17*. MoE.

Ministry of Education (MoE). (2018a). *Annual statistics abstract 2017/18*. MoE.

Ministry of Education (MoE). (2018b). *Annual statistics bulletin*. MoE.

Ministry of Education (MoE). (2018c). *Education statistics annual abstract 2017/18*. MoE.

Ministry of Education (MoE). (2018d). *Ethiopia education development roadmap (2018–2030)*. MoE.

Ministry of Finance and Economic Development (MoFED). (2010). *Growth and transformation plan I (2010/11–2014/15)*. MoFED.

Ministry of Finance and Economic Development, MoFED. (2016). *Growth and transformation plan II (2015/16–2019/20)*. MoFED.

Ministry of Labour and Social Affairs (MoLSA). (2009). *National employment policy and strategy of Ethiopia*. MoLSA.

Ministry of Science and Technology (MOST). (2012). *National science, technology and innovation policy of Ethiopia. Ministry of Science and Technology*. MOST.

MoSHE. (2020). *Research, technology transfer, University-Industry linkage and community services guideline*.

Organisation of African Unity (OAU). (1981). *The African charter on human and peoples' rights*. OAU.

Program for Research on Private Higher Education (PROPHE). (n.d.). https://prophe.org/

QS World University Rankings. (2018). https://www.qs.com/world-university-rankings-2018/

Rajab, R. (2018, February 9). Calls for quality over quantity in higher education. *University World News*.

Ranking Web of Universities. (2017, July). https://www.webometrics.info/en

Republic of Somaliland Ministry of Education and Higher Education. (n.d). *Somaliland's education sector strategic plan 2012–2016*.

Teferra, D. (2017). *Flagship Universities in Africa*. Palgrave Macmillan.

Teshome, T. (2015). *Higher education quality assurance for enhancement of higher education in Ethiopia: Achievements, challenges and some ways forward*. HERQA.

Tilaye, K. (2010). Rethinking institutional excellence in Ethiopia: Adapting and adopting the balanced scorecard (BSC) model. *Journal of Business and Administrative Studies, 2*(1), 22–53.

Times Higher Education World University Rankings. (2018.) https://www.timeshighereducation.com/world-university-rankings/2018/world-ranking#!/page/0/length/25/sort_by/rank/sort_order/asc/cols/stats

Transitional Government of Ethiopia (TGE). (1994). *Education and training policy*.

UNESCO. (1981). *Regional convention on the recognition of studies, certificates, diplomas, degrees and other academic qualifications in big bet education in the African States*.

UNESCO. (2005). *Guidelines for quality provision in cross-border higher education*. UNESCO.

UNESCO – Council of Europe. (n.d.). *Recommendation on criteria and procedures for the assessment of foreign qualifications*.

United Nations. (1990). UN Commission on human rights, convention on the rights of the child, 7 March 1990, E/CN.4/RES/1990/74. Retrieved March 3, 2021, from https://www.refworld.org/docid/3b00f03d30.html

United Nations. (2017). *The world drug report 2017*. UN.

United Nations High Commissioner for Refugees (UNHCR). (2012). *Education strategy 2012–16*. UNHCR.

United Nations High Commissioner for Refugees (UNHCR). (2015). *Ethiopia education strategy*. UNHCR.

United Nations High Commissioner for Refugees (UNHCR). (2019a). *DAFI annual report 2018*. UNHCR.

United Nations High Commissioner for Refugees (UNHCR). (2019b). *DAFI annual report 2019*. UNHCR.

United Nations Organization. (2010). Convention on the rights of persons with disabilities. Retrieved March 2, 2021, from https://www.un.org/development/desa/disabilities/convention-on-the-rights-of-persons-with-disabilities/convention-on-the-rights-of-persons-with-disabilities-2.html

University College of Addis Ababa. (1954). *University college charter*.

World Bank. (2003). *Higher education development for Ethiopia: Pursuing the vision*. World Bank.

World Bank. (2013). *Skills module survey of Ethiopia*. World Bank.

World Bank. (2014). *A decade of development in sub-Saharan African science, technology, engineering and mathematics research*. World Bank. http://documents1.worldbank.org/curated/en/237371468204551128/pdf/910160WP0P126900disclose09026020140.pdf

World Bank. (2015a). *Ethiopia economic update IV: Overcoming constraints in the manufacturing sector*. Africa region, World Bank.

World Bank. (2015b). *Enterprise survey Ethiopia*. http://www.enterprisesurveys.org/data/exploreeconomies/2015/ethiopia.

World Bank. (2016a). *5th Ethiopia economic update. Why so idle? Wages and employment in a crowded labor market*. World Bank.

World Bank. (2016b). *Ethiopia public expenditure review*. World Bank.

World Bank. (2018). *The cost of gender inequality*. World Bank.

World Bank. (2020a). *Doing business 2020: Comparing business regulation in 190 economies*. World Bank.

World Bank Group. (2020b). *The COVID-19 crisis response: Supporting tertiary education for continuity, adaptation, and innovation*. World Bank.

World Economic Forum. (2018). *The global competitiveness report 2018*. World Economic Forum.

World Health Organization (WHO). (2011). *World report on disability*. WHO.

World Health Organization (WHO). (2012). *The health workforce in Ethiopia: Addressing the remaining challenges*. WHO.

Yamada, S., Otchia, C. S., & Taniguchi, K. (2018). Explaining differing perceptions of employees' skill needs: The case of garment workers in Ethiopia. *International Journal of Training and Development*, 22(1), 51–68.

Zeng, Z. D., & Kayonde, S. (2016). *Assessing the potential for the electronics and ICT manufacturing industry in Ethiopia*. World Bank. https://openknowledge.worldbank.org/handle/10986/28408

Printed in the United States
by Baker & Taylor Publisher Services